THE SPIRITUAL JOURNEY OF NEWMAN

In Memoriam

MARY LUDDEN

1919-1985

The Spiritual Journey of Newman

JEAN HONORÉ

Translated by
Sr. Mary Christopher Ludden, S.C.

ALBA · HOUSE   NEW · YORK

SOCIETY OF ST. PAUL, 2187 VICTORY BLVD., STATEN ISLAND, NY 10314

Library of Congress Cataloging-in-Publication Data

    Honoré, Jean
      [Itinéraire spirituel de Newman. English]
      The spiritual journey of Newman / Jean Honoré : translated by Mary
Christopher Ludden.
        p.   cm.
      Translation of: Itinéraire spirituel de Newman.
      ISBN 0-8189-0654-5
      1. Newman, John Henry, 1801-1890. Cardinals — England —
Biography. 3. Spirituality — Church of England — History — 19th
century. 4. Spirituality — Catholic Church — History — 20th century.
5. Church of England — Membership. 6. Catholic Church — Membership.
7. Anglican Communion — Membership.   I. Title.
    BS4705.N5H6413   1992
    282'.092 — dc20   92-26405
                                                CIP

Produced and designed in the United States of America by the
Fathers and Brothers of the Society of St. Paul,
2187 Victory Boulevard, Staten Island, New York 10314,
as part of their communications apostolate.

ISBN: 0-8189-0654-5

Printing Information:

Current Printing - first digit   1   2   3   4   5   6   7   8   9   10

Year of Current Printing - first year shown

1992   1993   1994   1995   1996   1997

ACKNOWLEDGMENTS

*F*ROM THE BEGINNING, this work has been a providential and cooperative venture. When this book was first published, I received the French edition, *Itinéraire spirituel de Newman*, from my sister, Mary Ludden, who encouraged my interest in the cause of Cardinal Newman.

From the first reading and through all subsequent readings of this work, the ambitious thought of an English translation persisted. After many years, with a limited knowledge of French but with many years of Newman study, I conscientiously translated the book. Then, a providential meeting at a Newman celebration with Rev. Dr. Jacques P. Bossière, Ph.D., for which I am forever grateful, brought the project a step closer to reality. Father Bossière, an Episcopal priest, a French scholar, a theologian, and a retired professor from Yale University, carefully and minutely checked the translated manuscript for accuracy, all of which involved hours of labor.

The book became a reality when my dear friend, Margaret Petlicka, an excellent editor, spent countless hours in attempting to provide an interesting and readable account for the English public. Likewise, she entered the original translation on the computer and spent many more hours revising and correcting the text. Without her untiring work, this manuscript could never have been submitted for publication.

I would also like to thank those friends who reviewed the document and submitted editorial changes: Dr. Mary C. Sullivan, currently a Professor at Hunter College, who read and checked the final document, offering helpful suggestions in grammar and style that have been incorporated, and Sr. Bernard Quinn, RSHM, an English teacher at Cathedral Preparatory Seminary in New York, who offered pertinent changes to improve the work's readability.

My deep appreciation is extended to Brother Aloysius Milella,

S.S.P. and Father Edmund Lane, S.S.P. of Alba House for their careful reading of the manuscript and acceptance of it for publication, as well as to Father Benedict J. Groeschel, C.F.R., who has supported this project and recommended Alba House.

Likewise, I would like to express my gratitude to both Monsignor Richard Liddy, a great Newman scholar, who encouraged my interest in Newman from the very beginning, and to Rev. Vincent J. Giese, founder of the Friends of Cardinal Newman Association in the United States, who has kept interest in Newman's life and works alive through his newsletters and sponsorship of annual conferences.

The translator, Sr. Mary Christopher Ludden, Ph.D., a retired Professor from Hunter College and, thereafter, a teacher at Cathedral Preparatory Seminary, is most grateful to all of the above who helped in the publication of this book.

TRANSLATOR'S NOTE

*M*UCH HAS BEEN written about Newman — the prose writer, the poet, the philosopher, the educator and the theologian. But this book by Jean Honoré deals with another aspect of Newman's life — his spirituality.

In January 1991, Pope John Paul II, speaking for the Universal Church, declared John Henry Cardinal Newman, Venerable. This means that Newman practiced the Christian virtues to a heroic degree. Pope John Paul II urged that Newman's cause for Sainthood be promoted by spreading knowledge about his life and works.

As Archbishop Honoré maintains in this work, Newman's life is worthy of serious study because his spirituality was first experienced in a life before it was defined as a rule of life. Therefore, Newmanian spirituality can serve as a guide to many of us on our own spiritual journeys. His life and message can be especially inspiring for the priests of today who encounter so many problems from an unsettled society that rejects the Church's teachings, as well as her official representatives.

Beginning with his first assignment as a young Anglican assistant in the Church of St. Clement to his last years as a Cardinal in the Roman Catholic Church, Newman saw himself as a simple parish priest and Oratorian. From the age of fifteen onward, he had a vivid realization of his relationship with the Creator. He tried always to look beyond the human side of life and to live with a real appreciation of the invisible world. His trust in Divine Providence, his openness to God's will, and his faithfulness to prayer all strengthened him, especially when he was faced with suspicions, misunderstandings, trials, and failures.

Archbishop Honoré's work is a scholarly, insightful, and inspiring account of how John Henry Newman, led by a "kindly light" on his spiritual journey, reached the heights of holiness.

For the above reasons, this book has been translated from the original French and is being made available to the English speaking public.

TABLE OF CONTENTS

THE SPIRITUAL JOURNEY OF NEWMAN

CHAPTER I

THE CHILDHOOD OF NEWMAN

There is in most men's minds a secret instinct of reverence
and affection towards the days of their childhood.

II Par. VI, *The Mind of Little Children*, p. 265.

SOME, IN ORDER to understand themselves and to explain their destiny, return again and again to the mystery of their childhood. Newman was such a man. All his life, which was long, he remained faithful to the memory of his earliest years. Without doubt, because he lived them intensely, which is a child's privilege, always ready for wonder, wholly and entirely attentive to the call of everything around him, he discovered himself while discovering the world. Newman, the adult, had a need to reflect back on Newman, the child, to see himself more clearly.

The course of this spiritual journey will show that in Newman's eyes, no event in one's life is indifferent or without purpose. Indeed, unforeseen and unusual circumstances can have great influence on the course of one's personal history. They are the exterior framework of one's existence which, apart from their relationship to oneself, might seem incidental and insignificant. It was in his own inner soul that Newman relived the past which gave meaning and value to his life. His recollections of the past were transparent only to him because they were *his* memories. He alone knew the meaning of his life as it was prefigured in events of the past about which he was the sole judge and unique witness. No one person is another. Every attempt at self knowledge reveals the person to himself, in the depth of his own identity, which ultimately the wear and tear of existence both alters and protects. This self knowledge, Newman called his "egotism," adding that this "egotism was true modesty." This rightful

1

claim for each one to be understood only by himself, in the uniqueness of his singular destiny, is at the heart of the message that Newman transmits to the men and women of our times. It is in the reminiscences of our childhood years that we grasp the first contours of our personal inner nature.

As he went back to the sources of his past, John Henry Newman returned to the image of a huge house in the countryside near London, isolated in a field of greenery, illuminated in the evening with the fleeting glimmer of candles burning in honor of Admiral Nelson, the victor at Trafalgar.[1] It was Grey's Court at Ham near Richmond, some miles from the feverish city of London. The memory of this spacious and peaceful home, in a beautiful Hanoverian style, made such an impression on Newman that much later in life he maintained he was able to recall the slightest detail although he had only seen the house once or twice since his youth.

His father, a banker, probably decided to establish his residence at Ham in order to move his family from the restraints and noise of the city. Businessman though he was, he seems not to have had much success. Without doubt, he was more attracted by new enterprises than by a concern for financial security. Nevertheless, he was able to provide a comfortable existence for his family. Hard hit by the financial collapse which followed the campaign at Waterloo and the end of the war, Mr. Newman left the bank and managed a brewery. This created a great deal of disruption in the home, bringing to John Henry's childhood a measure of instability. In light of these circumstances, his attachment to Grey's Court is much more significant.

John Henry showed his father an affection tempered by the usual respect accorded the head of a family in those days. In his writings, he reveals some of his father's traits which attracted esteem without forcing admiration. Mr. Newman was close enough to his children to win their confidences, yet he kept enough of a reserve to ward off any and every excess of enthusiasm or feeling. He was an English gentleman, typical of the period prior to the Victorian era. His culture was that of a liberal member of the bourgeoisie of the eighteenth century. He was an avid lover of books and music. His religion was without doubt more conformist than profound, more sincere in its convictions than in its enthusiastic manifes-

---

[1] Letter to Miss Holmes, August 5, 1861, W. I., p. 607.

tation of them. His greatest merit was in orienting the studies of his children, especially in awakening a mind like John Henry's, which needed only the opportunity to express itself.

As for Mrs. Newman, she was a descendant of the French Huguenot refugees who had come to England at the time of the revocation of the Edict of Nantes. She was a thoroughly upright, well-bred, and honest woman who had something of a Calvinistic bent which expressed itself in a note of moral severity. This she transmitted to her children, and John Henry kept its mark all his life. However, she also shared with her husband a sense of religious moderation which expressed itself more in regularity of customs and habits than in any kind of emotional fervor. One of her sons-in-law, conjecturing much later on her narrowness of mind, sought to see in it an example of pure Evangelicalism as expressed in the austere doctrine of the eighteenth century English reformers. But her children always denied this interpretation: there was nothing odd in the religion which they received from their mother. It was a contented and tolerant Anglican religion, always somewhat restrained in its enthusiasm and formal in its rites; it was a religion that enjoyed the King James Bible, which they regarded as an ancient patrimony and which they guarded more with fidelity than with passion.

Six children were born into the home of the Newmans, three boys and three girls. John Henry, born February 21, 1801 on Old Broad Street in London was the oldest. Grave and artless, he assumed the burden of the eldest son, taking his role in regard to the little ones very seriously. In absolute contrast, the second son, Charles, was capricious and irresolute. Lured by the demons of his own personal daydreams and Lady Luck, he led the life of a wanderer, always dissatisfied and in pursuit of a new illusion. He remained a constant source of anxiety to his family until the day they gave up on him and let him follow his sad destiny. Francis, some four years younger than John Henry, was at first docile, following in the tracks of his older brother, perhaps in too servile a way. Because of this, once he had attained the age of manhood, he suddenly became jealously defensive of his own identity and chose to assert himself by assuming religous positions contrary to those of the brother whom he had sought to equal.

In this family, the three sisters also present contrasts. Harriet, two years younger than John Henry, had the charm of a witty woman, perhaps more pretentious than real. She prided herself on her writing ability, interested herself in everything, and spoke on any subject. She married a clergyman, the Reverend Thomas Mozley, a friend of Newman. Jemima, the second daughter, born in 1807, was quieter and deeper. She married the brother of Thomas Mozley, also a clergyman. Later, she became the chosen confidant of Newman, especially in the days of his distress. Mary, the youngest, was full of intuition and charm. Death came to take her in the fullness of youth, a few years after the death of their father.

Residing alone with her two daughters, Mrs. Newman was the heart of the home, which her eldest son loved to visit more out of affection for her than out of personal choice. There was always a lot of conversation in this feminine household. They predicted success for their elder brother and anticipated a brilliant ecclesiastical university career for him. Prospects for his marriage were even suggested. This little intimate circle of family and friends had eyes only for the already prestigious young man, whom all found imposing for his grave, serene, and reflective manner.

But now, it is Newman, the child, whom we must rejoin in the beautiful home at Grey's Court. He is ready to go to sleep on the eve of Trafalgar Day when the burning candles in the windows were beginning to dissipate the mystery of the night. The memory of this home abounds enchantingly in many passages of Newman's literary works. He celebrated it in several poems, and described it in several pieces of his correspondence:

> A large plane (tree), a dozen acacias with rough barks, as high as the plane — a Spanish chestnut, a larch. A large magnolia, flowering (in June I think) went up to the house, and the mower's scythe, cutting the lawn, used to sound so sweetly as I lay in a crib — in a front room at top.[2]

One can imagine here the poet, Rainer Maria Rilke, who recalled in his *Cahiers de Malte Laurids Brigge*, the image of a house from his childhood, "fallen on him from infinite heights it smashes itself into his very depth."[3]

Grey's Court remained for Newman the "familiar sanctuary full of affection and of promise"[4] which he sang about with such fondness. As a

---

[2] Letter to Henry Wilberforce, July 1853, W. II., p. 339.
[3] R. M. Rilke: *Les Cahiers de M. L. Brigge*, trans. Betz, p. 26, éd. Emile-Paul, 1947.
[4] *Lyra Apostolica*, ed. Derby, 1841, "Home," p. 2.

young child there, he experienced his very first impressions, the truest and the most lasting, those which were inscribed in the depths of the conscious mind and which were already shaping the man to be and forming his vision of the world. Are not the sentiments of plenitude and vitality which swell the heart of the little four-year-old lad, when the first perfumes of summer penetrate his bedroom, a preview of all the world's enchantments, joys, and charms? The Newman whom we will get to know is intensely susceptible to all the impressions of the external world and to nature's beauties, and he is fully aware of the power of their seductive charm to ensnare and keep one attached to the created universe. The man can already be discovered in the heart of the child who succumbs to the spell of a warm June morning. Still at an age when he is unconscious of his own happiness, he knows only the joy of innocent games; he looks about with eyes of wonder and is attentive to the marvelous bursts of light and of life.

Moreover, Grey's Court not only reveals to John Henry the magic of its colors and its scents, but here he also hears the first mixed calls of a world beyond the veil. In the dusk of the silent evenings in the village of the large suburb, the child perceives the stirrings of a hidden world full of marvels. The spirits whose presence behind the somber screen of the approaching night he guesses, do they not come from another world? This great circle of darkness which projects the shadow of the immense plane tree on the terrace, does it not conceal a strange, perhaps evil power, that prompts the child to bless himself with the sign of the cross when he goes into the night? And how are we to interpret the confession at the beginning of the *Apologia*, the book in which Newman reveals himself:

> I used to wish the Arabian Tales were true: my imagination ran
> on unknown influences, on magical powers, and talismans.... I
> thought life might be a dream.[5]

Already, at the heart of Newman's childhood, we find this inclination which later developed into a genius for transfiguring reality. He looks for the true nature of things in areas other than on the world's surface which reveals only outlines and appearances. For the child of Grey's Court, the imaginary world reached beyond appearances. Not that he sought to recreate piece by piece a marvelous and strange world, inclining toward

---

[5] *Apologia*, p. 14.

dream or fantasy. The mystery is not in external things; it is a part of reality itself. And it is in the depth of beings that it is found; it is here that it is necessary to seek it. It is not by some transmutation of reality that the invisible world manifests itself. Rather it is by a certain kind of outlook and by a type of questioning of our close and familiar universe. It is offered to us in all its obscurity, but too often our perception stops at the surface and does not go beyond appearances, which are only signs of the absolute reality which constitutes the very essence of beings and the truth of their presence among us.

Such an intuition about reality presumes an innocence and a disposition of heart, a certain quality of vision, which is often the privilege of childhood. It was because Newman knew the value of this discovery in the course of his early years at Grey's Court that he always considered childhood the supreme gift offered to human beings at the threshold of their existence to enable them to penetrate into the invisible world.

> We know it from our own recollection of ourselves and our experience as children — that there is in the infant soul, in the first years of its regenerated state, a discernment of the unseen world in the things that are seen; a realization of what is Sovereign and Adorable, and an incredulity and ignorance about what is transient and changeable. The child has this one great gift in that he seems to have lately come from God's presence, and doesn't understand the language of this visible scene, or how it is a temptation, how it is a veil interposing itself between the soul and God.[6]

There is something like a spontaneous accord between the outlook of a child and what is secretly hidden inside of things. The purity of a heart that has not yet been tarnished by contacts with the world is able to discover reality in its true dimension; this is not the reality that is perceived by the senses. The imaginary world which the child creates is definitively closer to the truth for it is the world where vision goes beyond the vast horizons of men and of nature and is given access to mystery and to the transcendent.

Such was his great discovery in those short years of childhood at Grey's Court. Newman, the adult, later knew how to fathom the experience lived by Newman, the child, in that dear home, bursting with life, with its

---

[6] II Par., VI, *The Mind of Little Children*, pp. 266-67.

green lawns and groves. In a life that too often would be subjected to the tension of his doubts and projects, his childhood at Ham was like a pleasant interlude, fresh and pure, which remained bright and clear on the horizon of all his memories. Newman recalled the day when he left Grey's Court with his family. It was in September of 1807; he was not yet seven years old!

Here we must mention the effect of the first lessons of "Bible Religion" on this imaginative child. He learned these lessons from his mother, aided by grandmother Newman and by his Aunt Elizabeth. Like all little English children, John Henry was introduced to the sacred texts, and the Bible remained the manual, par excellence, for all of his religious life. It is difficult to conceive the attraction exercised on a spirit like his by the strength and beauty of the biblical language which he discovered in the Anglican version of King James.

The text speaks as much to the eyes as to the mind, and the impressions which he received from it day after day, were of an aesthetic as well as of a religious order. Bible history revealed some strong and beautiful images to him. His memory collected them as precious symbols, burying them in the deepest recesses of his mind, in order that they might never be lost. Much later, they will spring forth from him spontaneously. Every sermon in St. Mary's at Oxford and at Birmingham is already present in germ because of this first initiation. The revelation of a personal God, living at the very heart of history, so rich in personages and heroes of all sorts, furnished his subconscious with all the richness of the representation of the divine, those precise evocations which give the Protestant soul nourished on the Bible such a vivid and sharp sense of the transcendent. Later studies somewhat blurred this initial certitude of faith. Newman's religious experience, which would be established in a decisive conversion at the age of adolescence, eventually recovered the sense of the Absolute. There is no doubt that his famous expression "God and myself," would not have found in him all its significance, had he not completely discovered the full mystery of God and himself in the course of his Bible readings during early childhood.

At the age of seven, Newman was a boarding student in a private school at Ealing, not far from Richmond. His father, who was fully conscious of the intellectual precociousness of his eldest son, enrolled him there, without realizing how trying it would be for John Henry to be surrounded by students too old for him to find real companionship. He remained there for eight years until December 1816, the date of his departure for Oxford.

The young scholar immediately impressed the director, the amiable Dr. Nicholas, who in all his scholarly life had not known a pupil so exceptionally endowed. On the pages of the private notebook in which John Henry wrote from day to day, we follow the many discoveries of a spirit open to everything, insatiable in its thirst for reading and exhibiting a joy in learning. He discovers the classics, notes with fervor his first encounter with these authors, falls in love with music, composes some librettos for an opera, scribbles some poems, and undertakes a journal.[7] His leisure activities were as refined as his tastes. He loved solitude. He had a repugnance for all athletic sports although he sometimes went swimming and horseback riding to please his father.

As the years went by, the frail, developing adolescent did not seem to have a very religious spirit, in spite of his great moral sensitivity. He inclined toward a sort of colorless deism, based on the humanistic and liberal model characteristic of the beginning of the century. Always thirsty for books, he ventured into the literary frontiers of the philosophies of the preceding century where the seeds of doubt flourished. He studied *The Age of Reason* by Paine. The rationalism of Hume did not appear to have frightened him any more than that of Voltaire, and he transcribed several verses of the latter.[8] His curiosity refused to be bound by any prejudice, nor did his spirit seem to be shocked by the most audacious critics.

A religious upbringing which seemed to be receding into the background, a critical spirit not yet cognizant of its powers, a moral disposition intimately experienced in an upright family, and a depth of superstition inherited from childhood,[9] — this is the Newman of 1816, an adolescent who is about to be touched by a first conversion.

---

[7] See the work of Maisie Ward, *Young Mr. Newman*, Sheed and Ward, 1948, p. 309.

[8] "When I was fourteen, I read Paine's *The Age of Reason* in which there were tracts against the Old Testament, and found pleasure in thinking about the objections which were contained in them. Also I read some of Hume's essays.... Also, I recollect copying out some French verses, perhaps Voltaire's, in denial of the immortality of the soul, and saying to myself something like 'How dreadful, but how plausible!'" *Apologia*, pp. 15-16.

[9] "I used constantly to cross myself on going into the dark." *Apologia*, p. 14.

CHAPTER II

THE FIRST CONVERSION

Myself and my Creator.

Apologia, p. 16.

ALL HIS LIFE, Newman kept the memory of himself as a fifteen-year-old adolescent who in the loneliness of a summer vacation experienced the most moving event of his youth and perhaps of his life, the moment of a religious conversion.

After he became a Cardinal, he confided to Anne Mozley, the editor of his correspondence:

> Of course I cannot myself be the judge of myself; but... I should say that it is difficult to realize or imagine the identity of the boy before and after August 1816.... I can look back at the end of seventy years as if on another person.[1]

For his family, the first months of 1816 were marked by the painful collapse of the bank which Mr. Newman directed. Mr. Newman had to remain in London with his wife to deal with matters concerning the liquidation which he wanted to carry out honorably for himself and his family. During this family crisis, the children were confided to Aunt Elizabeth. John Henry made a brief visit to the family in March when the drama unfolded and was sent away to the College at Ealing where he had to remain after the close of the school term in June.

---

[1] Mozley I, p. 19.

Spending much time by himself in the course of those summer
months, the adolescent learned to appreciate solitude. This was not
difficult for him. Except for the anxiety that the family situation caused
him, he was actually enjoying the happiness of being alone. For a young
man of his age, being alone offered the joy of thinking; it provided a quiet
time for reading and for considering the lofty desires which were filling his
heart. Always eager for knowledge, he was open to a maturity of spirit
which characterizes the gifted student. He was often intellectually stimulated by conversations with his masters who did not hesitate to spend time
with their best pupils.

As a matter of fact, at Ealing, he found a discrete and dedicated
scholar in the Reverend Walter Mayers who possessed a natural gravity
and firmness of manner, combined with a heaviness of style and dullness
of speech. This shy man, who had nothing about him to captivate the
young, nevertheless concealed some secret energies. He was above all a
man of God, preoccupied with the seriousness of the Gospel message,
which was perhaps lost on the thoughtless boys who were doubtlessly ever
ready to mock him. Mayers always had a yearning for a more apostolic
mission and for a pastoral ministry. He hid the simplicity and depth of his
faith under the austere appearance of the rigid professor, indifferent to
sympathy or success. Nevertheless, his example and the straightforward-
ness of his words earned him the esteem of the pupils who knew how to
look beyond his timidity and awkwardness. In religion, he was a convinced
supporter of Evangelicalism.

In the Anglican Church, whose doctrinal features are not easy to
define, the Evangelical stream represented the reforming tendency of the
Methodist movement inspired by John Wesley in the preceding century.
The goal was to bring souls to the purity and rigorous simplicity of faith.
This movement was conceived less as an adhesion to some dogmas than
as an experience of assured salvation. From this came the importance
given to the "conversion," the "new birth" which was to give to each one
the certainty of his own salvation experienced through the grace of Jesus
Christ. Accompanying this conversion was an austere moralism which
colored the piety and the conduct of true Evangelicals.[2]

---

[2] In the religious history of the eighteenth century, Evangelicalism, born of a need for
reform, stirred up by the preaching of John Wesley, blazed an austere path between the
current Methodists, from which it was derived and from which it separated itself, and

This religion, moreover, had its rites, its traditions, and its temples, where the initiates came seeking consolations and religious fervor. For numerous souls, conversion remained their highest ambition and in this experience, they discovered with luminous certitude that they had a divine enlightenment.

To the Methodists as well as to the Evangelicals, conversion was *the* supreme religious experience. Without doubt, the first group, the Methodists, experienced their conversions in the collective trances where they encountered the same kind of frenzy as that of the faithful penitents. The second group, the Evangelicals, were more modest and looked for an interior illumination accompanied by an absolute knowledge of having been elected to eternal salvation. But the two "conversions" are identical in substance because they call forth the same psychic responses and the same conviction of salvation by faith.

Vehemently or peacefully, according to the differences in nature or temperament, the feelings and the trances associated with the conversion are necessary for arousing the certainty of salvation, so desirable for the faithful. The essence of a "new birth" lies in the conviction of a singular predestination, acquired by a strong effort of the will and of the imagination. One should experience the certainty of God's pardon in a stirring intuition, which is necessary to reach the certitude that Christ has redeemed one from sin. This is a proof which is as absolute and as infallible as the fact of one's very existence. Yielding to a flood of emotions, the heart lets itself go in some touching avowal of gratitude and love for its God who has filled it from His most bountiful mercy.

At Newman's time in England in the 1800's, religious fervor was always measured by the interior upheavals of which John Wesley and his disciples had given so strongly an example in the preceding century.

---

the Established Church which it wished to renew and to which it claimed to remain faithful. In spite of its adherence to Methodism, it distinguished itself from it on two capital points: on the one hand, it denied the most rigid theses of Calvinism which inspired the first disciples of Wesley; on the other hand, it remained careful to keep the forms of ecclesiastical jurisdiction of the Established Church in opposition to Wesley and his followers who considered "the world as their parish"; they did not hesitate to defy the bishops and to worm their way in everywhere. It was this intrusion of the Methodists into their dioceses which sealed their break with the Established Church and led to the birth of a new sect, also designated by the label of *non-conformist*. On the origins and evolution of Evangelicalism, see Appendix I.

In opposition to the liberal stream born from the philosophy of enlightenment which was beginning to detach souls from religion, the mystique of the "new birth" was the temptation offered to all souls who were anxious for spiritual progress. In Wales, the Methodist "cenacles" were still numerous. The memory of the great preachers of the preceding age had not disappeared from the consciences which had been stirred up by the wind of reform. Charles Wesley, John's brother, left some hymns of a touching fervor which are still sung today.[3] Evangelicalism, which claimed to distinguish itself from Methodism, was itself inspired by his piety and his religious life.

A current of reform had even developed inside the Anglican Church which began to bear fruit during the first years of the century. Under the influence of William Wilberforce, the campaign against slavery was actively led; the missionary effort of the Evangelicals revealed to the Anglican Church a task which it had forgotten. All these endeavors seemed to be stimulating to the emotional piety which was the soul of this reform. The religion of the heart thus burst forth in all the fascination of a moral crusade.

In his autobiographical work, the *Apologia Pro Vita Sua* written in 1864, Newman recalled the circumstances which caused the profound change in his religious life and aroused his inner call to conversion. He recognized his debt to Mr. Mayers, whose words, advice, and suggestions about spiritual reading, introduced him to the strict way of Evangelical perfection and of faith. But the question is: What was the exact meaning of this first spiritual experience? In following the path opened by Mayers, was Newman accepting his beliefs? And was this religious change which Newman was experiencing in his conscience due to a conversion of the Evangelical type such as his master was able to reveal to him? This question is important for it concerns Newman's first religious orientation. Let us allow him to expand on it from his memories:

---

[3] On the spirituality of "new birth," its origin and nature, see the book of Swarts, *Salut par la Foi et Conversion Brusque*, Paris, 1931. Swarts studies the spiritual descendants of John Wesley: "The behavior of the Methodists all this time maintains a dramatic character, violent, extraordinary in the strongest sense of the term, which makes it so captivating...," p. 265. See also Penido, *The Religious Conscience*, Paris, 1938. On the spirituality of the hymns of Charles Wesley, see the short study of Msgr. Davis, "Christ in the Spirituality of the Non-Conformists," *Intellectual Life*, Oct. 1946, p. 29 ff.

When I was fifteen, (in the Autumn of 1816), a great change of thought took place in me. *I fell under the influence of a definite Creed, and received into my intellect impressions of dogma,* which through God's mercy, have never been effaced or obscured. Above and beyond the conversations and sermons of the excellent man, long dead, the Rev. Walter Mayers, of Pembroke College, Oxford, who was the human means of this beginning of divine faith in me, was the effect of the books, which he put into my hands, all of the school of Calvin. One of the first books I read was a work of Romaine's; I neither recollect the title nor the contents, except one doctrine, which of course I do not include among those which I believe to have come from a divine source, viz., the doctrine of final perseverance.

I received it at once, and believed that the inward conversion of which I was conscious (and of which I still am more certain than that I have hands and feet) would last into the next life, and that I was elected to eternal glory. I have no consciousness that this belief had any tendency whatever to lead me to be careless about pleasing God. I retained it till the age of twenty-one, when it gradually faded away; but I believe that it had some influence on my opinions, in the direction of those childish imaginations which I have already mentioned, viz. in isolating me from the objects which surrounded me, in confirming me in my mistrust of the reality of material phenomena, and making me rest in the thought of two, and two only, absolute and luminously self-evident beings, myself and my Creator, -- for while I considered myself predestined to salvation, my mind did not dwell upon others, as fancying them simply passed over, not predestined to eternal death. I only thought of the mercy to myself.[4]

In spite of its lucidity, this analysis which seems to have said it all appears simple only to the superficial reader. Like every autobiographical text of Newman, this one is not as simple as it appears. This straightforward account glides over all the profundity of the interior experience. A simple literary exegesis risks the worst misconception if it confines itself only to this single insight without recourse to the other sources which clarify the true meaning of the text in the *Apologia*.

---

[4] *Apologia*, p. 16 ff., author's underscoring.

Numerous signs would make one think indeed that Newman's conversion would be in all aspects similar to the type of Evangelical conversion that the enthusiastic apostles of the "new birth" were striving to arouse in the generous souls disappointed by the cold ways of the Established Church. In the account of his conversion, one can discern the same isolation of a conscience which appears to escape from the constraints of beings and things, the same sentiment of being alone and relying solely upon God, with the same assurance of knowing himself to be saved. Doubtless, we are not seeing the ecstatic upheaval found in so many conversions, but we know that this is not essential. Authentic Evangelicals like Thomas Scott had known conversion only as a tranquil and serene experience. Newman affirmed him in the *Apologia* as the one to whom "I almost owe my soul."[5]

It is then very natural to think that the conversion of Newman was of the same type he found among those who introduced him into their spiritual family. The adolescent quitting the vagueness of a religion more deistic than Christian anchored himself firmly in the Evangelical faith to which he had given a loyalty as spontaneous as it was decisive.

The numerous historians who, after Bremond, have studied the conversion of 1816 have not failed to emphasize the sincerity of the assent given by Newman to Evangelicalism. Although a change in sentiment occurred in the years that followed, no serious doubt was raised about his acceptance of Evangelicalism at the moment of his conversion.[6]

Or, is it precisely the steadfastness of this assent which one has the right to contest, for the account in the *Apologia* may lead into error. Newman did not try, when considering his conversion itself, to disassociate the elements which gave it its religious depth from those which were purely external. Indeed, the circumstances and external conditions in

---

[5] *Apologia*, p. 17. Thomas Scott, convert to Evangelicalism, was a pastor and writer: his most celebrated work, *Force of Truth*, 1779, is a classic in the spirituality which will exercise a considerable attraction on Newman.

[6] Henri Bremond, *Essai de Biographie Psychologique*, p. 191 ff. Bremond seems to think that the illusion of certainty regarding his salvation accompanied the wholly interior sentiment of conversion. It was only after 1821 that Newman came, little by little, to have his own doubts about it, accusing Evangelicalism of misinterpretation and denouncing finally the initial illusion through a kind of hidden "resentment." Having become so bitterly disappointed, he would then have broken in a definitive fashion with the Evangelical creed.

which the conversion took place risk concealing the profound nature of it. Appearances seem to favor the Evangelical thesis but the reality is, no doubt, more hidden and on the whole much simpler.

It is necessary to remember that this conversion concerns a fifteen-year-old adolescent and the conversion of any adolescent by reason of the feelings and emotions which it provokes will never have the same fullness nor the same clarity as the conversion of an adult. Without doubt, Newman, the boy, already revealed the trait of an exceptional precocity. He had long left behind him the simple games of childhood, but he still remained a young boy. Like all young people, particularly those who have a taste for hidden and secret thoughts, he was extremely open to the indistinct calls of living life to the fullest, calls that would lead him to an exceptional destiny. Addicted to his dreams and anxious about his freedom, the youth wished to conquer himself in the pursuit of an absolute of which he invented the forms at the same time that he received the calls. The adolescent relished the ideal, notwithstanding all the anxieties about perfection or about success; he created his own ideal even before discerning its demands. When, along his path, there appeared a master or a friend whose life and example were rich in the values to which he aspired, he was ready to be influenced, less by discussion and reasoning, than by the absolute need of an ideal. There is always a certain conformism in the admiration of young disciples who have found their master and it will often take years of patient searching and reflection to discover the way whereby one is finally his real self. Furthermore, the adolescent becomes the vassal of the model he has chosen. However, if the ties tend to come loose or unravel to the extent that the initial fervor of the association diminishes, still it retains nonetheless its undeniable riches; it allows for the nurturing of profound values to which the man of tomorrow will refer during the course of his whole life. Underneath the superficial responses which soon disappear, there subsists some durable foundation; this consists of the convictions and the certainties which are going to definitively direct his personal destiny.

Would not this evolution of feelings, so frequent in every adolescent anxious for an ideal and for security, have been Newman's experience at the time of his conversion? This young boy in his fifteenth year believes he has converted to Evangelicalism when in fact he has converted himself simply to God!

Behind the ambiguous forms of religion expressed by unquestionably respectable masters whom he wished to imitate, the adolescent had an illusion of acquiring the ideal of perfection to which he aspired without knowing too much about it.

Many confidences in the *Journal*, written at the time of his conversion, are indeed very significant for understanding Newman's state of mind. They throw light on the account in the *Apologia* and permit a comprehension of it with all its nuances.

There is a first admission that ought to hold our attention:

> I recollect, in 1815 I believe, thinking that I should like to be virtuous but not religious. There was something in the latter idea I did not like. Nor did I see the meaning of loving God.[7]

Thus, more than from a religious fidelity, the student of the Ealing school was anxious for moral perfection. The call from a sovereign God made less sense than the demands of a conscience characterized by sincerity and uprightness. Moreover, his readings drew him into the dangerous paths of a deism perfectly reconcilable with a certain moral strictness. Likewise, the adolescent discovered that virtue must be acted upon in order to be true. His conversion was going to change all of that, dissipating the fog of moralism in the ardent clarity of an encounter with God.

One can imagine the role played by Mayers, whose discreet presence in the course of those months of vacation in the empty school acted as an attraction for the young lonely boy. In the meetings which developed, the timid scholar was able to express his better self. He was going to succeed in gaining the confidence of Newman and soon revealed to him the true meaning of life, the seriousness of the call that God addresses to every soul, and the inestimable reward of conversion. Mayers, finding a receptive soul, perhaps succeeded in arousing and persuading him too much, for the docile pupil would obey before acquiescing. The grave warnings of Mayers detached him from a deism hardly realized and revealed to him the austere call of the narrow way of life. The young man was assuredly captivated; he knew the exhilarating and hidden exultation of one who has found his way and who has encountered the excitement of God's presence.

---

[7] M. I., p. 19.

It was his conversion! Newman had no doubt that his spiritual experience gave him the privilege of this "second birth" into which the strict Evangelicals were initiated. Mayers confirmed him in the feeling that he was an elect of God, and the adolescent was ready to let himself be convinced of this truth.

Nevertheless, during the time which followed, this enthusiastic certainty tended to fade away. All too clearly, the pupil was searching for an explanation of the grace with which he had been filled and which he was told was a sign of his predestination. He started raising some doubts and posing some questions. He wished to understand what God said to him and what was expected of him. A letter from December of the same year revealed Mayers' preoccupation with forming the pure Evangelical ideal in the disciple who already seemed to be distancing himself.

Indeed, in the month of December 1816, Newman left Ealing for Oxford. At his departure, Mayers gave him a work to read, the *Private Thoughts* of Bishop Beveridge. At the end of the month, the master wrote these very significant lines to the young student:

> On perusing it you will see that the opinions which we have discussed, though at present singular, are not novel, nor are they without authority, for they are deduced from the only authentic source. To that source let me direct your attention. Be more disposed to form your sentiments upon religion from that, than to adopt and interpret it to your opinions.[8]

This letter is a fundamental document for understanding Newman's conversion in the month of August. Several months had scarcely passed when Mayers, who had exerted his influence on an apparently docile pupil, betrayed a secret alarm in seeing the pupil free himself from his tutelage. Newman did not comply without reservation to the principles instilled in him with such great insistence and concern. He seemed anxious to keep his own originality, even at the risk of putting aside the counsels of the master when they appeared contrary or alien to his personal experience.

---

[8] *Correspondence with John Keble and others*, p. 115. One need not conclude that Bishop Beveridge was Evangelical. Having died in 1708, he is well before the reform of Wesley. But his doctrine based on the will to improve is a prelude to the ideas of the Evangelicals; and Mayers comments in this sense in *Private Thoughts*.

Nevertheless, in the years which followed, the disciple was not yet clearly conscious of such a divergence. In good grace, he submitted himself to Mayers' commanding directions. He read the devotional books which were recommended to him: Beveridge, Doddridge, Law, and Romaine, "all of the school of Calvin."[9] He listened to the sermons which led him towards predestination and efficacious grace.[10]

He even scribbled some writings, one of them drawn clearly from the Calvinistic inspiration: "These will be punished with eternal punishment."[11] More and more, the thought of predestination took possession of his spirit and an obsession with eternal salvation accompanied it. There are in these dispositions more of an apparent conformism than of any real adherence to the Evangelical faith. Newman was seeking to persuade himself that the conversion of 1816 really was the "second birth" which the books described and which an all too impressive master announced to him. He kept this illusion until much later when his inner life grew strong and when the realities of the pastoral ministry showed him the inconsistency of a doctrine so evidently contrary to true peace of soul.

Several testimonies from 1821 and 1826 are definitive:

> I speak of conversion with great diffidence, being obliged to adopt the language of books. For my own feelings, as far as I remember, were so different from any account I have ever read that I dare not go by what may be an individual case.[12]

In 1826, Newman was still more explicit:

> In the matter in question, that is conversion, my own feelings were not violent but a returning to, a renewing of principles, under the power of the Holy Spirit, which I already felt, and in a measure acted on when young.[13]

Hence, we discover the essence of Newman's conversion: it is the doctrinal character of a religious certitude more than of any feeling of

---

[9] If Romaine (+1795) affirms some of the most extreme principles of Calvinism, Law (+1761) by contrast jettisoned all rigorism and his moral doctrine carries on that of Beveridge.

[10] Sermon, June 29, 1817. M. I., p. 21.

[11] Ibid., p. 20.

[12] M. I., p. 109.

[13] Ibid., p. 109.

consolation. The young man received a shock to the spirit; a sense of submission and dependency filled his soul: "I fell under the influence of a definite creed, and received into my intellect impressions of dogma."[14] In contrast to Kant who, under the influence of Hume, "awakens himself from his dogmatic slumber," Newman at fifteen escaped the deism which held him captive until then and submitted to a revelation from on High.

The account in the *Apologia* thus appears clearer. The change of feelings as a result of the conversion is easily discerned. With the conversion to dogma, however clear and decisive it was, it had some Evangelical overtones, which risked falsifying the true nature of the conversion. In the books suggested by Mayers, the young boy searched for the key which would enable him to comprehend his astounding experience of the month of August:

> One of the first books I read was a work of Romaine's; I neither recollect the title nor the contents, except one doctrine, which of course I do not include among those which I believe to have come from a divine source, viz. the doctrine of final perseverance.[15]

This ambiguous doctrine disappeared many years later, and with it, the entire Evangelical system. Nevertheless, at this time, he still maintained some illusions about it. During the years which followed his conversion, Newman was seeking to copy exactly the models which were proposed to him. He applied himself to restricting his life within the limits of the narrow way; he made resolutions and cultivated virtue, not without giving the impression of being pleased with himself in the image of his own perfection. The spectacle which he offered to his family around him was one of a solitary soul, not understood. But everyone knows that misunderstanding by adults is the most efficacious ploy for adolescent heroism.

He reflected:

> Although it is far from pleasant to give my reasons, inasmuch as I shall appear to set myself up, and to be censuring recreations, and those who indulge in them: presenting my scruples with

---

[14] *Apologia*, p. 16.
[15] *Apologia*, p. 16.

humility and a due obedience to my parents; open to conviction,
and ready to obey in a matter so dubious as this is, and to act
against my judgment if they command, thus satisfying at once my
own conscience and them. [16]

The first and most tangible outcome of the conversion was the
shutting up of the young man within himself. The desire for perfection,
which was well in keeping with his temperament, was stimulated. There
is no doubt that the Evangelical spirituality had a lasting influence on
Newman, not so much because of certain of its doctrinal convictions which
fell away quickly enough, but because of the rigors of the moral conformism to which he subjected himself. Judgment on the sinful world, the
denying of himself, and the strict preoccupation with spiritual progress
were to be retained in the depths of Newman's religious sensibility. In the
first years of his student life at Oxford, he walled himself off in voluntary
isolation that revealed the image of a very withdrawn young person, too
much a stranger to the world, to the point of being indifferent to the society
of men who made it up. Perhaps, the first traits in the Newmanian legend
come from this isolation of a soul, which one respects but at the same time
fears. Nothing creates more anxiety and moral anguish than the isolation
of a man who lives among his fellow men and who does not live as they
do.

However, the true fruit of the conversion of 1816 did not consist of
a turning inward of a youthful conscience longing for perfection and
asceticism. Newman at that time overemphasized his personal desire for
holiness and underestimated revelation, which is the source of all true calls
to holiness. It was the beneficial discovery of a personal and living God in
the profound depth of his own soul which was the fundamental fruit of his
conversion. "Intimior meo mihi." ["Closer to me than I am to myself."]

For the first time, he experienced a "terrible and incommunicable"
relationship with a God who spoke to his conscience and revealed to him
His transcendence. It taught him his own proper condition as a creature.

---

[16] M. I., p. 19. (Manuscript 1817). But Newman maintains every assurance of being on
the right track. Thus this curious text of a personal note: "The reality of conversion, as
cutting at the root of doubt, providing a chain between God and the Soul, that is with
every link complete; I know I am right. How do you know it? I know I know." (M. I.,
p. 21).

Thus, his conversion consisted entirely of a recognition of the dependency of his own being with regard to the One who is the beginning and the Father of all that is. Singularly, that which appeared to him as the most inalienable and the least contested good was the understanding of his personal individuality, "myself and my creator." It is the same message, at the level of the experience of the believer, of the revelation in the desert, "I am who am."

If God is the Absolute, all existence justifies itself only in a relation of dependency, and the dependency of the soul calls for a submission of the will. The conversion of Newman was nothing other than his entrance into the realm of faith: the first step is in referring oneself to a Sovereign God, who is making Himself known. Henceforth, his destiny would find itself fixed. The Newmanian spirituality, which expresses itself in *self-surrender,* in the highest and purest form, manifested itself in these early outlines: God is present to my soul, inside of me and infinitely above me. My destiny is delivered to His guiding presence; it does not belong to me because I am not able to dispose of anything unless under His watchful providence. It is only for me henceforth to discern the signs in which I recognize the existence of my Creator and His nearness.

This is the whole practice of faith. The man who desires to live by faith has nothing else to do but to seek and discover the signs from God in order to grasp the pledge of certitude. The fulfillment of every destiny identifies itself with the total submission of the conscience to the interior Master. Henceforth, Newman's every effort was to detect in himself the living power of God, to see the marks of it in his soul, to recognize how his soul was invaded by His presence, and how it was filled with truth and driven towards its destiny. In his personal history, Newman had a presentiment of the mystery of God who probes the reins and hearts of every creature. The germ of the idea of Providence was in the experience of his conversion. Having seen God act in him, Newman understood how He acted upon others. Henceforth, the preacher of St. Mary's, Oxford, was to be attentive only to the mysteries of the human soul because there he recognized a Presence whom he himself felt with emotion in the days of his youth. Newman, who was to become a marvelous analyst of the feelings and realities of the conscience, always knew how to return to the event of his conversion, which revealed to him the mystery of his own existence at the same time that it revealed the mystery of God. Indeed, if God is a mystery, it is evidently necessary that the meeting of man with the

Creator also be a mystery. It is the principle of spiritual inwardness itself which is here at stake. "God's presence is not discerned at the time when it is upon us, but afterwards, when we look back t ）on what is gone and over."[17]

Newman did not know immediately the entire meaning of his conversion; but it is not too bold to affirm that his entire spirituality was already incorporated into this unique experience, so providential in this boy of fifteen.

---

[17] IV Par; XVII, p. 889, "Christ Manifested in Remembrance."

CHAPTER III

THE CALL OF GOD

Thou must hear the sound of
the still voice divine.

Verses, p. 25

AFTER SOME MONTHS of waiting at home with his family, Newman enrolled at Oxford in June of 1817, having left Ealing at the end of the previous year. During the month of December, his father enrolled him in Trinity College. He had a secular ambition for John Henry and already saw in him the great man of the family. Law seemed to Mr. Newman to be the surest step up on the ladder to a brilliant career, and he tried to influence his son along those lines.

Upon arriving at Oxford at the age of sixteen, still a young boy in every way, had Newman any suspicion that his life would be bound to the site and history of this ancient and prominent city for a long time, maybe forever? He was completely astonished and carried away by the admirable harmony of the college buildings, so different and yet so familiar in the variety of their styles. The intimacy and quiet of their sheltering walls, which maintained the traditions of the University, intrigued him. The city is situated in majestic peacefulness between the still banks of the Isis and Cherwell rivers, and the main streets, High and Broad, stand still in their past: noisy only in the hours of leisure and during holidays. The country in particular enchanted Newman; those charming rolling meadows, divided by groves, enclosed the city in isolation and rustic beauty like an incomparable jewel. From the very first day, Newman felt himself to be fully in accord with this city and the Oxonian tradition.

In *Loss and Gain*, one of Newman's novels, there is an account of a conversion to Catholicism. Several very revealing pages describe the charm which Oxford exerted on the hero:

> I am just going for a turn into the meadows... this is to me the best time of the year; everything is beautiful; the laburnums are out, and the may. There is a greater variety of trees there than in any other place I know hereabouts; and the planes (trees) are so touching just now, with their small multitudinous green hands half-opened; and there are two or three such fine dark willows stretching over the Cherwell; I think some dryad inhabits them; and as you wind along, just over your right shoulder is the Long Walk, with the Oxford buildings seen between the elms.[1]

Newman, indeed, always attached great value to a familiarity with things and persons. Such familiarity creates for every man the singular universe of his own existence. To the degree to which the adult wishes to remain faithful to all that which he had been, he is bound to the world of his childhood and his youth. The impression of things is never so decisive as it is during the stages of life which coincide with the unfolding of promise or potential. Each personal destiny manifests itself in searching for its own way, docile to all calls that seem to fulfill its desired goal. It is then that the bonds of affection establish themselves. A monument, a college, or a city are all symbols of a personal attachment that cannot be forgotten without betraying something of oneself.

Thus, Newman himself encountered the principle of "genius locorum," an interest in specific locations, which he later advocated in his *Idea of a University* as a way of providing balance and depth in the education of young people. He embraced this principle with devotion in this Oxonian city one day in June of 1817.

For Newman, Oxford was at first Trinity. This college is sheltered behind the high walls of prestigious Balliol, whose facade of ivy looks on St. Giles and the Martyr's Memorial. Closed off from view by its majestic-like iron gate, which gives it the look of a convent, its sixteenth century

---

[1] *Loss and Gain*, Newman, Longmans Green and Co., London 1898, pp. 6-7. Also, see the celebrated passage about the hero, Charles Reding, and his farewell to Oxford, p. 430.

buildings, with their beautiful Palladian-style chapel, nestle around the quadrangle as two wings of a cloister.

Under the direction of his tutor, Dr. Short, Newman prepared for his first examination, the Baccalaureate of Arts. His ambition was not limited to just obtaining this title, which was well within his reach. He desired honors, that is "passing with honors or distinction," the highest accolade conferred on the best graduates. Despite working hard for ten to twelve hours a day, he failed. The disappointment was so cruel that he was close to being discouraged.

However, he recovered quickly. Seeing in this failure a first mistake of only relative importance, he freed himself from the servitude of examinations and devoted himself for a while to personal studies. He was more preoccupied with enriching his educational development than in binding himself to an academic program.

In the months which followed, Newman was more and more tempted by the thought of consecrating himself to both an academic and an ecclesiastical career. Thus, he wrote in his notes on January 11, 1821: "My father said to me that I should decide about my future. So I chose; and determined on the church. Thank God, this is what I have prayed for." He envisioned himself becoming a fellow in one of Oxford's great colleges.

In Newman's time, nothing was more typical of life at an English university than the institution of fellows; they were the inheritors of a medieval tradition in which every cleric was both a man of the church and a man of learning. Each college had its own fellows who were chosen by competitive examinations. The fellowship was the most coveted title at the university, and the prestige of each college was measured by the quality and fame of its fellows. When he returned to Oxford in October, 1821, Newman aspired to the most prestigious fellowship, the least accessible of all, the one for Oriel College. In the sleepy Oxford of the beginning of the century, Oriel College stood out as a symbol of intelligence and culture. The Oriel men were conspicuous for the prestige of their talents and for the independence of their spirit, which made them veritable mandarins of letters and thought.

Because of his recent failure, Newman was not held in very great esteem, which was typical of the university world, so over-attentive to such matters. Therefore, Newman appeared to be too eager to attempt the impossible by deciding to enter a competition in which his chances of success were only one in a hundred. Nevertheless, he decided to take the chance with such firm resolution that his most intimate friends were disconcerted. He approached the task systematically and with discipline; he alone had the assurance that his efforts would be rewarded. And the marvel was accomplished: on April 12, 1822, the bell towers of the University rang out the election of John Henry Newman to an Oriel fellowship. The masters of Oriel did not hesitate to prefer Newman over all other contestants as they were attracted by the sagacity of his mind with its unexpected resources. The joy of the young man whose expectations were fulfilled was recorded in a simple note of his *Journal*: "Today, I have been elected fellow of Oriel." His future was now assured and he became aware that this would bring him a promotion which would place him among the elite of Oxford.

His religion was still strongly tinged with Evangelicalism. Since the time at Trinity, he had molded his religion strictly on the spiritual model defined by Mayers. As was the case in the days following his conversion, this predestined youth feared being false to his grace if he even deviated one inch from the lines stipulated by his master. From the first day, Newman shut himself off and refused the company and the excesses of student life, which almost appeared to him to be contaminated by the spirit of the devil. The common pleasures and the tradition of lax morals in a cloister-like milieu, which was typical of university campuses, was like a plague to him. He was disgusted by the "Gaudy," the traditional day of enjoyment when students indulged themselves in noisy drinking parties. He condemned these excesses and found in denouncing them a pretext for isolation. He acknowledged he was happy to live "like a hermit." In the notes and correspondence of this period, there is a rather irritating touch of inflexibility. John Henry looks at himself in a mirror of virtue which reflects an uptight image of himself. He keeps a strict account of his resolutions and of his progress. Without doubt, this is actually a part of the Newmanian character. It is a spontaneous inclination to clear-sightedness about himself and others, but there is surely also a good dose of narrow-mindedness and scrupulosity. One can imagine the youth having learned well the lessons of his Evangelical masters as he searched to recognize in the world around him their simplistic views. According to their teachings, there are only the good and the bad; the world breathes the odor of fire and brimstone; it is necessary to hold oneself apart; and the reward for such renunciation is the mercy of God. As early as June 16, 1817, he wrote about his first impressions to his father:

Besides, I did not know anyone, and, after having been used to a number about me, I felt solitary.... I am not noticed at all except by being silently stared at. I am glad, not because I wish to be apart from them and ill-natured, but because I really do not think I should gain the least advantage from their company.[2]

Much later, in the course of the long vacation of 1820, when he remained alone at Trinity, he was elated that his thoughts were "becoming more and more serious." Then, the soon to be recipient of the Oriel fellowship, gave up neither his daily practices nor his solitary thoughts. He was later to confide in the *Apologia*:

During the first years of my residence at Oriel, though proud of my College, I was not quite at home there. I was very much alone, and I used to take my daily walk by myself. I recollected once meeting Dr. Copleston, then Provost, with one of the fellows. He turned around, and with the kind courteousness which sat so well on him, made a bow and said, *"Nunquam, minus solus, quam cum solus."* ["Never less alone than when alone."][3]

Newman realized that he had an excess of timidity which gave him the appearance of being uptight. This aroused in those around him some doubts about his resources and possibilities. On several occasions, he noticed that he was "trembling within himself"; because of this, his failure to get honors at Trinity did not really surprise him much, but it did vex him. It brought this reflection from his mother: "Your fault is a want of self-confidence and a dissatisfaction with yourself."[4]

The moral rigidity of the Evangelical faith influenced the young man's judgment of himself and other things. It put a damper on all the joys of studying and on all his ambitions. While preparing for his examinations in August of 1820, he shared this confidence with his brother, Frank:

Here at Oxford, I am most comfortable. The quiet and stillness of everything around me tends to calm and lull those emotions which the near prospect of my grand examination, and a heart too

---

[2] M. I., pp. 26-27.

[3] *Apologia*, p. 25.

[4] M. I., p. 51. Same confidence in a letter to one of his sisters.

solicitous about fame and too fearful of failure are continually striving to excite.... How in my future life, if I do live shall I look back with a sad smile at these days! It is my daily, and I hope heartfelt prayer, that I may not get any honors here if they are to be the least cause of sin to me.[5]

When he competed for the Oriel fellowship several months later, the same cry surged from his troubled heart. He wrote on November 15, 1821, at the height of his studies: "How active still are the evil passions of vainglory, ambition, etc. within me... they spread and overflow and deluge me."[6] And several days later, "my heart boils over with vainglorious anticipation of success." On February 5, 1822, he scribbled this prayer: "O Lord! dispose of me as will best promote Thy glory, but give me resignation and contentment."[7]

The excitement and even the triumph of his election to Oriel did not take away his self-control. Having reached the enviable position of being able to enjoy the prestige "of living and dying a fellow of Oriel," Newman still seemed willing to escape the success and easy triumph. He confessed his shortcomings; he acknowledged the scruples of his conscience; he was obviously intimidated by his new prestige and the thought of sharing the life of important people. Although Newman's influence and sovereign power over hearts would not be long in coming to light, he shut himself up more than ever in his interior solitude by a sort of auto-defense mechanism. The *Apologia* gives us decisive testimony of such an emotional state;[8] letters tell us the same thing. They reveal his moral anxiety between the fear of human aspirations and the fear of apathy or lukewarmness which he denounced with unrelenting rigor. He would soon note, with great clarity of vision, that his moral austerity bordered on intransigence. It contained the germ of scorn and of arrogance:

> We are apt to get censorious with respect to others as soon as we ourselves have adopted any new strictness. At least, that is the case with me.... Humility is the root of charity.[9]

[5] *Ibid.*, p. 38.
[6] *Ibid.*, p. 59.
[7] *Ibid.*, p. 60.
[8] *Apologia*, pp. 18-19.
[9] M. I., p. 70.

Nevertheless, all these struggles of conscience were not in vain. They contributed to assuring fidelity to the ideal of a religious life, even if in this case, they were tinged by the Evangelical spirit. Newman, who was too strictly tied to Evangelicalism for far too long a time, would gradually discover at Oriel the gloomy vanity of a system which, under the cover of holiness and perfection, forced a man always to look at himself, at the risk of isolating him from the simple enjoyments of ordinary life and of maintaining him in a constant state of anxiety and spiritual tension. In entering into the very new world of Oriel, the young fellow permitted himself to gently enter into the spirit of the house. It was a sort of peaceful humanism, often bordering on intellectual dilettantism, which accorded more weight to original ideas than to their truth. Thus, Newman entered into another world, a world of the intellect, of paradox, and of culture. He was so intelligent and so virtuous that he could resist its allurement, but he was also clear-sighted enough to recognize the wisdom of those men who did not profess Evangelicalism.

Newman's faith would receive some rude blows from his colleagues in the Common Room of Oriel. Their influence would broaden the horizons of Newman's thought and spirituality and eventually a brief pastoral experience would completely eradicate the mystique of Mayers in his soul. Would this tempt him to deny all his past resolutions and efforts? Would he discard the system which had nourished an illusion for too long a time? Would putting the Evangelical ideal aside without any apparent crisis create in the young fellow a void which would expose him to a much graver and more subtle danger?

There is a certain inclination of the mind which, under the guise of "liberalism," espouses freedom of thought and denies every authority other than its own reason. Scarcely out from under the shadowy fever of Evangelicalism, Newman found himself confronted at Oriel with the first seductions of the "mal du siècle" [evil of the century] which were to have a destructive influence on many minds and which Newman would denounce with utmost vigor much later. Earlier, he had already experienced the power of doubt and the keen joy of dialectics. His lively intellect made him a thousand times more vulnerable to the fascination of liberalism than to the laborious constraints of Evangelicalism. The conversion of 1816 had for a time removed him from this danger but the temptation was to surge anew. The miracle of his youth was that he escaped from this danger at the very same moment that he freed himself from the Evangelical tutelage. In the *Apologia*, however, he was to judge himself severely with regard to this period of his life when he commenced "to prefer intellectual to moral excellence."[10]

One can well imagine that the still timid and hesitant young newcomer was attracted to those liberal minds which were unfettered in thought, subtle, brilliant and daring. This group of intellectuals was given the bizarre name of "Noetics." The very name is synonymous with the Oriel Common Room. The Noetics declared themselves enemies of all conformism, whether it was religious or philosophical. They combined independence of judgment with the rigors of thought; they speculated on everything audacious but they were more apt to entertain skepticism than to create a new order of thinking. The absence of positive and concrete responsibilities made the Noetics more dilettantes than realists.

It was said of Whately, the most sagacious and most paradoxical among them, that he used the minds of his disciples as an anvil with which to forge ideas. Alongside him, Hawkins was the principal representative of the group at Oriel which continued the scholarly reforms that had been started by the humanist Eveleigh, a man of the preceding generation.[11]

In spite of Newman's modest and unimpressive appearance, Whately certainly surmised his hidden merits and his authentic value. He became his mentor and attempted to make him bloom, helping him to leave his shell and to find a place among the aristocracy of the gifted.[13] The young "fellow," now less attached to Evangelicalism, allowed himself to be won over without too much resistance. Thus, he manifested an overt sympathy for the Noetics during those years. In 1826, he became a tutor of Oriel and this function gave him direct responsibility for some of the students entrusted to his direction. When discussing this period in the *Apologia*, he accused himself of sacrificing too much to the mood of the times and of expressing a secret scorn "for Christian Antiquity."[14] He was caught at his

---

[10] *Apologia*, p. 24.
[11] On the influence of the Noetics at Oriel, see the note of Newman on liberalism at the end of Appendix to the *Apologia*, p. 216. To the celebrated names of Whately and Hawkins, it is necessary to join also those of Copleston, Arnold, Hampden, and Blanco White. This last was closely bound to Newman, although he followed an opposite path from the one of his friend: an adventuresome spirit, he began in Catholicism only to end up, after a romantic enough career, in the frontiers of the most vaporous liberalism.
[12] *Apologia*, p. 22.
[13] *Ibid.*, p. 24.

own game and, certain of his pupils astutely discerned donnishness in him. He succumbed to an academic posture — a gravity of manner on the part of the master who takes everything too seriously and assumes a high-brow manner in making the slightest remark.[13] However, these are only sins of youth, if sins at all. Too many witnesses attested to the fact that during those years of searching, Newman showed an indisputably strict conscience and a very real desire for moral progress.[15]

On June 13, 1824, he received the diaconate in the Anglican Church and secured a post as vicar in the poorest parish in Oxford, Saint Clement's. He was kept very busy meeting his parishioners and visiting the sick. The result of these contacts was to loosen his last bonds to Evangelicalism and to dispel his last doubts which were born of prolonged solitude.

His pastoral care and his concern that his activities should have an apostolic sense were reflected in the way he organized his studies and his teaching at Oriel. In a very significant note sent to Mrs. Newman in response to a glowing letter of congratulations for his first sermons, he said: "There is always the danger of the love of literary pursuits assuming too prominent a place in the thoughts of a college tutor."[16]

He did not wish to see himself teaching at Oriel as an orator who distilled knowledge. Rather, he envisioned himself as a teacher with moral and religious sensibilities, who had a responsibility for the souls in his charge as well. With several colleagues, he shared the ideal of being accountable before God for the students assigned to him. This ambitious ideal, which was far from the custom, soon aroused prejudice against him, and it put Newman in direct conflict with the authorities of Oriel. It was even to be the occasion of a painful crisis which ended in his being deprived of the tutorship.

But from the first year in which he became a tutor, his academic work became more spiritual, and it had a truly ascetic dimension. His was no longer the hard work of a candidate concerned with successful achievement. He discovered the condition for true influence, the one which he was already exercising and which, in time, would continue to grow and flourish. A highly spiritual wish, in a letter of November 26, 1826, testified

---

[14] An unpublished page in the *Apologia*, cited by Bouyer. *Newman*, pp. 80-81.
[15] Brilioth, *The Anglican Revival* (p. 112, note i) is right to point out the limits of the influence of the Noetics on Newman.
[16] M. I., p. 114.

to his soul's uprightness: "I trust I am placed where I may be an instrument for good to the church of God."[17]

Thus, in spite of the dangers in the intellectual milieu, Newman's soul always harbored a major concern about its mission. In fact, he did not acquiesce to Whately's liberal guidance any more than he had acquiesced to Mayers' advice: "Something from within was resisting,"[18] and told him that this was not his way. Returning to his own quest in solitude, he disengaged himself from an excessive greed of the intellect and shielded himself from outside threats. He again found the God of his conversion. God spoke to him in a secret dialogue, and His voice created strange resonances.

The soul, which was awaiting its destiny, was confused by various calls — some seemed to announce a higher vocation, away from vulgar mediocrity; others, more precise and also more intimate, invited it to sacrifice and suggested a greater detachment of the heart.

We perceive an indistinct echo of these calls in some poems of 1827. In one of them, "Snapdragon," October 2, 1827, Newman explained the symbolism of the flower which he had chosen for his personal emblem:

Snapdragon

I am rooted in the wall
Of buttress's tower or ancient hall;...
Humble — I can bear to dwell
Near the pale recluse's cell,
And I spread my crimson bloom,
Mingled with the cloister's gloom....

Pleasure, wealth, birth, knowledge, power
These have each an emblem flower;
So for me alone remains
Lowly thought and cheerful pains....

Mine, the Unseen to display
In the crowded public way,

---

[17] *Ibid.*, Letter to Rickards, pastor of Ulcombe, p. 127.
[18] This is what he wrote to Whately after the separation when Whately became Anglican Archbishop of Dublin. See *Apologia*, correspondence with Whately, p. 283. Also see the text in Chapter VI, footnote 4.

> Where life's busy arts combine
> To shut out the Hand Divine....[19]

This poem expresses the secret wish for a hidden and studious life in the calming shadow of silence and solitude, which is often brightened by reflections from another world. The retreat was sufficient for the young tutor whose profound ambition was "to live and die in the college cloister."

Another poem from the month of October takes up the theme of solitude. Being shut off from the world of appearances, the soul opens itself to the realities of an invisible world:

> The Trance of Time
>
> Then what this world to thee, my heart?
> Its gifts nor feed thee nor can bless.
> Thou hast no owner's part
> In all its fleetingness.
> The flame, the storm, the quaking ground,
> Earth's joys, earth's terror, nought is thine,
> Thou must but hear the sound
> of the still voice divine.[20]

The meaning of these strophes is not yet totally clear. There are the vague aspirations of a soul which is jealous of its purity, the grief of a heart which fears being bruised by the sharp edges, and the unformulated wishes of a secret and withdrawn conscience. One can guess, by the indefinable accent of disenchantment, the fears and struggles of a man who did not accept solitude without some nostalgia for the joys which he was sacrificing.

However, the direction taken by his soul, no matter how mysterious, did not leave him any doubt. Invincibly, it proceeded towards a higher destiny, safeguarded against the attacks of the world by an intense need for

---

[19] *Verses on Various Occasions*, p. 21. The circumstances of the composition are curious enough. In September and October of 1827, Newman experienced with a friend, Robert Wilberforce, the joys of the hospitality of his friends, the Rickards, at Ulcombe. Mrs. Rickards asked her guests to compose several poems for an album of flowers. Newman chose the symbol of the snapdragon. Cf. M. I., p. 146; *Apologia*, p. 183.

[20] *Verses*, pp. 24-25.

silence and for moral integrity. This need contained a very precise call and the exigencies of this call gradually revealed themselves. Already, in the days following the conversion of 1816, the young man had understood the secret invitation to the sacrifice of celibacy.

A very brief note in the *Apologia* mentions this unique call, but this note does not tell it all. In order to make of the *Apologia* a defense (rather than a biography) and also in order not to expose too intimate events from his youth, Newman had withdrawn from the definitive edition a long and forceful page at the beginning, which explored the history of his vocation to celibacy.[21]

We cite this page in its entirety because it sheds light on the spiritual development of Newman during the first years at Oxford:

> I am obliged to mention, though I do it with great reluctance, another deep imagination, which at the time, the autumn of 1816, took possession of me, — there can be no mistake about the fact; viz. that it would be the will of God that I should lead a single life. This anticipation has held its ground continuously ever since, and it has been closely connected with that feeling of disassociation from scenes about me, of which I have already spoken. I had a strong persuasion that offenses against the rule of purity were each of them visited sharply and surely from above: I have still extant prayers and memoranda of the years 1816 and 1821, showing my distress at the thought of going to dances or the theatre.
>
> This imagination, which I will speak of once for all and then dismiss, was not founded on the Catholic belief of the moral superiority of a single life over the married, which I did not hold till many years afterwards, when I was taught it by Hurrell Froude. It arose from my feeling of separation from the visible world, and it was connected with a notion that my mission in life would require such a sacrifice as it involved. When I was first on

---

[21] We are obliged to Father Tristram of the Oratory at Birmingham for the communication concerning these notes, ranged among the intimate papers of the Cardinal, unedited prior to the publication of *Newman* by Father Louis Bouyer. These notes have a great biographical interest, for they confirm many details about which one can already guess in the poems, the letters, and even the Sermons of St. Mary's. Father Louis Bouyer published them in his *Newman*, p. 27.

the Oriel foundation, it was associated in my mind with the Missionary employment, or with duties at Oxford.

(In 1824, at the death of my father, I find this remark): When I die, shall I be followed to the grave by my children? My mother said the other day she hoped to live to see me married, but I think I shall die within college walls, or a Missionary in a foreign land.

And in 1827, in some verses I wrote for a friend's album, after comparing myself to the "Snapdragon" fringing the wall opposite the rooms in which I spent my first solitary three weeks at the College in June, 1817, and I express a hope that I may "in college live and die."

To continue, that which had been only an impression before became a preference. The idea is obscure in my soul during one month or another during the years preceding February, 1829, but since this date, I have always had the will and the resolution, with the grace of God, to live and die a celibate.

I decided to be a pale pilgrim attached to the rude cincture of Paul. I add this: while considering these details from the past, I have found by chance this note from the same year, with the date, September, 1828. "For me, at Oriel, advancing kindly... led by the hand of God blindly, without knowing where he leads me; all is right."[22]

This page which retraces the history of his vocation to celibacy reveals also its setbacks and progress. It discovers some sort of secret movement in the soul of Newman, stirred up, even bruised by a tenacious spur. For it is all too clear that the progress and the drawbacks concerning celibacy alternate with the rhythms of his conscience, sometimes more lucid and open than at other times with regard to his ultimate vocation.

After the first call to conversion, the idea of celibacy continued in Newman, while he was immersed in the severe moralism of the Evangelical spirit, which was still alive at that time. We noticed earlier his spiritual difficulties during the days following his conversion: he was afraid to appear too narrow-minded among his own people, and he was keeping himself as open as possible.[23] Here, the impression of moral strictness

---

[22] See *Apologia*, p. 19; Bouyer, pp. 27-28, 99; *Journal*, p. 203.
[23] M. I., p. 19.

which refuses to compromise with sin or even the occasion of sin is confirmed. At the same time, he discovered in himself a very lively sense of the danger which weighs on every guilty conscience too complacent about vice.[24]

Nevertheless, the call to celibacy is not born of an anxious or timid conscience; it certainly does not come from a servile fear, engendered by the single thought of a possible offense. But it derives from a more generous and calming sentiment. It is a vocation which is both an abjuration and a commitment.

With disconcerting precision, Newman noted the bonds which linked his first anticipation of celibacy — on the one hand, a giving up of earthly things, and on the other, a religious mission. The sacrifice appeared to him as the pledge of better and more lasting blessings in the invisible world than those of the visible world. Furthermore, it seemed to announce the precise way in which he was to fulfill his destiny. Thus, Newman's call to celibacy coincided with his presentiment of his priestly mission.

The years of the young tutor were intense and full. He shared his time between the guidance of his pupils and the diverse responsibilities which were given to him at the university. During the vacation of 1827, he set himself the task of systematically reading the Fathers of the Church. He had a beautiful edition which his friend, Pusey, sent him from Germany. But he worked so much that he became depressed and this, in turn, forced him to rest for some weeks. This "illness" served to accent his need for solitary meditation and inner detachment.

A decisive event was to precipitate Newman's spiritual evolution. It would attach him to the world of supernatural reality which was his true homeland. On January 5, 1828, came news of the unexpected death of Mary Newman, the candid, favorite youngest sister of John Henry.

---

[24] This extreme moralism due to the Evangelical influence is going to carry over into his preaching at Oxford and to inspire several sermons with an unwavering strictness. See IV, Par. III, "Moral Consequences of Single Sins," p. 750; I, Par. IV, "Secret Faults," p. 31 ff.

CHAPTER IV

THE DEATH OF MARY

Joy of sad hearts,
And light of downcast eyes!

Verses, p. 28.

*I*N THE FACTUAL and clear style characteristic of the *Apologia*, Newman evoked the memory of his trials: "I was drifting in the direction of the liberalism of the day. I was rudely awakened from my dream at the end of 1827 by two great blows: illness and bereavement."[1]

The illness was a depression due to intellectual overwork which he brought on himself by assuming the burden of becoming a tutor. The temptation to take on too many responsibilities remained with him for most of his life. Already in 1820, when he competed for honors at Trinity, he experienced a distressing lassitude, symptomatic of a state of extreme cerebral fatigue.[2] The remedy was simple; it was to go out, take some exercise, and walk in the open air. In the course of his walks, which he most often took alone, Newman's thoughts wandered. He was often preoccupied with the image of his sweet and lovely youngest sister, Mary, whose unexpected death came as a shock to him. Her memory absorbed him more and more.

Between Mary and John Henry, there had existed a bond which was very deep and is difficult to define. It was special, as it was born in an intimacy of kindred spirits, unknown even to the family. The few letters of Mary Newman to her brother, John, or to her older sister, Harriet, reveal

---

[1] *Apologia*, p. 24.
[2] M. I, pp. 151-152. Letter of December 11, 1827.

a deeply sensitive soul who knew how to hide her impulsive heart with artless whimsy.[3] One understands the immediate harmonious agreement of John Henry with such a delicate and intuitive soul. At first, he guided his young sister in her early studies. In spite of all his professorial seriousness, the influence of the older brother did not stop at the academic level. In Mary's open and upright soul, John Henry's deep interior life engendered a sort of fascination. Long before her brother's future friends recognized his talents, Mary discerned something of the genius which hid behind his solitary demeanor. She communed with Newman in some sort of mysterious way, attracted as she was by his otherworldly or meditative spirit. Their common partaking of the same profound reality of God produced a bond that death itself was not only unable to dissolve but which actually strengthened it in a renewed fidelity.

Concerning this communion of souls, we have scant evidence from Mary. There are just a few letters where, with the juvenile emotion of a blushing girl,[4] she expressed her admiration for her brother, and even more, for the influence he exerted on her: "Well, I really think I have found out the secret of my difficulty in writing to you. It is because I never told you the difficulty. At least, I find I write much easier since my confession."[5] A few weeks before her death, she wrote with the same abandon: "How I long to see you! I can fancy your face — there, it is looking at me."[6]

No one in the family suspected this intimacy between the elder brother and the youngest sister. After Mary's death, Jemima, the second of the three sisters, was almost astonished at Newman's preoccupation in treasuring all the memories of the departed. She wrote: "... how you delighted me once when you said she was so singularly good! I never heard you speak so much about her, but I was sure you thought so; and indeed we, John, know more of her than you could know; I especially, who have been always with her."[7]

Did Mary's mother have any idea of the nature and the degree of the intimacy between these two children? In a serene letter written to her son a month after Mary's death, she stated: "It is delightful to think that your

---

[3] *Ibid.*, pp. 117, 119, 121.
[4] The expression is from Father Bouyer, p. 104.
[5] Letter of May 5, 1826; M. I., p. 117.
[6] Letter of November 27, 1827; *Ibid.*, p. 150.
[7] M. I., p. 159, March 7, 1828 to Jemima.

dear departed sister owed so much of her religious and right feelings to you; her knowledge of her own insufficiency, and her submission and fitness to obey her awfully sudden call."[8]

In this letter, Mrs. Newman not only affirms the brother's influence upon his sister but with a maternal instinct, she discerns something more: a close communion of souls in the sharing of a common religious ideal. This communion with Mary sustained Newman after her death. His remembrances of her drew him to the very threshold of the invisible world and made him even more attentive to the presences who inhabit it. Thus, did bereavement purify the Oriel tutor's soul, deepening his sense of the world beyond and renewing his interior life.

Newman's first reaction to so brutal and unexpected a tragedy was one of shock.[9] But not for an instant did he express any feelings of inquietude or bitterness. This death did not cause him any anxiety. He did not ask himself any useless and unanswerable questions about it. More to the point, it was her death which resolved for him the problem of his own destiny. Very quickly, John Henry understood that Mary's death was not an end but a beginning and it inaugurated a new order of relations between them.

A much closer communion began to establish itself. Thanks to the mysterious presence of his sister, the survivor discovered a long procession of invisible presences in a world other than the concrete world of appearances, this "veil" in which we live.

The utter suddenness of Mary's death revealed the presence and action of the living God in its terrible majesty. The event had been so rapid and so unexpected that it allowed no room for conjectures or misgivings. Death came alone without preparation and accomplished its end with disconcerting ease, as if it felt quite at home with men. It was precisely death's off-handedness, its striking at the door without anyone's being prepared for it, which captured Newman's attention. In it, he saw the sign of God, absolutely and peremptorily seizing for Himself a life which belonged to Him. Thus, Mary's death was a witness to the mystery and power of the Almighty.

---

[8] *Ibid.*, p. 157. Letter of February 18, 1828.

[9] He writes to his sister, Harriet, April 21, 1828, and sends her his poem, *Consolations in Bereavement*: "May I be patient! It is so difficult to realize what one believes, and to make these trials, as they are intended, real blessings." M. I., pp. 159-160.

In an event in which God has been so manifestly the only actor, man is nothing. Thus, Newman saw Mary's death as a sort of theophany, a revelation of the living God. If the death had not been so rapid, if human skills had delayed or prolonged it, this revelation of God would not have been so apparent. If she had been able to evade her destiny by the intervention of humans, the soul of Mary would not have attained this consecration which came entirely from the hand of God; she would not have entered into the mystery of the invisible world as a pure and spontaneous offering.

The suddenness of Mary's death, which revealed a Divine action, constitutes the theme in a poem composed several months after the separation:

Consolations in Bereavement

Death was full urgent with thee, Sister dear,
And startling in his speed; —
Brief pain, then languor till thy end came near —
Such was the path decreed,
The hurried road.
To lead thy soul from earth to thine own God's abode.
Death wrought with thee, sweet maid impatiently: —
Yet merciful the haste
That baffles sickness; — dearest, thou didst die,
Thou wast not made to taste
Death's bitterness
Decline's slow—wasting—charm, or fever's fierce distress.[10]

Thus, this event brought the revelation of God's action to Newman and helped him understand that the presence of God in his life was always as real as on the day of his conversion. During the weeks of bereavement, another sentiment was also expressed in his continued meditations. It was the precariousness of this world and by way of contrast, the absolute certitude about another world, which was just as real, but so much less fragile and less deceiving. Of course, one may say that this conviction had

---

[10] M. I, p. 159. The suddenness of unexpected death constitutes the theme of each of the other strophes: "Death came unheralded"; "Death urged as scant of time"; "Death came and went." This same sentiment of suddenness is found in another poem of January 5, 1830: "Epiphany Eve." (*Verses*, p. 52 ff.).

nothing original about it and that it ought to constantly feed and nourish the thoughts of all believers. Nevertheless, Newman's conviction about the invisible world was so real that it came close to constituting one of the most basic foundations of his spirituality. Mary's death was incontestably the event which contributed the most to the clarity of vision which made the preacher of St. Mary's the prophet of otherworldliness.

In several instances in the correspondence of 1828, it becomes clear that Newman's memories of Mary provoked in him a more or less conscious disenchantment with the world which is born from his seeing it as both ephemeral and vulnerable. Thus, in a letter in May, Newman wrote to his sister, Jemima:

> Thursday, I rode over to Cuddlesdon.... The country too, is beautiful; the fresh leaves, the scents, the varied landscape. Yet I never felt so intensely the transitory nature of this world as when most delighted with these country scenes. And in riding out today, I have been impressed more powerfully than before I had an idea was possible with the two lines:
>
> ... Chanting with a solemn voice
> Minds us of our better choice....
>
> I wish it were possible for words to put down those indefinite, vague, and withal subtle feelings which pierce the soul and make it sick. Dear Mary seems embodied in every tree and hid behind every hill. What a veil and curtain this world of sense is! beautiful, but a veil.[11]

This page is typically Newmanian. It reveals the transparent quality of his sentiments which are far removed from any affectation and any despair. Likewise, it reveals his ability to grasp the profound depth of being behind the mask of appearances. This was Newman's most constant and, perhaps, most fundamental intuitive trait.

Indeed, his inner suffering expressed itself in serene images which pour forth in a veritable incantation. The literary magic of these sighs ought not to alter the nature and significance of Newman's deep and personal loss. It was not primarily the desire to revive some very sweet emotions

---

[11] M. I., p. 161. Letter to Jemima, May 10, 1828.

which inspired Newman's confident poem. It would not be correct to accuse him of aestheticism. In no way was he the sensitive artist who is sometimes described as caressing his interior vision lovingly. The weight of memories only paralyzes those who are over eager to draw out of them emotional wealth rather than to comprehend the content of their truth. For Newman, his "reminiscence" of Mary had meaning only to the degree that it strengthened the bond between them and that it clarified the meaning of his own life.

When he evoked the memory of Mary, what interested him and what captured his heart was less the delicate, sorrowful emotion produced by the vision from the past, but rather the moving reality of an existence which still continued on and which became for him the mystery of his own destiny. The past is never totally abolished; it projects itself into the present. But this reality is of another nature than the one which is perceptible to our senses. This reality is in an existence beyond time. In this super-spatial existence, the profound identity of spirits and of persons is determined. The past only contains images as fleeting and fragile as present-time appearances. However, since our remembrance of the past allows us to grasp the identity of beings who live beyond time, the past is profoundly meaningful: it is the messenger of the invisible world.[12] It involves the reality of living persons much more than that of lifeless remains, and it brings them very close to us. "Not one half-hour passes but dear Mary's face is before my eyes," wrote Newman in June, 1828 to his sister Harriet.[13]

Several of his poems explain his vision of a mysterious presence and of a happy life beyond death:

> Dearest, gentlest, purest, fairest!. . . .
> Paradised in the inmost shrine.
> There thou liest, and in thy slumber
> Times and changes thou dost number.[14]

---

[12] The conception of the invisible in Newman is strictly bound to the metaphysical problems of time and eternity. Time localizes memories. But these are not simply symbols of reality because they refer to a wholly personal presence in a time beyond space.

[13] M. I., p. 163.

[14] From the poem, "A Picture," *Verses*, p. 29. See Bouyer, "A Picture," in *Memorials of the Past*, pp. 107-108.

Newman had a presentiment of a blessed and serene life in the world beyond. It is in God that it takes birth and is achieved:

> A sea before
> The Throne is spread; its pure still glass
> Pictures all earth-scenes as they pass.
> We on its shore
> Share, in the bosom of our rest,
> God's knowledge, and our blest![15]

In the above poem, the death of Mary conveys its definitive secret. To Newman, the event brought confirmation of a mysterious reality of which he already had an intuition. There definitely exists a spiritual and invisible universe which, in spite of its invisibility, is truer and more real than the visible world. In this universe, each destiny finds its own consecration. Physical existence is transformed into a spiritual presence that permits a more profound encounter and a more authentic communion between souls which cannot be reached by the power of the senses. During the trying days of bereavement, Newman's silent, brotherly memories brought his prayerful meditations to the very frontiers of the invisible world. In order to understand Newmanian spirituality, it is important to comprehend the depth of his vision of the world beyond, a vision reached only by faith.

Newman's mind inclined towards an idealistic and Platonic conception of the universe. The unity of being and truth were not to be sought for in things which belong to an ephemeral and fleeting world.

Things are at best only symbols of a reality which escapes our perception because it belongs to another existence. Newman's spirit assuredly found more truth in Plato's myth of the cave than in the realism of Aristotle. Indeed, such an inclination was not without danger: it could lead to the creation of an abstract world in which reality consisted of purely the formal and the ideal.

It becomes clear, however, that the death of Mary helped Newman to reject these phantasms of idealism forever. It was a universe of persons and not one of ideas and things which would nourish Newman's contem-

---

[15] *Ibid.*, pp. 108-110. It is the poetry of the invisible world which expresses itself with such depth in this verse.

plation. It was the world of faith, a world beyond this world, a world wholly immersed in the sovereign glory of the living God, enlightened by "presences," with whom Newman's soul was able to sustain a secret and continuous dialogue. Among those presences, Mary Newman revealed herself to her brother with a particular glow: "Joy of sad hearts, and light of downcast eyes!" She restored the vision of John Henry. In purifying his sight, she had introduced him to the threshold of the mysterious world where his contemplation would find its decisive pole. The future poet of the *Dream of Gerontius* was now able to follow an enlightened intuition that was guided by faith.

Newman was about to undertake his patristic studies with a fervent discovery of the Alexandrian school. His mind and heart were prepared to welcome their teachings. Clearly and lucidly, they portrayed for him the invisible world, which henceforth remained the true home of his heart.

So it appears that the death of Mary was a decisive event in Newman's life, occurring as it did during his early years when he was awaiting his destiny and the great tasks that lay before him. Therefore, one can understand the force of the author's expression in the *Apologia*, when he spoke of "two great blows: illness and bereavement," which freed him from any illusion about the attractions of this world.

Let us not be surprised at the unexpected emphasis given to a familial event which seems banal enough if one envisions it only as an anecdotal reality. It is an event, however, which carries a great deal of weight when considered in light of one's personal destiny. It is especially significant in the life of a young man when he is not yet definitively engaged in works and undertakings which will confer on him a sense of achievement. At the threshold of his thirtieth year, Newman's life was still in the making; he was experiencing the last respite which preceded the great struggles of the mature man who was intended for an exceptional role. The respite was a solitary novitiate where he studiously pursued his scholarly readings in great silence. It was probably during this time of intense reflection that his inclination to celibacy grew. His resolution, that was to become his definitive response to the call of celibacy which he heard in the course of the preceding years, was strengthened. This call of celibacy consecrated Newman totally to his mission in the Church.

The daily walks in the fresh air, recommended for his health, had the added advantage of taking him away from the excitement of the common room, while providing him with more time for personal reflection. "It is so great a gain to throw off Oxford for a few hours," he wrote to Jemima.[16] But in a letter to Harriet, there is an even more significant acknowledgment:

> My ride of a morning is generally solitary; but I almost prefer being alone. When the spirits are good, everything is delightful in the view of the still nature which the country gives.... A solemn voice seems to chant from everything. I know whose voice it is — her dear voice. Her form is almost nightly before me, when I have put out the light and lain down. Is not this a blessing? ... How desirable it seems to me to get out of the stir and bustle of the world, and not to have the responsibility and weariness of success! Now, if I choose to wish a scheme, and in my solitary rides, I sometimes do, I should say, "Oh, for some small curacy of a few hundreds a year, and no preferments, as the world calls it!" But, you know this is wishing for idleness, and I do not think I shall have this obscurity because I wish for it. Yet, see I talk of the comfort of retirement — how long should I endure it were I given it? I do not know myself.[17]

With these personal musings, Newman betrayed a concern for perfection, which was easier to achieve in obscurity and silence than in the excitement of Oxonian life. More than ever, he distrusted the seductions of the intellectual and academic world. He knew that the magical spell of the intellect was able to stop the flight of the soul more than the servitude of passions. All human ambition must go, including the more subtle form of ambition, a desire for influence. It is significant that at this point, Newman was cautious about the promise of a career which would have provided him, as he knew already, with an opportunity to exert considerable influence over students. He had written to Harriet about his not too convincing desire for an obscure country parish. This will not be the last time that he will be tempted by such a need for escape.[18] A letter in July 1839 to his friend, Rickards, is even more to the point than his comments to his sisters:

> I will but say it is now many years that a conviction has been growing upon me (say since I was elected here) that men did not

---

[16] M. I., p. 161.
[17] *Ibid.*, p. 172.
[18] In 1828, beside his work as tutor at Oriel, Newman was Vicar of St. Mary's. The temptation was great during the Oxford Movement.

stay at Oxford as they ought, and that it is my duty to have no plans ulterior to a college residence. To be sure, as I passed through a hundred miles of country just now on my way to and from Brighton, the fascination of a country life nearly overset me, and always does. It will indeed be a grievous temptation should a living ever be offered me, when now even a curacy has inexpressible charms.... One thing I have earnestly desired for years and I trust in sincerity — that I may never be rich; and I will add (though here I am more sincere at some times than at others) that I never may rise in the church. The most useful men have not been the most highly exalted.[19]

After this spontaneous acknowledgment to a dear and ever indulgent friend, Newman began to define what true influence is:

Men live after their death — they live not only by their writings or their chronicled history, but still more in "remembrances not writings"[20] exhibited in a school of pupils who trace their moral parentage to them. As moral truth is discovered, not by reasoning, but by habituation, so it is recommended not by books, but by oral instruction.[21]

Thus, it was not an immediate and conscious influence that Newman sought at Oxford. His intellectual gifts contributed to the life of this city but he achieved his real and personal mission through an ever deepening purification of his interior life. Unyielding to the most sensual seductions, his conscience guarded him from a too tempting desire for prestige and influence. Not only did Newman shun it, he also admitted to himself that he knew he had a mission in the Church. In 1830, this mission was not all too clear. But being aware of his astonishing possibility for influence was enough to prevent the tutor of Oriel from being pleased about it or about achieving it.

All these considerations were leading Newman back toward the bent of his heart. Quiet and peace were asserting themselves over the deceits of the world and the distress born out of a premature bereavement. Suffering

---

[19] This idea receives a very beautiful development in II, Par., I. This sermon, "The World's Benefactors," (Feast of St. Andrew, p. 227) is one of this same period, November 1830. Cf., M. I., p. 202.

[20] In the Greek, "unwritten remembrances."

[21] M. I., pp. 202-203.

had detached his mind and spirit from "vanitas," the attractions of the world. His purified soul was more attentive to God, more aware of the spiritual progress accomplished in him. Should his soul be surprised to hear a new call inviting him to sacrifice? Celibacy as a way of life had been an option he sensed since the days of his first conversion. But now before committing himself, Newman awaited a more precise call.

He recognized the call during the months which followed his ordeal, during the long period of quiet and solitude which was imposed on the tutor of Oriel by bereavement and illness. It was in February 1829, as the *Apologia* tells us, that the uncertainty ceased and preference was given to the commitment to celibacy.[22]

Newman did not elaborate on the circumstances which motivated his commitment to celibacy. We know serious motives calling him to such a vocation characterized his inner life ever since the conversion of 1816, but we do not know the precise role certain events played in the decision itself.[23] It is reasonable to guess that the sudden and unexpected death of his sister, Mary, enlightened his mind and strengthened his will toward a more complete separation from this ephemeral world. Mourning his sister led him to a greater spirit of detachment from all that this world has to offer and made his personal call to holiness more apparent.

Newman's decision was reinforced by another circumstance: his intention to spend his life within the narrow boundaries of his college. We already know that the basic motive in taking a vow of celibacy was his total dedication to teaching and/or missionary work.[24] It seems clear that around 1828, Newman became more and more persuaded about the meaning of his personal destiny. As a tutor of Oriel, he became increasingly aware of his responsibilities towards the students entrusted to his guidance. He was soon to lead a rude assault against the routine which stifled a true education, going so far as to battle directly with the provost, Hawkins.[25]

---

[22] Compare above, unedited note in the *Apologia*, "that which had been only an anticipation becomes a preference."

[23] The correspondence of February 1829 does not show that Newman had experienced then a strong kind of interior crisis. A letter of February 8th to his sister, Jemima, contains several very personal avowals, but nothing very positive. M. I., pp. 174-175. The letters of this period shed scarcely any light on his inner life. However, several of the poems are more explicit on this point.

[24] See text in Chapter III re: celibacy.

[25] On this reform of the tutorship, see "Autobiographical Memoirs," Chapter IV, pp.129-140.

Dedicated to his task as an educator, he clearly perceived the loftiness of a vocation to celibacy. His resolve to live a solitary life is explained by the acceptance of a call to a higher vocation. Thus, in 1829, we find the two demands that had been revealed to Newman at the time of his first conversion, which explain the true meaning of his idea of celibacy: First, the need for detachment from the world, and second, the demands of an apostolic or missionary vocation.[26] The death of Mary and his tutorship somehow crystallized these aspirations. Under great pressure, his soul consented to this ultimate sacrifice.

Several poems of 1829 manifest the sentiments that filled his heart. In September, evoking the merits of some of the saints of whom "Christ seizes the heart in order to make of it his throne, far from the vainglories of the world," Newman meditated on the singular election which gives to faithful souls the privilege of purity and glory.

> God sows in waste, to reap whom He foreknew
> of man's cold race; ...[27]

Several weeks later, the poet recalled all the Lord's blessings that surrounded him and he murmured a prayer of abandonment to God:

> And such Thy tender force be still,
>   When self would swerve and stray,
> Shaping to truth the forward will
>   Along Thy narrow way.
> Deny me wealth; far, far remove
>   The lure of power or name;
> Hope thrives in straits, in weakness love,
>   And faith in this world shame.[28]

---

[26] Among the Anglican clergy of this period, celibacy was quite exceptional. The fellows of the colleges would lose their privileges on marrying. In fact, with the exception of R.H. Froude, all the friends or companions of Newman were married.

But one should not confuse the idea of the vocation to celibacy with the vow of celibacy itself. To his friend, Froude, Newman will write on January 9, 1830: "I have thought vows (e. g., celibacy) are evidences of want of trust. Why should we look to the morrow? It will be given us to do what is our duty as the day comes." M. I., pp. 193-194.

[27] *Verses*, XIV, "The Hidden Ones," p. 43.

[28] *Ibid.*, XV, "A Thanksgiving," p. 45 ff.

CHAPTER V

THE PATRISTIC SOURCE

Before me the Fathers were
surging anew.

M. I., p. 229.

AT THE RISK OF anticipating events that are to follow in the life of Newman
and of specifying prematurely the great traits in Newmanian spirituality,
we ought, nevertheless, to stop at this stage in his career, the years 1826-
1830, and follow the young tutor of Oriel in his patristic investigations
which date from this period. Indeed, from the beginning of his tutorship,
he heard the call from those whom he described as "my huge fellows,"[1] in
a letter to Mrs. Newman. He devoted himself to studying them with
meritorious perseverance. The readings from the Fathers inaugurated a
patristic loyalty in Newman which never diminished. The richness of their
teachings happily prolonged the great lessons of spiritual detachment and
otherworldliness for which prior events in his life had prepared him. In
view of the fact that he lost his tutorship, he now had the leisure for such
studies.

What is the origin of Newman's great interest in the patristic
tradition? What direction does it take, and what common elements can be
discovered in the Fathers?

At the time of the schism and in the course of its entire history, the
Anglican Church never neglected the tradition of the Fathers of the

---

[1] Letter to his mother, October 18, 1827, M. I., p. 148.

49

Church. Various generations of theologians tried to discover in the patristic writings, which always held a place of honor in the Anglican Church, a basis for an authentic apostolicity. In fact, Oxford always prided itself on the inclusion of works which joined the solid erudition of the Fathers with an exclusively Anglican piety in its Alma Mater. Such writings won for its dons an incontestable reputation.[2] Newman found, then, in this specific university the most favorable milieu for the study of the Fathers. Besides, he seems to have been drawn to it by a fascination which needs no justification, considering how enthusiastic he was about it. Although he hardly knew of the Fathers' existence and entertained only summary notions of their achievements, he was dissatisfied with his status as a neophyte and was hungry for greater knowledge. He wanted to know more and guessed that it would be necessary for him, one day, to apply himself to the work. He faced the task of going through this immense body of literature in a systematic fashion, a task that likely would have discouraged most other neophytes.

At the time of his conversion in 1816, an introductory work on the early Church stimulated his appetite. The book, entitled *The History of the Church* by Milner, was dedicated to Christian antiquity.[3] Milner, an eighteenth century historian with an Evangelical background, was more anxious to recover an account of the spiritual life of souls than a summary of doctrines from past patristic history. He revealed to his avid reader some particular images and portraits of the great Fathers, which were always to fascinate the young convert:

> Since my youth, reading "The History of the Church" by Joseph Milner turned my thoughts toward the primitive church, and above all, towards the early Fathers. I have never lost, nor allowed to disappear the deep impression and so sweet that the portraits of St. Ambrose and St. Augustine made on my soul. Since then, the vision of the Fathers became for my imagination, I should say like a paradise of delight for all the times my work permits it.[4]

---

[2] This word for university students designates the Scholars or university professors.

[3] On Milner, see *Apologia*, p. 18.

[4] "Diff.," p. 324. See also "Autobiographical Memoirs," M. I., p. 112. One cites most often the celebrated text from the *Apologia*: "I read Joseph Milner's *Church History*, and was nothing short of enamored of the long extracts from St. Augustine, St. Ambrose, and the other Fathers which I found there. I read them as being the religion of the primitive Christians." p. 18. But the text of the "Difficulties," conferences delivered

Nevertheless, in spite of this early fascination, the examples of the early Christians would fade from his memory for several years. Around 1823, some academic studies were getting under way in the area of the early Fathers[5] but Whately was not kindly disposed toward those undertaking such studies and he referred to them as "the old dogmatics."[6] The young disciple appeared for the moment to have sacrificed his newborn fervor to the influence of his liberal mentor. When he again picked up his patristic studies in 1826, he published some superficial sketches of the Fathers which gave rise to the suspicion that he was influenced by Arianism. Thus, it appeared that he had a "certain disdain for Christian antiquity."[7]

But this disdain was too unconscious to be conclusive at the time. In fact, his patristic vocation was really searching for itself through those imperfect sketches. From time to time, some brief note in his *Correspondence* clearly shows that the tutor of Oriel was invincibly drawn towards a world of thought and prayer, the depth of which he saw and the complexity of which he feared.[8]

During the vacation of 1828, the grand exploration in patristics began with the venerable *Defensio* by Bull as a guide. Newman tells us years later that after having occupied himself with the history of Arianism, he set himself to study the Fathers. He read them with Bull's *Defensio*

---

at the Oratory in London in 1850, renders much more explicitly the vividness of the impression which is being felt again by Newman. In the *Apologia*, he signals one other influence of Milner "that upon the visible church come down from above, at certain intervals, large and temporary effusions of divine grace." *Ibid.*, p. 31. This conception of the history of the Church is of a cyclical development of divine graces, effusions of the Spirit at diverse times which renews the miracle of Pentecost. In the Evangelical manner, Newman would take this conception of history back and modify it some little bit in his historical tableaux. See *Historical Sketches*, II, "The Mission of St. Benedict," p. 365. *Var. Occ.* XII, "The Mission of St. Philip," p. 228. Religious history is presented as one vast fresco renewed at different periods by powerful spiritual currents.

[5] Newman points them out on one page in his "Autobiographical Memoirs," M. I., p. 112.

[6] Thomas Mosley, *Reminiscences of Oriel*, I, p. 110.

[7] *Apologia*, p. 24.

[8] Thus, in the letter to Smedley, of the 27th of January, 1826, Newman defines the line of his studies. M. I., p. 113. Some comments in the "Correspondence" with the sisters of Newman are significant; such as the simple question that Jemima poses to him in May 1826: "What is meant by 'the Fathers'?" M. I., p. 118. Likewise, the desire of Mary to know the "uses of reading the Fathers." M. I., p. 119. For the history of this patristic vocation of Newman, see the little book of Denys Gorce, *Newman et les Pères*, Paris, 1933, pp. 17-41.

serving as his key.[9] It is Bull who helped to show him "that antiquity was the true exponent of the doctrines of Christianity."[10]

However, Newman did not take long to progress in his researching the patristic sources all by himself. The vacation of 1828 showed him as "hungry for Irenaeus and for Cyprian."[11] Soon, he was going to discover his dream, the Alexandrian school in all its unique splendor. The text of the *Apologia* celebrates an enthusiastic hymn to Clement and to Origen. This hymn sings in our memories, just as the allegories of the Alexandrian school sang in Newman's:

> The broad philosophy of Clement and Origen carried me away; the philosophy, not the theological doctrine; and I have drawn out some features of it in my volume, and with the zeal and freshness but with the partiality of a neophyte. Some positions of their teachings, magnificent in themselves, came like music to my inward ear, as if the response to ideas which with little external to encourage them, I had cherished so long. These were based on the mystical or sacramental principle and spoke of the various Economies and Dispensations of the Eternal. I understood these significant passages to mean that the exterior world, physical and historical, was but the manifestation to our senses of realities greater than itself. Nature was a parable; Scripture was an allegory.[12]

As a result of his early patristic studies, Newman published his first theological book: *The Arians of the Fourth Century*. He had undertaken this work at the suggestion of two theologians, Hugh Rose and William Lyall, who were recruiting some "writers for a theological library."[13] In

---

[9] *Diff.*, p. 325, Fr. trans., Gondon: *Conferences de l'Oratoire*, p. 161.

[10] *Apologia*, p. 33. "I do not know when I first learnt to consider that Antiquity was the true exponent of the doctrines of Christianity and the basis of the Church of England; but I take it for granted that the works of Bishop Bull, which at this time I read, were my chief introduction to this principle."

[11] Letter of June 25, 1829, M. I., p. 184. Then, in 1827, Newman received from Pusey, then in Germany, the patristic series which he requested, and in 1831, he was to receive from his friends some beautiful editions of the Fathers which filled him with joy.

[12] *Apologia*, p. 34.

[13] *Ibid.*, p. 33. Newman received an offer to collaborate toward the end of 1830 or the beginning of 1831. In a letter of March 28, 1831, in response to the request of Hugh Rose, he mentioned his acquiescence. (M. I., p. 210). But the two men only met much later in June, 1831 by means of an intermediary, William Palmer, of Worcester College. (M. I., p. 229). The Oxford Movement was then in the air!

this work, the author argued at length for the Platonism of the Early Fathers, especially Origen's. One senses that Newman was in complete sympathy with the Alexandrians. His religious thought was beginning to mature and it was not too long before it would produce its fruit. His interest in patristic studies never stopped growing, and the charm of the old saints continued. Their image ever lived before his eyes, their harmonious words rang ever in his ears, and their words were never absent from his tongue.[14] His intellectual vocation had found its true home in the Fathers of the Church. Their faith and their prayers would always echo in the theological and religious thoughts of John Henry Newman.

In the *Apologia*, he recalled how much his own doctrine owed to the Fathers of the Church, particularly to the Alexandrians. In them, his philosophy found a firm support; his theology regarding the economy of faith and the development of dogma received its first clarification; his method of exegesis encountered some potentially rich principles for the interpretation of Scripture. Hence, the doctrinal gains from his patristic studies were, indeed, considerable.

His spirituality deepened, broadened, and matured. The study of the Fathers brought support and structure to his first intuition, which he acquired during his first conversion and which needed structure. In the years ahead, his spiritual principles would be marked by a definite content and his spiritual world would be more clearly defined. His conscience was thirsty for truth and harmony, and the patristic studies revealed to him the profound unity among the doctrines of the Church which was necessary to nourish any truly enlightened faith. Henceforth, an astonishing impression of total security and of proud assurance was demonstrated every time Newman spoke about his religious convictions. He knew he was backed by those seriously committed; he knew he was in profound and essential agreement with those whose authority it would be foolish to contest, for to do so would be to undermine the very structure of the faith and of the Church. After becoming a Catholic, Newman responded to those Anglican friends seeking to quarrel about Marian devotion: "I am not ashamed about relying upon the Fathers and I wish never to abandon them."[15] Not without

---

[14] *Diff.*, p. 340.

[15] *Diff.*, p. 376, Fr. trans., not available commercially: *Du Culte de la Sainte Vierge dans l'Eglise Catholique*, 1942.

[16] *Ibid.*

a little irritation, he added: "The Fathers made me Catholic and I will not throw away the ladder by which I have come to the Church."[16]

The first fruit of his patristic readings revived in Newman his "sense of the faith." He knew well that Christian faith required a submission and an adherence to a body of truths surpassing human understanding, but not until he studied the Fathers and became acquainted with the literature of the great writers of Christian antiquity did he come to understand with certainty the need for that ultimate step which requires first the fidelity of the heart before soliciting the submission of the spirit. Faith is a gift; it contains a call.

In his response to the voice of God, man does not bargain about his assent. He acquiesces before demanding some reasons. In his daily contact with the Fathers, Newman perceived instinctively this interior resonance of the faith, which is expressed in the motto: *"Standum firmiter per fidem."* ["Lean firmly on faith."] These words of Saint Hilary[17] at the beginning of his *De Fide*, symbolize in their concise vigor the most radical lesson that the young student of patrology was to receive. Wherever he turned, it was always the same refrain and the same request. If he looked towards Alexandria, it was Athanasius who was striking like a battering ram at the heart of the Arian heresy. If he turned to the Churches of the West, it was Hilary of Poitiers and Ambrose of Milan who were bringing to an end opposing stubborn opinions. If he glanced towards Africa, it was Augustine who was unraveling one by one the threads of the Pelagian heresy's subtle weavings. Everywhere, the persistent cry of the primitive faith reverberated like an echo.

Clearly, Newman imagined the history of Christian antiquity as a series of large frescoes depicting a distressing epic: on the one side, the faithful witnesses, the defenders of the faith, men with bare hands who were resisting, backs against the wall; and on the other side, the rebels, prophets of denial, who kept surging in continuous waves in the name of reason in order to undermine the Christian edifice. The stake in the conflict was the man in revolt versus the man saved. Newman discovered the irreconcilable opposition between two tendencies, two mentalities: one based on rationalistic pretension, concerned only with criticism and controversy; the other, penetrated by circumspection and piety, inclined

---

[17] Saint Hilary of Poitiers, fourth century Doctor of the Church.

towards obedience and fidelity. It was not that Newman contested the part of reason in faith but he did not wish to see in reason, the final arbiter of religious commitment.[18] Besides the doctrinal divergences, it was ultimately the quality of the heart and the rightness of conscience which are the grounds for such commitment. In his first book, *The Arians of the Fourth Century*, published in 1830, Newman returned constantly to the idea that heresy is born of controversy and of critical freedom, while faith is built up in silence and prayer. The taste for controversy begins and ends by ruining religious sentiment. It is to be encountered in all the intellectual groups which favored the Arian heresy.[19] A striking sentence by Hooker, the theologian, was to be used by Newman in order to contrast the two tendencies: "The one, because they enjoyed not, disputed; the other disputed not because they enjoyed."[20]

Thus, Newman found in the Fathers both "an authority and a guide."[21] That which he liked in the primitive Church was the living testimony of a religious conscience, in full possession of its faith and its divine privileges. The patristic writings revealed to him the dispositions and approaches that faithful Christians should adopt: absolute adherence to the Divine Word, a spiritual submission and dependence, a profound respect for the Christian mystery, and an appreciation of silence and fervor in prayer.

> If the early church regarded the very knowledge of the truth as a fearful privilege, much more did it regard that truth itself as glorious and awful... the most solemn truths... being attainable only by the sober and the watchful, by slow degrees, with dependence on the Giver of wisdom, and with strict obedience to the light which has already been granted.[22]

---

[18] Every theological work of Newman aims to justify the assent of faith with regard to reason which can exercise its critical role only within faith. Cf. *University Sermons, Grammar of Assent.*

[19] See in *The Arians of the Fourth Century* the pages dedicated to the School of Antioch (p. 19 ff.); those on the Sophists (p. 15 ff.); on the Eclectics (p. 100 ff.). See also in *The Essay on Development* (p. 248 ff.) where Newman defines the common character of the Christological heresies of the first centuries.

[20] Citation from Hooker, "Ecclesiastical Polity," in *The Arians of the Fourth Century*, p. 19. The work of Hooker, an Anglican writer of the end of the 16th century, was re-edited by Keble in 1836.

[21] *Lectures on Justification*, London, 1840, p. 123.

[22] *The Arians*, pp. 136-137.

When it came to the primacy of obedience in the development of faith, the patristic imprint was indelible. Such a manner of seeing is the antithesis of that of Whately, from whom Newman had separated definitively. Henceforth, for all his life, he was to lead the battle against liberalism, which constantly threatened to reduce dogmatic convictions to the rank of simple opinion under the banner of safeguarding the rights of freedom. In this persistent combat against the heresy of the century, Newman continued the tradition of the Fathers which had as its primary aim the protection of the faith of the Church against the assaults of reason. One may wonder if the accusation of fideism which has occasionally been brought against Newman would not have come from his seeming docility to conform to the example of the Fathers. It was the Fathers who had always adopted a tutiorist or protective attitude in order to defend the Creed; they were more eager to guarantee the absolute truth of the tradition handed down by the Apostles than to produce a rational justification of it. Newman followed them on this terrain: his first sermons on faith tended to minimize the pretensions of reason.[23]

As his studies progressed, his thought was to take on a much loftier tone and he was to discover a balance rarely found among the theologians of faith. Nevertheless, the first direction toward which he inclined after reading the Fathers was to reclaim the faith, something which required first and foremost, a submission to the truth of God. Is this not a commentary on the feelings he experienced on the day of his conversion and which were expressed in the following lines?

> The search for truth is not simply the satisfaction of a curiosity; this knowledge has nothing of the excitement of a discovery; the soul is always below the truth and not above it, and it is held not by reasoning about it, but by respecting it.[24]

There is another aspect in Newman's religious synthesis where the influence of the patristic readings was important, although it is much more difficult to be precise about this. It lies in the strengthening of his

---

[23] *University Sermons*, see the commentary of M. Nédoncelle in the French edition of 1955, *Sermons Universitaires*, p. 18.
[24] *Essay on Development*, Fr. trans., L. Boyeldieu d'Auvigny, Paris, 1846, p. 316.

Christological thinking. It is not certain that Newman himself was aware of this influence which, however, is undeniable.

Indeed, if one scrutinizes his writings from his youth — his letters, intimate notes, and poems — one cannot resist the impression that his religion is more inclined toward the biblical God of creation and of judgment than toward the Christ of Christmas and Easter. The prayer of the youth seems to be more spontaneously open to the divine mystery of God's grandeur and transcendence than to Christ's redemptive love. This is not to say that the spirit of the Gospel is absent: the Evangelical faith would have reminded the disciple of Mayers that his singular election had come from the merits of the Cross. Yet, if Newman had a conviction about it, he hardly mentioned it in his prayers and reflections. Without wishing to give too much importance to the accusations of Arianism which some partisan judges claimed were expressed in his early theological writings, it is, however, legitimate to think that faith in Christ, as mediator and savior, remained more implicit than explicit in the young man. Thus, the early *Parochial and Plain Sermons*, written before 1830, focus almost entirely on moral subjects and their Christology is weak.[25]

It appears that the conversion of 1816 disengaged the adolescent from the inconsistent deism which was beginning to mislead him, and it revived the religion of the Bible, which had impregnated the years of his childhood so strongly: God is the Creator, Lord, and Master of all that exists; He is coming to meet with man, offering the grace of salvation in His word; He directs the history of men, and all events are the signs of His powerful hand; in His presence, there is for the creature no other alternative than consent or refusal; all men are under the frightening judgment which is present every day of their lives; submission is earned by fidelity in adoration; refusal is a mark of ignorance and of condemnation.[26]

With the study of the Fathers, a new aspect of spirituality was revealed. Here in the living patristic tradition, Newman discovered an expression of the great truths of the "Credo," truths he had already recognized although not explicitly. Henceforth, Newman was to have the clear possession of a synthesis of faith, and his thought could sustain itself on that which he was to call a religious system. By this he meant he had a

---

[25] See in particular the themes developed in the first volume of the *Parochial and Plain Sermons*.
[26] *Ibid.*

clear vision of faith, a sort of "Weltanschauung," which provided a coherent solution to all the problems of the world, a solution which was not just a matter of opinion, but an external fact which penetrated the history of the world, which resulted from it, derived from it, and was inseparable from it. To be a Christian meant to submit oneself to it and be made a party to its system.[27] This system is none other than the Apostolic tradition of faith that Newman came to recognize in his patient effort during his patristic investigations.

At the heart of this tradition, the keystone of the entire synthesis, is Christ revealing Himself — the Word made flesh. The mystery of the Incarnation is precisely the historical event. It is objective and absolute and holds everything together because everything leads to it and depends on it. It is this essential truth that Newman discovered as soon as he courageously tackled the systematic study of the Trinitarian heresies in his first book. In the tangled maze of scholarly discussions, he immediately saw that what was at stake was a decisive battle for the Catholic faith. It was a question of definitively accepting or rejecting the mystery of Christ, the most absolute and the most non-negotiable mystery. Behind the Arian denial of the divinity of the Word was the denial of the reality of the Incarnation and with it the entire structure of the Creed. Newman did not hesitate for an instant. He was on the side of Athanasius defending an orthodoxy which was at risk of being constantly sacrificed or mutilated by the partisans of pure dialectics. From the very first pages of the *Arians of the Fourth Century*, he denounced the Judaic influence of the school at Antioch with its narrow and sterile rationalizations.[28]

Further along in the book, he attacked all those who in their discussions maintain that the Scriptures offer nothing at all concerning the mystery of the nature of God.[29]

The Fathers of Alexandria taught him that all Scripture is prophetic: God is reached through the analogy of the signs which reveal Him. The exegesis of the sacred texts seeks less to explain the letter than to understand the texts in their most profound and total meaning: the revelation of the Son of God. Faith in Jesus Christ is the requisite for

---

[27] *Diff.*, p. 322.
[28] *The Arians*, p. 19 ff.
[29] *Ibid.*, p. 211 ff.

deciphering the prophecies: all lead to Him but it is necessary to know Christ first in order to comprehend them. Newman remembered this lesson from the Fathers when he wrote: "The principal subject of Scripture is none other than that of treating of the Man-God, of Jesus Christ, not only in the New Testament, but also in the Old."[30] In Jesus Christ, Word Incarnate, is found all grace and all holiness. His humanity is made holy by the anointing of the Word, and in it He is mediator of our salvation. In the indomitable Athanasius, Newman saw both the defender of the divinity of the Word and the Doctor of the grace which divinizes men. Much later, Newman was to develop this very close rapport between Christology and the doctrine of justification.[31]

Finally, it is the mystery of Christ which gives unity to all the truths of faith. All his life, Newman was to be sensitive to this principle which the reading of the Fathers had rendered evident to him: Christian dogmas find their significance and intelligibility in the "coherence of the whole." Discursive reason is powerless to offer anything but fragmentary explanations for each of the articles of the Creed. It is the totality of Revelation, resting upon the fact of Christ, which gives meaning to all dogmatic truths. Catholic doctrines are members of one family. They are related among themselves, explaining themselves, confirming themselves, and mutually clarifying each other. The Incarnation is the principle of Mediation and both are the highest manifestations of the sacramental principle, and of the merit of the saints.[32]

This principle in Newman's theology becomes axiomatic in his thought and gives his Christology a vigor and a depth which added much to his preaching. The Newmanian catecheses found in his Oxford sermons were so piercing and enlightening only because they made continual reference to the central mystery of the Creed. From then on, the tutor of Oriel had a doctrine and a structure at his command. The sermons at St. Mary's, during the coming years, would more and more base their theme on a Christology which had grown very strong.

---

[30] *Ibid.*

[31] See *Lectures on Justification*, published in 1835.

[32] *Essay on Development*, p. 142. This aspect of synthesizing the Christian mystery unified in Christ, comes again in many parts of the theological works of Newman. See above all: *Lectures on Justification*, p. 230 ff.; *Essay on Development*, p. 365 ff.; *Grammar of Assent*.

Newman was no longer fearful and hesitant in his religious thinking because the mastery and balance of his doctrines were rooted in the Fathers of the Church, who had revealed to him a key to understanding Scripture and had allowed him "to draw the image of Christ in his own soul."[33] Thus, it is not an exaggeration to think that Newman owed much to the patristic tradition.

Another characteristic of Newmanian spirituality that seems to draw upon the patristic heritage with much vigor and precision is its "otherworldliness," the certainty of the existence of another world more real than our own. From his childhood, Newman allowed his imagination to wander to the frontiers of an invisible world, populated with mysterious beings whose existence he suspected without giving them too precise an image. The death of Mary, as we have seen, revived this intuition and his fidelity to the memory of his departed sister found support in the teachings of the Fathers. The reading of the Fathers, most especially the early Alexandrians, was going to strengthen his spiritual vision of the world beyond. What appeared to him as the fruit of a natural sensibility was going to become for Newman a religious certainty which had for its guarantee the faith of the Fathers. The Alexandrian Fathers taught Newman that his childhood dreams were not pure fiction: there really was a mysterious other side to our world.

Can it not be said that the apparent accidental character of our destinies in this fragile world is nothing but the ephemeral side of an existence in a universe infinitely more real and more stable? Are not the realities which surround us in the present world, with their enticements, less stable and meaningful in their accomplishments than in their mysterious relation to the invisible world of which they are the symbol?

A page from the *Apologia* specifies with a great deal of clarity the influence of the patristic studies on the genesis of the Newmanian metaphysics during the Oriel period:

> It was I suppose to the Alexandrian school and to the early church, that I owe in particular what I definitely held about the Angels. I viewed them not only as ministers employed by the Creator in the

---

[33] This beautiful expression is found in one of the celebrated works of Newmanian eloquence: "The Humiliation of the Eternal Son," III, Par., XII.

Jewish and Christian dispensation, as we find on the face of Scripture, but as carrying on, as Scripture also implies, the Economy of the Visible World. I considered them as the real cause of motion, light, and life, and of those elementary principles of the physical universe, which when offered in their developments to our senses, suggest to us the notion of cause and effect, and what are called the laws of nature. This doctrine I have drawn out in my sermon for Michaelmas Day, written in 1831. I say of the Angels, "Every breath of air, and ray of light and heat, every beautiful prospect is, as it were the skirts of their garments, the waving of the robes of those whose faces see God." Again I ask what would be the thoughts of a man who "when examining a flower, or an herb, or a pebble, or a ray of light, which he treats as something so beneath him in the scale of existence, suddenly discovered that he was in the presence of some powerful being who was hidden behind the visible things he was inspecting; who though concealing his wise hand, was giving them their beauty, grace, and perfection as being God's instrument for the purpose, — nay whose robes and ornaments those objects were, which he was so eager to analyze?" And I therefore remark that we may say with grateful and simple hearts with the Three Holy Children, "O all ye works of the Lord etc., etc., bless ye the Lord, praise Him and magnify Him forever."[34]

It is not an exaggeration to recognize in this passage his closely-knit relationship with Alexandrian thought and with Origen's angelology in particular. Indeed, we find in Newman the conception of a mission imparted to the angels in the providential design of creation and in the Christian economy of salvation, which is familiar to the author of *De Principiis*.[35] In both works, the mission of the angels is envisioned as an essential reality in the order of rapport between God and the world. These rapports are described by Origen as developing on a twofold level: first, at the level of individual destinies: every one who is engaged in the way of salvation is assisted by the mediation of an angel appointed as his guardian and his support;[36] then, at the more general level of the order of the world,

---

[34] *Apologia*, p. 35.
[35] See the study by Danielou, *Origen*, Paris, 1948, pp. 219-242.
[36] *Ibid.*, p. 237 ff.

where the angels are the spiritual agents whose role it is to secure harmony in all the realities which constitute the cosmos.[37]

It is precisely this double account of the angels' action among us that Newman was to develop with predilection in his catechesis from St. Mary's. Part of it was to make present to his listeners the certainty of an invisible world, filled with these mysterious presences, who were the habitual objects of his contemplation. For him, the supernatural gifts received by the Christian allow him to participate directly in this other world which is more real than ours.[38] The destiny of every soul is transparent in the presence of angels, who are messengers from God destined to participate in our lives, revealing the existence of a particular providence.[39] On the other hand, the world in which we live is too full of strange happenings and enigmas for it not to be the theater of secret influences, although we see only the setting and the appearance. It would be unintelligible and disconcerting if this world did not evoke a more profound reality, the reality of an invisible world always present to our existence.[40]

Thus, the attentive study of the Fathers contributed to reviving Newman's thought about the invisible world. He was to become the

---

[37] "Concerning the angels presiding over all things, including the well-being of the earth and fire, that is to say of the elements." Hom. Jer. X 6, cited *Ibid.*, p. 223.

[38] "At baptism, the neophyte is in communion with God, the invisible world, the angels." IV, Par. XV, "The Moral Effect of Communion with God" p. 869, II, Par. I, "The World's Benefactors," p. 227. See in Origen himself this relation between baptism and celestial angels: Hom. Jos., IX 4 P. G., XII, 874, cited by Danielou, *op. cit.*, p. 238.

[39] III Par., IX, "A Particular Providence As Revealed in the Gospel," p. 552.

[40] See the entire sermon, "The Power of Nature," the one designated by Newman in the page of the *Apologia*, already cited: II, Par., XXIX; this sermon is from September 29, 1831. The influence of Origen shows itself in another point of the Newmanian angelology: the rather curious thesis which attributes to some intermediary spirits the particular character of diverse institutions (races, nations, societies, political and religious). Newman explains this in the text of the *Apologia* which follows the one cited: "I thought these assemblages had their life in certain unseen powers. My preference of the Personal to the Abstract would naturally lead me to this view." (*Apologia*, p. 35). Yes, it is precisely such a conception of intermediary spirits, which is developed by Origen, interpreting a biblical tradition: see Danielou, *op. cit.*, p. 223 ff.; *Les Anges des Nations*. This conception of angels and the notion of history which follows are clear enough in themselves to range Newman among the most faithful and most recent disciples of the author of *De Principiis*. He did not, however, follow him in the most audacious thesis, the one about the pre-existence of spirits; but he is closely inspired by him for all the religious themes which could clarify his vision and guide him in the exploration of the invisible world.

confident prophet of this other world in his preaching only because he perceived the deep echo of the Fathers' testimony concerning a stable and permanent order of things that the eyes of the flesh are powerless to discern. Henceforth, the spiritual vision of the soul was to reach beyond the vague frontiers of the present world, finding in the invisible world the milieu of peace and light which constitutes the true pole of our thoughts and desires. The mysterious hosts that Newman encountered led him unquestionably to recognize the presence of God, radiant with all the luminosity and glory of the blessed spirits. How many sermons and prayers would owe their sublime inspiration to this secret and ineffable vision of the invisible world in the city of the angels and the saints. The angels are revealed to us to help us fix our thoughts on the heavens.[41] The angels are the witnesses and the living images of the Invisible. The spiritual vision of Newman makes us think of the poet, Rainer Maria Rilke, but Newman's thought has much more depth. His is not the fruit of an imagination anxious to let man escape from all worldly constraints and deceptions to which he is susceptible, but rather Newman's vision is an expression of an absolute fidelity to the biblical and patristic tradition.

All his life, Newman was able to return to his early masters, taste their "cheerful images," and hear the "harmony of their discourses." The patristic source spread itself before him as a great source of light. He was always able to draw from it, especially in his hours of anguish and doubt. It was to the holy Fathers that he would continually return in order to gain comfort. And that well never dried up.

---

[41] II Par., XXIX, "The Powers of Nature," p. 451.

Chapter VI

THE MEETING OF FRIENDS: FROUDE AND KEBLE

What a wonderful grace for me:
God gave me such a faithful friend.

W. II, p. 412.

Too perfect an image creates a myth, and the image of Newman lost in solitude, while attempting to fulfill his vocation in a jealous fidelity to himself and to God, has perhaps become too mythical for us to have any chance of correcting it. Yet, nothing is less true than that Newman's inclination to solitude became an irreversible trend. All his life, he was surrounded by sympathy and friendship. From his childhood and youth, he always enjoyed the tender admiration of his family. Furthermore, he never lacked friends, who were his steady and faithful companions.

During his first years at Oxford, Newman met John Bowden, the great friend of his youth. Bowden's early death in 1844 was one of Newman's deepest sorrows. His years at Oriel soon taught him that he had the gift of being empathetic. He had a strange power of attracting people at the very time that he believed he was giving up all human affections. Indeed, it is difficult to imagine the wide circle of friends that surrounded Newman during the noble and formidable years of the Oxford Movement and who supported him in his battles and trials. After his conversion to Rome, certain bonds were loosened, but the memory of them with their hopes and shared joys remained sacred. At the twilight of his life, during his long years of voluntary seclusion at the Oratory in Birmingham, his faithful disciples confounded him by the continued delicacy of their affections. Their devotion represented to him an ideal of tenderness and human warmth.

He evoked this joy in friendship in a poem in 1829. It is a homage of gratitude to all the confidants of his youth: "Blessings of friends, which to my door unasked, unhoped have come."[1]

In the *Apologia*, he truly vindicated himself against the accusation that he solicited influence and sympathy without giving anything in return:

> My habitual feeling then and since has been that it was not I who sought friends, but friends who sought me. Never a man had kinder or more indulgent friends than I have had but I expressed my own feelings as to the mode in which I gained them in this very year 1829.[2]

That Newman had an uncanny power of attracting others to himself is a fact too obvious to be contested. But it is equally an indisputable trait of his personality that he preserved a sovereign liberty over his affections and his feelings for others.[3] To tell the truth, we have a thousand reasons to think that he never denied the deep friendships entwined in the intimacy of his heart. "Cor ad cor loquitur" ["Heart speaks unto heart"]: his motto as Cardinal, expresses completely the secret of these attachments. But, assuredly, how rare were those who crossed the border of his heart.

There is, for example, his relationship with the "Noetics" of Oriel, especially with the most influential of them, Dr. Whately. In spite of frequent and familiar exchanges between the two men, there remained an

---

[1] "Thanksgiving" in the collection, *Verses on Various Occasions*, p. 45.
[2] *Apologia*, p. 25.
[3] The best pages on these two aspects of friendship in Newman himself have been written by M. Nédoncelle. In a penetrating analysis which illustrates an understanding of friendship in general, the author explains the secret of the influence of Newman: "The gift of almost universal sympathy of which Newman had the secret is explained by the fact that each one discovered in him his own idealized self. He offered them the intuition of that which they desired to find in the depth of their own soul. Without his or their knowing, this purified hidden self became a reality and this is why he had for them an invincible attraction. This unknown self was at the same time newer and yet older than all the masks of existence. And this communion did not prevent his friends from being different from him." (M. Nédoncelle, *La Réciprocité des Consciences*, Paris, 1943, p. 71.)

undefinable reserve between them that neither Newman nor Whately was able to surmount: "Something from within me resisted."[4] The young fellow knew he was not himself when he sought to follow Whately in his grand and overreaching strides. What stopped Newman was not so much his refusal to submit to the influence of another person because he jealously wished to protect his own liberty, but rather it was the feeling that Whately's influence was not absolutely convincing. It was too dominated by logic and paradoxes and not enough by virtue and spiritual strength. Was this an intolerant rejection by a young man still enmeshed in his own Evangelical prejudices? This is not certain. The "fellow," Newman, began to lose some of his timidity and scruples; he tried to cope with the intelligentsia of Oxford; he felt full of promise and waited for the occasion to put himself forward. But he had never lost the desire for spiritual perfection. The Noetics were decidedly too attached to the speculations of their minds. Thus, their discussions in the common room could not help but turn into intellectual dilettantism. It is not that these men were without scruples or were free from all authority. On the contrary, they were straightforward churchmen, with a keen sense of duty and a mixture of austere gravity. They also had a discrete humor which made them attractive and respectable. Nevertheless, Newman's heart remained unsmitten. His attitude toward them, no matter how real it was, never went beyond esteem, and possibly admiration for their intellectual performances. How different was his attitude toward men like Keble, Froude, and Pusey. He shared a communion of the soul with each of them. The key to Newman's friendships is only to be found in the sharing of a common spiritual fidelity in the pursuit of a common ideal.

The Example of Froude. It was Richard Hurrell Froude who revealed to Newman the secret blessings of a lasting and deep friendship. The young man, son of an archdeacon from Devonshire, had been brought up in the purest Tory and High Church tradition, which was that of his paternal home and county. Prematurely deprived of a mother, he received a strict

---

[4] Letter to Whately, then Anglican Archbishop of Dublin, *Apologia*, p. 283. "I can feel no reluctance to confess, that when I first was noticed by your Grace, gratitude to you and admiration of your powers wrought upon me; and, had not something from within resisted, I should certainly have adopted views on religion and social duty, which seem to my present judgment to be based in pride of reason and to tend toward infidelity...."

education from the archdeacon, which possibly contributed to exacerbat-
ing a difficult temperament. Froude found it arduous to master his too
easily excitable impulses. His natural fiery temperament carried him into
the most diverse enthusiasms: the frenzy of a galloping horse, the excitement of a boat race at sea, or the contagious fever of an intellectual debate
where he could use his passion for logic to his heart's content. These
contrasts in his character revealed in Froude a very attractive personality.
At the same time, he looked like a gentleman weighed down with tradition,
as well as an ancient hero doomed by fatality. Some historians, sensitive
to his aristocratic manners and his chivalrous sense of values, saw Froude
as a survivor from another age. Others saw in Froude, who was touched by
a cruel destiny which deprived him of his mother's tender love by her
untimely death, the anguish of another Pascal, if not the morbid anxiety of
a Hamlet, vainly battling against himself and death. But we can also think
of him as a young prophet, whose oracles were to be stifled even before he
could open his mouth, a sort of contemporary rival to Lamennais from
across the Channel, but a Lamennais still at the age of promise, a Lamennais filled with dreams and desires.

Possessing all these prophetic, intellectual, and religious insights, a
temperament such as his could have easily gone to extremes if it were not
for the influence of one man who managed to bring him the peace of mind
he needed. This man was John Keble, senior to Newman and Froude, who
became the common bond between the two young men. Before joining
Newman at Oriel, Froude had been Keble's pupil for a long time. When
Keble left Oxford, he retired to a country parish. Froude followed him as
a private pupil and the pastor's moral authority soon produced positive
results. Keble radiated the serenity and innocence of the just. He was
ambitious for much more than earthly honors and university titles. He was
a man of silence and prayer, and everything about him exuded peace and
the interior life. His example succeeded in exorcising the demons which
were challenging the vulnerable conscience of his disciple. John Keble
showed Froude the way of true renunciation. Tearing him away from his
dark humor, Keble taught him how to fight against himself and to free
himself from the somewhat narcissistic constraints which bound him.

Keble's direction allowed Froude to exercise his exceptional gifts.
Far from destroying Froude's spontaneous humor and native exuberance,
Keble helped refine and spiritualize them.

Resisting the morose tendency to turn in upon himself too much,

Froude mastered his multiple gifts in an astonishing way. When death felled him in 1836, Newman and Keble edited the papers left by their friend. The intimate notes of his *Journal*, which dates from 1826, testify to the staggering rigor with which the young fellow had seriously taken the call to holiness. This included a merciless discipline exercised in fasting, in sleeping on bare boards, in restricting his spending, and in seeking for purity of intention even in the least significant act. This was the daily bread of the young Anglican. Richard Hurrell Froude recalled the demanding law of the Sermon on the Mount to his Church that was tempted to forget it.

This kind of ambition in a man who was only able to choose the absolute, all or nothing, would not fail to surprise or provoke a scandal in his circle of friends. In fact, the personality of this young man of Oriel was of such youthful vigor that it appeared bold and impetuous. He immediately took the side of the rebels. He was resolutely on his guard against the numerous cohorts of the righteous believers. Against all prejudices, unconstrained vis-à-vis all social constraints, titles, and honors, Froude disguised under a calculated impertinence his unswerving attachment to a tradition which represented true authority.

Inheritor of the Toryism which had forged the British soul and a loyal son and lover of the High Church, Froude was too solicitous of true greatness to spare political or religious leaders whose only preoccupation was to establish alliances or agreements with the promoters of liberalism, which was already spreading fast. The defense of the Established Church was an absolute belief for him. He thought that the State should protect and serve it. Denouncing the most secret faults in himself uncompromisingly, Froude was not less categorical in stigmatizing the concessions and compromises of persons in power.

The bond of friendship between Newman and Froude tightened as they became involved in a reform of the educational discipline in the existing role of the tutor. Froude, who had been elected tutor in 1826, was inclined to share the ideas of Newman, his senior, and to follow him in undertaking a reform. Newman wrote about the traditional system:

> There is much in the system which I think wrong; I think the tutors
> see too little of the men, and there is not enough direct religious
> instruction. It is my wish to consider myself as the minister of
> Christ. Unless I find that opportunities occur of doing spiritual

good to those over whom I am placed, it will become a grave question whether I ought to continue in tuition.[5]

The election of a new provost at Oriel in 1827 stimulated the hopes of many for reform. To succeed the former provost, Copleston, who became Bishop of Llandoff, two names were suggested: Keble and Hawkins. Hawkins was vicar of St. Mary's and had Newman's support, while Keble found a passionate supporter in Froude. In spite of his admiration for Keble, Newman thought he was cut out neither for administration nor for the practical duties involved in directing a college. "It is not a question of electing an angel, but a provost," he said ironically. Since his early days at Oriel, Newman knew Hawkins well and believed him to be open to reform. To Newman, Hawkins appeared to be infinitely more realistic than Keble. Ultimately, Newman's opinion prevailed, and Hawkins was elected. But a phenomenon occurred which is not all that rare in men who attain an authoritative position. The former liberal lost his audaciousness and became unbendingly authoritative. To the great disappointment of those who had elected him, he resolutely opposed every reform.[6] From that time on, conflict became inevitable between Hawkins and the young fellows which resulted in the termination of their duties as tutors. Newman felt the rupture most deeply.[7] But at least, he earned the lasting friendship of Richard Hurrell Froude, the confidant of his hopes and the accomplice of his efforts.

In the *Apologia*, Newman tenderly drew a silhouette of the cavalier[8] Tory, as one who never retreated before obstacles be it as much in a discussion as in the chase. At the same time, Newman recognized his debt to his young friend with these words:

> He taught me to look with admiration towards the Church of Rome, and in the same degree to dislike the Reformation. He

[5] M. I., p. 133.

[6] See in Bouyer, *op. cit.*, pp. 90 ff., the account of the election of Hawkins and its consequences.

[7] However, the teaching of Newman with his pupils will engage him until the summer of 1831, while Froude and Wilberforce had ceased earlier. In his *Autobiographical Memoirs*, M. I., p. 140, Newman writes concerning this theological movement of Oxford: "Humanly speaking, that movement never would have been, had he not been deprived of his tutorship."

[8] *Apologia*, p. 31.

fixed deep in me the idea of devotion to the Blessed Virgin, and
he led me gradually to believe in the Real Presence.[9]

While the *Apologia* dwells discretely on Newman's profound feelings for his friend, a truer understanding of the depth of his feelings, rooted
as they were in the intimacy of his heart, can be discovered in the
spontaneous confidences found in his letters and in his poetic expressions,
which were inspired by the memories of Froude. Indeed, it is in the
correspondence and poems that we are able to recognize the real influence
of Froude and his astonishing power.

Upon the death of Froude on February 28, 1836, Newman added
several verses to a poem of 1833, "Separation of Friends":

> Ah! dearest, with a word he could dispel
>   All questioning, and raise
> Our hearts to rapture, whispering all was well!
>   And turning prayer to praise.
> And other secrets too he could declare,
>   By patterns all divine,
> His earthly creed retouching here and there,
>   And deepening every line.
> Dearest! he longs to speak, as I to know,
>   And yet we both refrain:
> It were not good: a little doubt below,
>   And all will soon be plain.[10]

In these last verses, the poet delicately traces the mysterious bond
which attached him to his departed friend: "he longs to speak as I to know."
Newman could not have better explained the reason why he found
Froude's example so compelling and absolute.

First of all, on the spiritual level, Froude was a witness to a sanctity
which was characterized by a simple and sincere conscience, always
anxious to bridge the gap between life as he lived it and that which he
expected of himself. Froude's impetuous nature carried him to extremes
in his spiritual combat. Incapable of controlling himself on the road to

---

[9] *Ibid.*, p. 32.
[10] *Verses*, CXV, pp. 195-196.

perfection, which he had uncompromisingly chosen, he expressed a radical dissatisfaction with himself. From Froude, Newman learned that there is always a risk in having too many ideas, particularly when they are beautiful and generous. These ideas can fill us with ourselves and shut us off from the demands of reality. Ideas can be sterile if they are not acted upon in everyday life. They put the conscience to sleep and end in self-deception. They can be deadening and deceiving and lead us away from the truth. The absolute need for truth, which burned like a fire in Froude, is seen in the *Remains*, published after his death. It had a salutary effect on Newman and helped lead him away from a risky intellectual impasse. He always saw his friendship with Richard Hurrell Froude, as well as his own illness and the death of Mary, as the means of leading him away from the influence of the Noetics.

Froude's influence exerted itself on still another level, hidden and less easily discerned. This influence had to do with the different attitudes each of these two young men manifested in the face of conflict. Without doubt, Newman had all the qualities of a man of action. His entire life testifies to this. He knew his objective, knew how to decide for himself, and he weighed the means and possibilities. His future would show that he was capable of the most blatant audacities. He put to work a heart so passionate that it even disconcerted him. But, with his gift of intuition without which he would not be Newman, he detected situations to be dealt with and calculated the risks involved. He foretold and guessed the reactions of others. He was never entirely indifferent to the opinions or suspicions of others. Not as favored as the angel of the Lord who could descend into the pool of Bethsaida without soiling its wings,[11] Newman could not jostle with men without experiencing fear of hurting them. Froude's attitude in dealing with men was entirely different. He stood firm before public opinion with the same boldness with which he disciplined himself in secret, and he was equally unconcerned whether he caused alarm or aroused enthusiasm. He never looked back at the fire he set and moved on as a precursor, lighting the way, and not bothering to pace his steps to the cadence of others. Newman said he had solidly anchored first principles, and his clear perception of their value rendered him relatively indifferent

---

[11] This quotation illustrates one of his sermons, "Scripture: A Record of Human Sorrow," I, Par. XXVI, p. 206.

to the revolutionary action which accompanied their application in a given situation.[12] Such serenity strengthened him in the face of opposition or ill-will and his determination was strengthened by the very scandals he provoked. His obvious sincerity, his open and direct manner toward other people, and his very inimitable free style, both frightened and stimulated Newman at the same time.

Won over by Froude's contagious vitality and ardor, Newman learned how to overcome his own reserve and timidity, and he surmounted his tendency to be alarmed by rumors and criticism.

In the rough battle that became the Oxford Movement, Newman, supported by Froude, was able to become engaged with a firm spirit and a strong heart. After Froude's death, the survivor cherished his memory. Moreover, a tangible bond tied them together. The presence and affection of Froude's spiritual director and teacher, John Keble, helped preserve his memory and bridged the loss imposed by death.

The Influence of Keble. It was to Froude that Newman owed his friendship with Keble. Since Froude had pierced Newman's reserve and became his friend, he wished to bring him together with Keble, and to dissipate the doubts which he suspected existed in the relationship between the two men. "Do you know," wrote Froude in his *Remains*, "the story of the assassin who had done only one good deed in his life? Well, if I was asked what good action I have done, I would say that I brought Newman and Keble to understand each other."[13]

Froude realized that in spite of the mutual suspicions which prevented an encounter between his High-Church teacher and the disciple of the Noetics, a profound affinity of thought and sentiment existed between the two men. Froude only had to bring them together for a common spiritual bond to be forged.

From the time of his arrival at Oxford, it was Keble's name which Newman heard uttered, with greater respect than admiration.[14] With

---

[12] *Apologia*, p. 32. In this same book, Newman gives another picture of his friend: "He took an eager courageous view of things on the whole. I should say that his power of entering into the minds of others did not equal his other gifts; he could not believe for instance, that I really held the Roman Church to be anti-Christian.... He seemed not to understand my difficulties."

[13] "Remains," I, p. 438, cited by Newman in the *Apologia*, p. 27.

[14] *Apologia*, p. 26; cf. *Essays Critical and Historical*, II, p. 445 ff.: "The Influence of Keble."

obvious emotion, he recalled in the *Apologia*, the shock he experienced
when he came face to face with Keble, when he first met him on the street
and then later in Oriel's common room during the presentation ceremony.

Keble then enjoyed incomparable prestige at Oxford; when he was
very young, he had obtained the highest honors of the University.[15] But the
honor flowing from such an enviable success had altered nothing of the
simplicity, the sweetness, and the modesty which came from "the patriar-
chal atmosphere of his paternal home."[16] Indifferent to the path of honors,
John Keble was ill at ease in the somewhat dry intellectual climate of the
university town. He soon resigned his fellowship to join his father's parish
and to allow his mystical and poetic talents to blossom with the peaceful
activities of his pastoral ministry.

As soon as he was elected to Oriel, Newman was able to measure
clearly the exceptional influence of this brilliant senior fellow. The
enthusiastic admiration which Newman then experienced was equalled
only by the timidity which he demonstrated on becoming one of Keble's
close associates in the common room. Writing to his friend, Bowden, he
confided his first impressions to him:

> I had to go in great haste to the Tower in order to receive the
> congratulations of all the fellows. I had suffered it just until Keble
> shook my hand, then I felt myself so confused and so unworthy
> of the honor which had been conferred on me that I would have
> wished for the earth to swallow me up.[17]

However, in the first years, Newman yielded only a little to the
positive influence of Keble. He told us that his reserve was then so
excessive that it prevented him from opening up. Besides, his critical mind
was drawn more towards the Noetics than to Keble. In the common room
where secret influences were forged, Keble had some idea, before returning to parish life, of his young colleague's intellectual orientation, influ-

---

[15] *Ibid.*, p. 26. A student of Corpus Christi College, Keble had taken a "double first," i. e.,
first prize in two different disciplines; then, he obtained a fellowship at Oriel. Cf., M. I.,
p. 66; letter of Newman to his father, May 16, 1822. See also Church, *op. cit.*, p. 23.
[16] The expression is from Dawson. Thomas Keble, his father, was rector.
[17] *Apologia*, p. 27; cf. M. I., p. 63.

enced as it was by Whately's liberalism and by his apparent attachment to the Evangelical creed.[18]

Since Newman did nothing to change Keble's impressions of him, Keble left Oxford taking those views with him. Keble represented the ecclesiastical tradition of the High Church in its most sincere and dogmatic form. Devoted to the Established Church from his birth, Keble was firmly protective of its rights. Since 1823, he was afraid of the threats to the Church posed by the growth of liberalism on the one hand and the Evangelical movement on the other. Not given to supporting his thinking with rigorous logic, Keble had an intuitive mind whose manner of expression was, as M. Nédoncelle said, "poetry, and his poetry a prayer." Yet, he had enough influence on two of his disciples, Froude and Isaac Williams, to inspire them with a resolutely hostile attitude toward liberalism and with a determination to defend the sovereign rights of the Anglican Church.

Thereafter, in 1827, Keble agreed to publish a collection of his poems, *The Christian Year*,[19] and this only after the pressing entreaties of his friends. In this collection, he reminded religious souls of the peaceful joys of prayer and of the moving beauty of the Anglican liturgy. Without ever striving for the sublime, nor for the originality of a personal lyricism, the genius of Keble, although it was touched by a romanticism which brought him close to Wordsworth's themes, nevertheless had the merit of combining religious sentiment with poetry.

He shed light on the providential harmony of the world when he evoked the beauty of creation. At the same time, he showed the existence of mysterious correspondences in the human soul. Inspired by the *Book of Common Prayer*, which is the liturgical book of the Anglican faith, the poems of *The Christian Year* had no other aim but to restore the richness of its prayer life and to inspire the desire for perfection. Keble published his poems at a time when naturalism was depriving religion of its sense of mystery and Methodism was offering the sentimental and ambiguous suggestion of a "rebirth."

---

[18] It is that which Newman confesses: "He was shy of me for years in consequence of the marks which I bore upon me of the evangelical and liberal schools. At least, so I have ever thought." *Ibid.*, p. 27.

[19] "The hymns of Keble had just been published on May 30, 1827. I have merely looked into them.... They seem quite exquisite." M. I., p. 144.

On reading these poems, Newman was deeply moved. He wrote to his mother on June 10, 1827 about his admiration for them. Some of these hymns were to bring him a salutary message of peace and resignation after the death of Mary. They acted upon him in the manner of a litany. On May 10, 1828, he wrote to his sister, Jemima:

> In riding out today I have been impressed more powerfully than before I had an idea was possible with the two lines:
>
> > Chanting with a solemn voice
> > Minds us of our better choice.
>
> I could hardly believe the lines were not my own and Keble had not taken them from me.[20]

After his first visit on August 10, 1828 to the home of Keble, then at Fairford, Newman again confided to his sister: "Keble's verses are such that 'My head ran so upon them that I was every minute in danger of quoting them.'"[21]

It was not Keble's poetic and musical insights alone that attracted Newman, but his happy resonance with Bishop Butler's *Analogy*, a book familiar to Newman for many years.[22]

---

[20] M. I., p. 161. The verses are extracts of the hymn for the First Sunday after Epiphany, in *The Christian Year*, ed. Longmans, 1909, p. 34.

[21] M. I., p. 167.

[22] These two principles which he defines in the *Apologia* under the name of the "sacramental system" and of "antecedent probability" were to become of exceptional importance in Newman's religious philosophy. They were going to help him to prove the existence of an invisible world and to justify faith with regard to believing. Newman is the disciple of Plato and of the Alexandrians and he simply applies the principle according to which the physical world is essentially the symbol of a world much higher and more real.

As for the second principle that we mention, it tends to justify faith in demonstrating that the act of faith presupposes moral dispositions which allow one to recognize and receive the revealed truth.

These two principles are based on a Newmanian intuition that we shall call the law of connaturality; if there is a harmony between the two worlds, it is because there is a relationship which, for want of a better word, we call a connaturality between these two worlds; if moral dispositions are required for faith, it is because the conscience which endorses these dispositions has a natural affinity for religious truth. The philosopher, Maurice Blondel, has adopted and developed this idea of connaturality, which seems to him to be the basis for religious knowledge. See, "Le Problème de la Mystique," in *Cahiers de la nouvelle Journée*, Paris, 1929.

Without doubt, these readings did not suffice to forge the bonds of friendship which both men mutually wanted. At least, they were one step toward a harmony of thought which would produce fruit in time. At the close of 1827, as we have seen, the young tutor did not discern in Keble the authority and practicality that would make him an excellent college provost, although he admired his high moral sense. But soon after, when Hawkins' disappointing performance as provost brought Newman and Froude together in their attempt to reform the tutorship, Newman quite naturally remembered Keble, whom he had sacrificed too quickly. Under the influence of Froude, the last reserve between the two men disappeared.

In the course of the years that followed, there were numerous contacts between the two men. Subsequently, it was Newman who visited the poet in his parish at Gloucestershire and returned enchanted with some moments of intimate sharing; another time, it was Keble, who in an affectionate letter, testified to his warm feeling for his young friend.[23]

A correspondence started which expressed their identical views, hopes, and ambitions. In 1829, the campaign against Peel for the seat of deputy representative from Oxford to Parliament brought Newman closer to Keble, who had been an adversary to the reelection of Peel from the beginning.[24] At the same time, it consummated Newman's rupture with Whately and Hawkins, who were strong supporters of Peel.

Soon, their intimacy was great enough for the two men to confide in

---

[23] Letters from Keble to Newman from August 20, 1828 and from August 24, 1831: "You are a real honest man." M. I., p. 216.

[24] He had come to Oxford with a petition signed by him and addressed against Peel. (M. I., p. 175: Letter from Newman to his sister, Harriet.)

Robert Peel, representative from Oxford, had convinced Parliament to vote for the emancipation of English Catholics, overpassing the limits of the mandate that had been confided to him by his electors; he had previously presented himself as an adversary of the Emancipation Act. In 1829, he resigned his mandate and proposed himself anew for the vote of his electors. Newman, who was at heart a partisan of emancipation, saw in this maneuver of Peel, a threat to the authority of the Established Church because the liberals, defenders of the law, were animated much more by a spirit of neutrality and religious indifference than by any benevolent concern with regard to the Catholics of their country. See the correspondence of Newman: Letter to his sister, Harriet, Feb. 17, 1829 (M. I., p. 175); to his mother, February 28th and of March 1st (*Ibid.*, pp. 176-177). He wrote notably after the fall of Peel: "We have proved the independence of the Church and of Oxford" (*Ibid.*, p. 177). The candidacy of Peel, in effect, failed thanks to the vigorous campaign. On this phase of the religious history, see Thureau-Dangin, *Renaissance Catholique en Angleterre au XIX siècle*, I, p. 48.

each other about their projects: Keble was elected to the chair of poetry at the end of 1831, when Newman was writing his book on the Arians.[25] There is no doubt that in those years of expectation, Keble and Newman, stimulated by Froude, were together pondering the principal reforms for the Church. When Newman was in Rome in 1833, he wrote to his sister, Jemima, of his hopes for the future of the Anglican Church, as envisioned by Keble, "a second Ambrose."[26]

From then on, complete confidence existed between the two men and this trust created a climate of optimism, enthusiasm, and boldness which characterized the beginnings of the Oxford Movement. Suspicions of former times had fallen away completely; the superficial disagreements which probably existed between the former disciple of the Noetics and the delicate poet of *The Christian Year* disappeared under the skillful influence of Froude. John Keble's radiating candor was in perfect harmony with Newman's ardent moral sincerity. We shall see much later how in the dark hours of the Oxford Movement, the friendship between these two men matured into a profound religious communion of thought. But we must now discuss the nature of this friendship which bloomed on the eve of the Movement.

On August 27, 1837, Newman wrote to Keble, who had invited Newman to the consecration of his church at Hursley in his new parish:

> Thank you for wishing for me at the consecration... and I should have liked it. I think I am very cold and reserved to people, but I cannot ever realize to myself that any one loves me. I believe that is partly the reason, or I dare not realize it.[27]

In this confidence, Newman displays a disposition which seems to characterize the nature of his relationship with the pastor of Hursley. It was hard for him to realize that he could be Keble's friend and confidant. One searches in vain in the correspondence with Keble for the lively spontaneity or playful freedom that one finds in the letters to Froude or to Bowden, his friend from his earliest days. In the affectionate portraits of Keble

---

[25] Letter from Keble to Newman, January 16, 1832 (M. I., p. 224).
[26] Letter of Newman to his sister, March 20, 1833 (*Ibid*, p. 331).
[27] M. II., p. 216, underscored in the text.

which Newman sketched, there is always that element of respect and veneration.[28] A legitimate familiarity never developed in their relationship, which was henceforth enhanced by a mutual confidence and an equal sincerity. Furthermore, the spirit of openness, which is the gauge of real friendship, did not affect the reserve and intimate discretion which Newman and Keble maintained toward each other. In one of his sermons, Newman defined certain conditions of friendship which seem applicable to his relationship with Keble:

> How differently we feel and speak of our friends as present or absent. Their presence is a check upon us; it acts as an external law, compelling us to do or not to do what we should not do or do otherwise, or should do but for it.... When a person... should be present, we qualify our words... we observe a deference and a delicacy in our conduct towards him.[29]

This passage reveals a puritanical note. It is possible that by insisting too much on fear and on respect, a friendship in its most delicate and

---

[28] These portraits are scattered throughout the works of Newman; and such dispersion shows well how lively he preserves the memory of Keble in every period of his life. See note A of the Appendix of the *Apologia*, p. 219; *Essays Critical and Historical*, II, pp. 421-453; *Idea of a University*, p. 158. See also the last testimony in W. II, p. 96, which relates an account of the visit of Newman to Hursley some time before the death of Keble.

Once, however, his praise does not prevent him from expressing some reservation about the too timid character of the poet. It is in Newman's article on the *Lyra Innocentium* (edited in *Essays Critical...*). This article of 1846 takes into account a collection of poems that Keble had just published. With a measure of tact, but in a firm manner nevertheless, Newman, who had just converted to Catholicism, criticizes Keble for shielding his poetry from the needs of the hour and for taking refuge in the evocation of a past devoid of a sense of history. While the first poems, those of *The Christian Year* (1827) and of the *Lyra Apostolica* (1836) denounced the evils and sufferings of the Church without hesitation, those of the *Lyra Innocentium* did not do a thing to come to the rescue of the Church, torn by liberalism. Beyond a simple quarrel of ideas, Newman denounced in Keble a typical weakness in his character, his dread of taking too strong positions, and his fears, that Bouyer called "a provincialism, not to say a very timid narrowness, almost an intellectual cowardice."

[29] V Par., II, p. 959. "Reverence, A Belief in God's Presence." Newman, in this sermon, urges respect and religious silence as the highest signs of love and faith. This is one of the most cherished ideas of the Vicar of St. Mary's; true religion is not a simple familiarity with God, it ought to join fear to love. Cf. I Par., XX, "Forms of Private Prayer," p. 163. VII Par., I, "Reverence in Worship," p. 1557.

balanced form can never be attained.[30] But, this is not the point here. In
spite of, or more so because of his reserve towards Keble, Newman truly
knew the privileges of a friendship which was an authentic communion of
souls. This reserve was based on the mysterious power of Keble, on his
moral purity, and on his intense spiritual life. This explains why, in the
difficult times ahead, Newman ultimately turned to Keble, seeking from
the poet some appeasement for his troubled conscience, if not a light
without shadows. Later, we shall address the advantages as well as the
disadvantage of this spiritual direction.[31]

It was neither at an intellectual nor a doctrinal level that Keble's
influence was most profound. His teachings, taken on the whole, were not
new to Newman who had already recognized their limits. Besides, Newman
had less need for teachings than for a living witness. In Keble, Newman
had the serene example of a man who had judged the promises of the world
according to their true value and who was dedicated to another way, the
way of sanctity.

In a poem which he published in the *Lyra Apostolica*, Newman
expressed the emotion he always felt in Keble's presence: "The glory of
the living God aurioles about him — a saint, it is a saint."[32]

Newman had drawn inspiration for his poem from the memories of
his early encounters. He had preserved wonder and admiration in his
memory. The impression that Keble made upon Newman's spirituality
seemed to develop around two themes: the first gave him a model in which
the orders of nature and grace were reconciled; the second helped him to
discover the requisites for exercising a true moral influence.

Newman's moral austerity was still colored with traces of Evangelicalism, and he had some difficulty in accepting the possibility of harmony

---

[30] This danger is particularly evident in a milieu open to some puritanism. One knows
about the affectation of English preachers at the beginning of the nineteenth century,
and Newman early denounced the "cant," which replaced true eloquence with
affectation and a lack of simplicity. This absence of frankness was also able to affect
the means of relating: On cant, see Newman, *Lectures on Justification*, p. 141.

[31] See text Chapter X, "An Ineffectual Spiritual Direction."

[32] *Lyra Apostolica*, p. 72. In this poem composed at Zante in the course of the voyage on
the Mediterranean, January 8, 1833, the allusion to Keble is clear:

  I saw thee once and nought discerned
    For stranger to admire
  A serious aspect, but it burned
    With no unearthly fire.

between natural and supernatural gifts. His first sermon at St. Mary's carries the indelible mark of a spirit defiant of too human values.[33] He was more inclined to recognize a radical separation between nature and grace than to seek a possible alliance between the two orders.

Keble, in whom the splendors of grace were reflected in a luminous manner, denied none of the talents with which a generous nature had endowed him. He had clearly rejected the honors of a successful career. Retired to his country parish, he incarnated the religious ideal which attracted Newman's conscience. Nevertheless, the saint was also a poet; his asceticism had preserved in him all human values and his poetical inspiration was joined to an authentic mystical experience. In Keble, with his singular powers of influence, we have a religious model in whom were reconciled the beauty of both intellect and grace.

Newman recognized in Keble that which he soon called the beauty of sanctity, the unique privilege of saints who influence solely by the presence of the divine grace which transfigures and elevates their natural gifts into a spiritual unity. Henceforth, Keble appeared to him as the witness of true humanism, introducing poetry into prayer and beauty into religion.[34] The pastor of Hursley cast over the inborn austerity of his friend a note of peace and joy.

Confined within the Anglican climate, Keble's mystical aspirations were not able to reach their fullness: they lacked a firm dogmatic base. Yet, his disposition offered Newman a type of perfection that he would constantly try to emulate. Much later, when Newman entered the Catholic Church, he would again discover this special type of sanctity which would transfigure and elevate his own nature. This type of spirituality decidedly drew Newman to saints like Philip Neri or Francis de Sales, whose humanism and simplicity reminded him of John Keble[35] and brought the full brilliance of the beauty of holiness before his very eyes.

---

[33] II Par., XXX, "The Danger of Accomplishments."

[34] See this expanded in *Essays*, II, p. 442.

[35] It is Newman himself who noticed the likeness between Keble and Saint Philip Neri: "This great saint reminds me in so many ways of Keble, that I can fancy what Keble would have been if God's will had been that he should have been born in another place and age; he was formed on the same type of extreme hatred of humbug, playfulness; nay, oddity, tender love for others, and severity, which are lineaments of Keble." M. II, p. 424, a letter to Mrs. Mosley, January 26, 1847.

However, Keble not only reconciled the movement of the heart with those of prayer in his spiritual life, he also knew how to master a culture, very largely humanistic and most original, while purifying it in his personal care of souls.

Voluntarily confined to a country parish, he was completely taken up with his pastoral concerns. And this retreat, which seemed to turn him away from Oxford, in fact kept him more alive with a spiritual prestige more enviable than all other titles. His influence became more profound and effective because his presence was distant. Keble's generous renunciation was the start of a new influence, one which surpassed all material and immediate bonds, to nourish souls in the depths of their hearts and wills.

At the time of Keble's departure, Newman was caught by surprise; then, he understood that true influence does not remain at the intellectual level but reaches out into a different sphere, which is nothing less than the sphere of sanctity.

In the *Apologia*, he elucidated the specific nature of Keble's influence:

> Keble was young in years, when he became a University celebrity, and younger in mind. He had the purity and simplicity of a child. He had few sympathies with the intellectual party, who sincerely welcomed him as a brilliant specimen of young Oxford. He instinctively shut up before literary display, and pomp and donnishness of manner, faults which always will beset academical notabilities.... He went into the country; but his instance serves to prove that men need not, in the event, lose that influence which is rightly theirs, because they happen to be thwarted in the use of the channels natural and proper to its exercise. He did not lose his place in the minds of men because he was out of their sight.[36]

To Newman, Keble's influence appeared all the more profound when it was less sought after, all the greater when it was more hidden, all the more effective when it was despoiled of the artifices of nature. Newman

---

[36] *Apologia*, p. 219.
[37] Letter to Rickards, July 20, 1830, M. I., p. 202; A personal note in M. I., p. 91.

never forgot this lesson. He saw a certain type of saint in Keble; he saw in him a model of an Apostle. He did not go as far as to follow in his footsteps. If he never sought an isolated parish following the example of his new master, he sometimes felt a longing for it, especially during moments of crises in the Oxford Movement.[37] Perhaps, we should attribute Newman's recurring desire to leave Oxford and England to become a missionary in a foreign land to the value of Keble's example.[38] At least, Newman would know how to draw from Keble's example a spirit of detachment and serenity when it would become necessary for him to leave Oxford. Going beyond a personal renunciation, Newman would learn also the true meaning of an influence that would hereafter mark his personal spirituality and preaching. Newman always regarded his spiritual influence as a free gift by which divine grace recompenses the work of all those who, like Keble, do not sacrifice to ambition, power, or human rewards.

---

[38] *Autobiographical Memoirs*, Chap. IV (M. I., p.129); *Apologia*, p. 19: "My calling in life would require such a sacrifice as celibacy involved; as for instance missionary work among the heathen, to which I had a great drawing for some years."

Chapter VII

ILLNESS IN SICILY

The night is dark and I am far from home.
Verses, p. 156.

AT THE POINT WHERE we are now in the spiritual journey of Newman, we are able to discern the various roads he traveled since his conversion of 1816. Detaching himself from Evangelicalism with which he was so little in accord, Newman avoided the snare of intellectual ambition and skepticism. Rude ordeals, which deeply shook him, helped him in the first stage of detachment; some shared friendships, dedicated to the pursuit of the same religious ideals, fortified him in his renunciations.

Yet, in order to be perfectly available to the call of God, Newman still needed to detach himself from what was left of his youthful self-confidence and intellectual presumptions. Conscious of all the gifts and promises that he was carrying within himself, the senior tutor was perhaps a little too eager to share a measure of those gifts. A final trial was necessary in order to discover, on the sharp cutting edge of spiritual combat, the true condition of a complete interior fidelity and total sanctity. Conversion can bring about profound changes which shake the very foundation of an individual's existence. But let no one be deceived here; conversion cannot fully reach its potential for renewal as long as one's liberty, of which the Apostle speaks, has not been totally surrendered into the hands of God, who alone leads us and gives us His commandments: "Another will take you and lead you where you do not wish to go."[1] The innermost recesses

---

[1] John 21:18.

of one's very self, one's own selfish will, is what is finally in question; it rebels and is most in need of being subdued. In spite of an avowed sincerity and a desire for progress, Newman still needed to ι ake this discovery. It seems that his spiritual destiny, on the eve of the great enterprises which were awaiting him, was calling for such a decisive trial by which the soul, well aware of the vanity of its desires and of its own will, was to put itself completely into the hands of God. It is the classical desert experience to which the great masters of the spiritual life were subjected from their youth: John of the Cross in the prison at Toledo; Francis de Sales, tortured by the idea of predestination; and many others who experienced this purifying state of the soul.

It was during the course of a voyage in the Mediterranean, in the feverish solitude of a springtime in Sicily, that Newman was confronted with such a spiritual transformation. It was for him a terrifying encounter with the hidden demon of his own will, a dark night of the soul, the combat of Jacob with the angel, but he discovered in the end the promise of a resurrection; his spiritual agony found peace in a burst of confidence and abandonment to the saving God. He wrote to Keble in June of 1844: "... but what most impresses itself upon me, is the strange feelings and convictions about His will towards me which came to me, when I was abroad."[2]

More than any other event in his life, his illness in Sicily confirms the repeated observations that we are able to make about all the events which stand out as milestones in his religious destiny. The event is rich in premonition, for it reveals the signs of a personal vocation which is about to unfold; but it is also a crucifying event, for it discloses that he was not yet ready to submit to such a rigorous yoke.

It was not without hesitation that Newman agreed to embark on the Mediterranean voyage proposed to him by the Froudes in the summer of 1832. The Archdeacon, always anxious about the precarious health of his son, Richard Hurrell, took the advice of the doctor who recommended a cure with sun and relaxation for the young man.

Invited to be a party to the voyage, Newman was spontaneously attracted by his friend's offer. He had just completed his first book, *The Arians of the Fourth Century*, and he felt a need to take some rest; moreover, his responsibilities as a tutor were over, and he felt totally free.

---

[2] K., p. 315.

Nevertheless, he did not answer the invitation immediately; he weighed the pros and cons with such seriousness that he gave the impression that he wanted to be asked a second time.[3] He was tempted, no doubt, by the wonderful chance to escape, a chance "he may never know again" but he deplored the absence of several months from his work. He was uneasy about the very idea of a vacation and even speculated about the risks of his contracting an illness far away from his family! Two weeks later, he was more confident, seeking to justify the reasons for such a voyage: "But it may be a duty to consult for one's health, to enlarge one's ideas, to break one's studies."[4] Finally, he made his decision and embarked with the Froudes. But before leaving the English coast at Falmouth on December 8th, he needed to justify himself once more to his mother.[5] Throughout the entire crossing, which led him from Gibraltar and Malta to Corfu, then to Naples and Rome, the numerous letters he sent to his family testify to the same scruple of justifying himself by listing a thousand and one reasons for leaving:

> So that I have good hope I shall not be unsettled by my present wanderings. For what are all these strange sights but vanities! ... So that I really do think that the hope of benefiting my health and increasing my usefulness and influence, are the main consider-ations which [cause me to] absent myself from you and Oxford. Yet even [such] thoughts do not reconcile me to the length of time I shall be away... it is of course an habitual feeling with me which I now express.[6]

In another letter dated December 25th, addressed to his sister, Harriet, we again find the same regret: "After all, it is a great waste of time when life is so short."[7]

Thus, his soul remained divided: the enjoyment of the voyage, along with its relaxation, did not fully succeed in stifling the scruples of a conscience which was never quite sure it had not ceded too quickly to the fantasy of evasion. The undeniable enthusiasm which Newman experi-

---

[3] Letter to R. H. Froude, September 13, 1832; M. I., pp. 241-242.
[4] Letter of October 4th; M. I., p. 243.
[5] "The voyage... for the only cessation from labour to which I may look without blame." Letter to his mother, December 3, 1832, M. I., p. 248.
[6] *Ibid*; p. 266. Letter to his mother, December 19, 1832.
[7] *Ibid*; p. 274.

enced in the face of the magnificent sights did not subdue him to the point where they erased his nostalgia for the time lost and the interrupted labors; the memory of Oxford, although already distant, was always present.

When one examines and studies the vast dossier of letters and poems written in the course of the voyage, keeping in mind the background for the dramatic event which would soon take place in Sicily, one cannot fail to discern in the destiny of the voyager a sort of fatality. Numerous notes, confessions, and confidences reveal an undefined anxiety, never at rest, which the crisis in Sicily would bring to its highest degree of intensity. In contrast to the sudden and unexpected conversion of 1816, the trial experienced by Newman in the desert of Leonforte seems to us to be the climax of a hidden crisis about which we are able to detect many signs in the course of the preceding months.

Two sentiments in particular seem very significant: in the first place, the more or less conscious refusal of the voyager to be subdued by the fascinating beauty which surrounds him; secondly, the certainty, although still an undefined premonition, that he is singled out for a unique mission to which he should dedicate his life. We shall find these two sentiments even more strongly expressed during the terrible crisis in the Sicilian springtime.

Indeed, it seems that the Mediterranean voyage, which revealed to Newman the beauties of a sumptuous nature, had the unexpected consequence of reviving his irrepressible need for interiority. He rejected, all the more jealously, the mirages of the world which deployed its pomps with the most seductive ostentation. In displaying all their prodigious beauty, Greece and Italy revealed to him the dangers of a creation which subdues one by its charms and at the same time irreparably distracts him from his end. To the degree that he appeared to succumb to the paroxysm of admiration before the fantastic spectacle which revealed itself each day, Newman experienced something like panic, a fear of being under a spell. As much as the voyage was a discovery, it was also a challenge: he had to face the beauty in created things, which symbolized for him the "world," with all its charms and temptations.

From time to time, he could not contain his cries of ecstasy. Such was his enthusiasm at the enchanting sight of Taormini: "I never saw anything more enchanting.... I never knew that Nature could be so beautiful."[8] He

---

[8] Letter to Harriet, April 27, 1833; M. I., p. 349.

expressed his admiration; nevertheless, he noted, "though I am so much pleased, I am not interested.... I shrink involuntarily from the contact of the world."[9] He went so far as to denounce with some vehemence the ambiguous fascination of travel in general:

> I no longer wonder at younger persons being carried away with travelling and corrupted; for certainly the illusions of the world's magic can hardly be fancied while one remains at home... but I think it does require strength of mind to keep the thoughts where they should be while the variety of strange sights... are passed before their eyes, as in a tour like this.[10]

Furthermore, Newman's attention went beyond the pleasures experienced by the incomparable variety of sights along the banks of the Mediterranean to the patrimony of Christian history, of which the silent and inviolate nature was a witness. An emotion born of faith filled the soul of the traveler who contemplated as a pilgrim those lands where the vestiges of pagan legends mingled together with memories of the ancient Church. The poems which he wrote for the *Lyra Apostolica*[11] reveal an intensely religious soul, retired from the world, but dazzled at first by the austere clarity which comes from centuries of faith and seemed to project a strange light on the mysterious route which opened before him.

Indeed, Newman admits in the *Apologia* that the weight of a heavy presentiment was upon him at that time. He carried within himself a confused vision of his future accomplishments: "I wrote verses about my Guardian Angel, which begin with these words, 'are these the tracks of some unearthly friend?' and which go on to speak of 'the vision which haunted me':— that vision is more or less brought out in the whole series of these compositions."[12] Several times in the course of the voyage, he felt a need for solitude and peace, which was not only the fruit of years of solitary studies at Oxford but it corresponded to the more radical need of a soul anxious to capture every possible sign of God's grace and protection.

---

[9] Letter of January 4; *Ibid.*, p. 282.
[10] Letter to Harriet, December 18, 1832; *Ibid.*, p. 261.
[11] *Lyra Apostolica* is a collection of poems published in 1836. Newman and his friends, Keble, Froude, Williams, Henry Wilberforce, and Bowden all collaborated in it. Newman contributed about 40 poems.
[12] *Apologia*, p. 38.

More and more, Newman wished to assure himself that he remained in the
hands of God. What is called his "accord with the supernatural" is nothing
other than Newman's vigilance in recognizing the actions of an always
active Providence, multiplying the mysterious signs, which he would one
day decipher. Thus, he was to interpret events which were insignificant
only in appearance: the familiar chant of psalms in a church, the unusual
sounds during the night in Malta, and the unexpected declaration that he
had a mission to fulfill in the course of an unscheduled dialogue with the
Rector of the English Roman Catholic Seminary in Rome.[13]

Newman always associated his illness in Sicily with a divine
punishment for having been too capricious and self-willed.[14] In a letter to
Keble, he explained his culpability:

> When I went down to Sicily by myself, I had a strong idea that He
> was going to effect some purpose by me. And from Rome I wrote
> to some one, I think Christie, saying I thought I was to be made
> something of in His Hands, "though if not, the happier for me."
> And when I was in Sicily by myself, it seemed as if someone were
> battling against me, and the idea has long been in my mind,
> though I cannot say when it came on, that my enemy was then
> attempting to destroy me. *A number of sins were committed in the*
> *very act of my going down by myself — to say nothing else, I was*
> *willful, and neglected warnings — from that time everything went*
> *wrong.*[15]

This text, in which we italicized a revealing passage, contains an
allusion to some past faults. Clearly, among those hidden faults was the
fanciful and sudden decision to return to Sicily but his conscience pushed
him to recognize other faults. In the notes of the *Memoirs* edited by
Newman during various periods in his life, we find again the allusion to a

---

[13] This prelate is the famous Dr. Wiseman. "I began to think that I had a mission. There
are sentences of my letters to my friends to this effect.... When we took leave of
Monsignore Wiseman, he had courteously expressed a wish that we might make a
second visit to Rome; I said with great gravity, 'We have a work to do in England.'"
Apologia, p. 40.
[14] M. I., p. 363. "I felt it was a punishment for my wilfulness in going to Sicily by
myself."
[15] K, p. 315. The author is stressing this point.

precise culpability. These particular notes, by reason of their intimate character, were not published by Miss Mozley in Newman's correspondence but they have since been published by Father Bouyer, who transcribed them from the Oratory papers at Birmingham.[16] We see here that Newman established his guilt by returning in his mind to two precise actions from his own personal past: a certain negligence at the Communion Service and, above all, his obvious hostility to the provost of Oriel.

But these admissions were made only in the delirium of a fever. When Newman decided on his expedition to Sicily, he was thinking only of the pleasure it would afford him. It was the desire to know more about the enchanting places which he had only started to discover in the course of his Mediterranean voyage with the Froudes which made him decide to leave them at that time. They were returning to England by way of France while Newman was setting out to return to Naples and Messina. On April 11, 1833, the voyager wrote to his sister, Jemima, from Naples:

> I have lost my companions, and I was going among strangers into a wild country to live a wild life, to travel in solitude, and to sleep in dens of the earth — and all for what? for the gratification of an imagination, for the idea of a warm fancy which might be a deceit, drawn by a strange love of Sicily.[17]

The irony of these lines hardly veils the anxiety which was to grow in the course of the following days. As we said, the pleasure of the voyage never totally brushed aside his unexpressed scruples of conscience. The decision to leave for Sicily alone and to part company with the Froudes, served only to clarify and magnify the doubts of his conscience. As long as Newman remained with his friends, he was reassured: he found a guarantee against his fancy in the fact of having accepted once and for all the conditions of a voyage shared with others which could be considered a legitimate relaxation. After the departure of the Froudes, this guarantee vanished. If he undertook the previously unplanned expedition to Sicily, it was in order to satisfy his own personal desire. The fever which was soon

---

[16] Father Bouyer in his book, *Newman* (p. 139 ff.) restored texts that Miss Mozley had deleted from the correspondence.

[17] M. I., p. 337.

to overtake him brought an increase in the sentiment that he made his
decision capriciously. It was, indeed, a delirious fever which awaited
Newman in the land of Sicily. For a whole month, he was to be completely
prostrated in a terrible state of despondency.

Following an excursion of several days in Naples, he took a boat for
Catania. The spectacle of Taormini brought forth the most ecstatic expression of admiration from him, which he attempted to communicate to his
sister, Harriet, in a letter of April 27th, written from Syracuse.[18] Nevertheless, already assailed by fever, he decided to go back to Catania on an
inland expedition. Accompanied by the picturesque Gennaro, his Sicilian
servant and guide, Newman, not without pain, reached the village of
Leoforte, a hundred miles from Palermo. After a sleepless night, he was
overwhelmed by his disease without finding a suitable remedy to fight it.
Two or three days later, realizing that his state was getting progressively
worse without hope of rapid improvement, he decided to take to the road
again in the hope of reaching, at any cost, a place where he would be in a
better position to receive care. A few miles later, he was forced to stop
anew. A doctor, met by chance, took him to the village of Castro-Giovanni,
where he was to remain for nearly three weeks in a precarious state
between life and death. It was only on the 29th of May that he finally set
out again en route to Palermo where he was forced to wait until mid-June
before he was able to embark for home.

Such were the circumstances of a voyage which seemed from the
beginning to be dominated by the capricious veil of a somber Nemesis. By
throwing Newman into a state close to agony, this illness was the occasion
of a terrifying encounter with himself. It was a dramatic confrontation with
the obscure forces which are inside each one of us, the permanent traces
of original sin. The sting of sin remains menacing, as long as we have not
exposed and gotten rid of it.

In a letter intended to console his friend, Thomas Mozley, who was
nailed to his bed by illness, Newman had written a year earlier:

> It is one especial use of times of illness to reflect about ourselves...
> had it pleased God to have visited you with an illness [serious]...
> it would seem a rebuke for past waste of time. I believe that God

---

[18] Letter to Harriet, April 27, 1833. M. I., p. 349.

cuts off those He loves and who really are His, not interfering with
their ultimate safety, but as passing them by as if unworthy of
being made instruments of his purpose.[19]

The austere reflections made to Mozley were probably now present
in the mind of the depressed voyager, languishing in a poor Sicilian inn.
His physical weakness stirred up a sorrowful examination of conscience;
the mounting fever accentuated the need for self-examination, while the
delirium made former scruples reappear. That which most strikes the
reader of the Sicilian documents, now published in their entirety in spite
of Anne Mozley's fears, is the extraordinary lucidity of the patient at the
height of the crisis which he was experiencing.

His conscience emerged from a zone of indecision where it no longer
exercised its power of control, where dreams were surging at the height of
the fever, giving life and substance to the most hidden and unavowed
specters. The psyche experienced a loss of control; the will failed to
express itself with clarity; and scruples, after a long inhibition, reappeared
even more forcefully. Delirium turned to a pitiless introspection which
revealed in the light-darkness of a subliminal conscience the clear contour
of past weaknesses and faults. All the incidents of his moral life were
projected in a sharp light which uncovered scruples and deceptions, regrets
and remorses, promises and graces. The plunging into the hidden recesses
of truth seemed to bear the mark of a personal chastisement: "I am coming
to think almost that the devil seeing that I have the means of rendering
myself useful, was seeking to destroy me."[20] God seemed to abandon his
servant to the worst of temptations, the one of the desert, which revealed
the image of his own self-will, along with the threat of a spiritual failure
that was beyond repair.

This menace became more apparent when he was detained at
Leoforte during the most critical phase of the crisis. Newman alluded to it
in a memoir written some eighteen months after the event; it constitutes
one of the most moving documents in the autobiographical literature of all
times:

---

[19] Letter of May 13, 1832; M. I., p. 228.
[20] Unpublished document.

> Next day the self-reproaching feeling increased. I seemed to see more and more my utter hollowness. I began to think of all my professed principles, and felt they were mere intellectual deductions from one or two admitted truths. I compared myself with Keble, and felt that I was merely developing his, not my convictions. I knew that I had very clear thoughts about this then, and I believe in the main true ones. Indeed, this is how I look on myself; very much (as the illustration goes) as a pane of glass, which transmits heat being cold itself. I have a vivid perception of the consequences of certain admitted principles, have a considerable intellectual capacity of drawing them out, have the refinement to admire them, and a rhetorical or histrionic power to represent them; and having no great (i.e., no vivid) love of this world, whether riches, honours, or anything else, and some firmness and natural dignity of character, take the profession of them upon me, as I might sing a tune which I liked — loving the Truth, but not possessing it, for I believe myself at heart to be nearly hollow, i.e., with little love, little self-denial. I believe I have some faith, that is all.[21]

Such a rigorous examination of conscience is beyond all commentaries, and we would be tempted to add nothing if we were not anxious to elucidate all the data of the spiritual drama which resulted in this masterpiece of introspection.

In this text, the remembrance of Keble seems very significant. This is not the first time that Newman felt the need to evoke the noble and austere figure of the pastor of Hursley to contrast it with his own conscience. He believed he lacked the inner sincerity, the "accord with the self," as modern thinkers say, which was the very charm and source of his friend's influence. He was not able to realize, with regard to himself, this marvelous accord, this sort of natural symbiosis between truth and sentiment, grace and life.

This spiritual trial which tortured the ex-tutor tore his heart apart in two different directions: Newman was attracted by a moral beauty which remained too remote from him, almost inaccessible; at the same time, he

---

[21] M. I., p. 366. This confession of Newman is of December 28, 1834, a month and a half after the event. *Autobiographical Writings*, p. 124 ff.

was avidly open to the truth with the fear that he could not always grasp all its requirements. It was not blindness, for "he had not sinned against the light," nor a failure of his conscience too distracted by aesthetic pleasures to make spiritual progress. When Newman recognized that the Lord was battling against him,[22] it was not in connection with the renouncement of earthly pleasures. These, he admits, never attracted him: "I do not love the world, its riches, nor its honors." Much more was at stake; it was a question of Newman's renouncing his own self-will and any secret passion which could take him away from a destiny where God ought to remain the Master. This self-will was made up of a certain independence of judgment and a certain impatience of heart which sometimes was unable to master his passions. In the background of the Sicilian drama, one can imagine the anxieties and scruples which revealed the struggles of past years to his conscience. A spiritual fire threw light on his most intimate sentiments, those which dared not manifest themselves; it was as if his conscience were subjected to a spectral analysis which did not spare any secret. The memories and images of the past appeared in a new light which burned away that which it revealed; the conscience knew the impurity of its acts and thoughts; the resulting remorse made it condemn any trace of self-will.

Two recollections in particular came back in sharp relief; the battle against the provost of Oriel[23] and his inner struggle to accept the call to celibacy.

Newman had fought against Hawkins for good reasons; it was for a just cause and his intentions were pure. But in the course of the conflict, how much bitterness, obstinacy, and arrogance! As for the call to a solitary celibate life, if it had its grandeur, it was not without its sufferings; it was not without anxiety that Newman had accepted this heavy sacrifice. So his impatience, his excessive arrogance in the battle against Hawkins and too human a fear associated with the renunciation of marriage, did not all this

---

[22] M. I., p. 365. "I felt God was fighting against me, and felt — at last I knew why — it was for self-will." M. I., p. 365.

[23] As stated in an unpublished text, December 28, 1824; see M. I., p. 366. Another confession can be found in an original document, August 31, 1834, in *Autobiographical Writings*, p. 121. "I seem to see, and I saw, a strange providence in it. At the time I was deeply impressed with a feeling that it was a judgment for profaning the Lord's Supper, in having cherished some resentment against the Provost for putting me out of the tutorship; though this impression has now faded away."

testify to a burdened conscience? Was it not the sign that his soul was losing its serenity? It believed it was free but circumstances showed clearly that it was not free from itself at all. Self-will prevented his soul from freeing itself from the narrow circle of its own preferences and attachments; such attachments were neither recognized nor accepted. Newman was discovering them only because of the extreme lucidity brought about by his fever. Until now, he had hardly checked elusive scruples; he was, so to speak, in the driver's seat and from time to time, since the day of his first conversion, he had recognized the presence of God in some particular signs which showed him without doubt that the way was sure.

But when illness struck, a deep questioning spirit came to throw a true light on his spiritual journey. In spite of many rigors and self-denials, in spite of the security of a divine presence which give him light, his journey was less the work of grace than of nature. It was less a revelation of God than a performance by Newman; the pilgrim had chosen for himself his own Jerusalem; he had elected his own star. Far from abandoning himself to a power from on High, he believed he could anticipate it, and the narrow path he thought he was following was the one of his own ambition; it was not a given grace.[24]

When he discovered the vanity and illusion of his spiritual life, Newman experienced something like the shipwreck of his soul with great anguish: "I seemed to see more and more my utter hollowness. I felt more and more how much my soul was empty." He confessed to not being able to describe his intense misery in the course of the following day. To cut short such painful reflections, he counted the number of stars and flowers[25] "in the pattern of the paper on the walls" to occupy himself in his sick room.

---

[24] See, for example, the poem "Sensitiveness."

> Time was, I shrank from what was right
>   From fear of what was wrong.
> I would not brave the sacred fight
>   Because the foe was strong...
> Such dread of sin was indolence,
>   Such aim at heaven was pride.

Verses on Various Occasions, LX, p. 113. The above poem is from January 13, 1833. The last lines are very significant.

[25] M. I., pp. 366-367.

At least, such a trial accomplished the necessary purification; the will for a more complete abandonment into the hands of the Lord (at last disengaged from all illusions) filled his soul. The pilgrim at first had chosen his own way, forgetting about divine grace, but this way was sincere and the Master would eventually make Himself known. Newman had not sinned against the light; his route, indeed, had been the road to truth:

> I had a strange feeling on my mind that God meets those who go on in His way, who remember Him in His way, in the paths of the Lord; that I must put myself in His path, His way, that I must do my part, and that He met those who rejoice and worked righteousness, and remembered Him in His way.[26]

Newman felt that this full encounter with the Lord was ready to come; yet somehow, it was already there, since in the midst of the crisis, he had kept a distinct awareness of being an elect of God: "One time I had a most consoling, overpowering thought of God's electing love, and seemed to feel I was His."[27] A major spiritual turn around was taking place amid his suffering. A new sentiment penetrated him and pacified him: a sense of abandonment to his Creator, a feeling in his soul that it was to abdicate its own ambitions in order to allow the soul to bloom in the faith and love of God. When the fever left Newman and he was able to respond anew to life, a last crisis jolted him. He wrote that this manifested itself in a burst of salutary and liberating tears: "I was very weak. When I got up the morning of the 26th or 27th, I sat some time by the bedside, crying bitterly, and all I could say was that I was sure God had some work for me to do in England."[28] Moreover, this certitude never left him during his illness even at the height of the crisis. The delirium might have been able to heighten his feelings of powerlessness and to sharply reveal his past scruples but it had also stimulated a new hope and brought with it a new promise. The mysterious vision evoked in his poem, written at the time of his departure from England and which inspired other compositions in the

---

[26] M. I., p. 368.
[27] M. I., p. 365.
[28] M. I., p. 376; see *Apologia*, p. 40.

Lyra Apostolica,[29] had never ceased to be present in the spiritual vision of the voyager. In spite of the somber recommendations made to his servant and guide to be prepared for the possibility of his death, the certainty of his survival never departed from him for a moment.[30] The punishment might be merited: it would not be final. God did not abandon His servant; He preserved him for a necessary mission in His Church.

Indeed, Newman was fully prepared for the mission which was soon to involve him completely. Before dedicating himself to the almost superhuman task of reforming the Church, before traveling along the long and unknown road that would unknowingly lead him into the total light, Newman's soul had need of this experience in the desert. He was not to pass through this dark night without the purification well known to spiritual men, which empties the conscience and creates in it the void that God alone is able to fill. Such is God's way of preparing souls for the great works of His Kingdom.

If up to this point Newman had chosen his own way, he would now have to banish all vanity and attachment to his own self-will. Henceforth, it was up to God and God alone to open to him the way and to lead him towards his destiny in the midst of suffering and joy. This desire for total abandonment to the will of God, which the student at Ealing had experienced in his first conversion and which manifested itself on other occasions, was now going to become effective. Like the pilgrim he had celebrated not so long ago in his poem, entitled "Our Future," with the line, "A pilgrim pale, with Paul's sad girdle bound," Newman had now abandoned the choice of the route and of the means to the Lord.

---

[29] These texts are a comfort to spot in the *Lyra*:
    No. XXXIX, p. 44:   But now there reigns so deep a rest
                             That I could almost weep . . .
    No. CLXVI, p. 226: Wait the bright advent that shall loose thy chain!
    No. CLXXVI, p. 238: Blest scene! thrice welcome after toil.
    No. V, p. 5:   Lord, grant me this abiding grace,
                             Thy Word and Son to know;
                             To pierce the veil on Moses' face,
                             Although his speech be slow!

[30] M. I., pp. 353, 358, 363, 367. Same mention in the letter to Keble, June 8, 1844. Nevertheless, the conviction that he would survive the ordeal did not go without agonizing thoughts which compelled Newman to make his last will in case of his death. Thus, among the unpublished papers, a note, written September 22, 1850, indicates the terms of his last will which empowers Froude with the care of his personal affairs and the responsibility to communicate the news of his death to his family.

Thus, surrender to God, which for him took place in the desert of Sicily, would become the surest, if not *the* decisive foundation of Newmanian spirituality.[31] We shall soon see how his abandonment to the will of God, marked by a supernatural indifference with regard to that which was about to happen to him, humanly speaking for better or worse, would be the sole and finally the most secure attitude that Newman would try to preserve all his life.

In the history of Christian spirituality, Newman is placed with Francis de Sales, Lallemant, and Thérèse of Lisieux among the great witnesses of spiritual abandonment. God knows better than we what suits us. The only task for the soul is to empty itself of all passion and of all vain anxiety in order to allow itself to be guided by the interior motion of the grace of God. Moreover, God guides us with great wisdom; he leads us step by step. Time is needed in the course of a human destiny for the work of the Lord to be accomplished. Every event has a spiritual dimension and reveals the continuity of the divine will, provided that our religious conscience is attentive to discerning its value and significance and situates it within the range of a personal fidelity which for all men coincides with the mysterious trace of the vocation assigned to him in the plan of God.

This royal way of total surrender to God was discovered by Newman at the price of a profound humiliation but also with the light of a filial confidence. Divine Providence watched over His faithful servant at every moment; it prepared the way for him; it led him with enough light, day by day, and with "manna," with which the Hebrews in the desert should have satisfied themselves. The voyager was reassured on this journey in which he was engaged, which was about to conduct him "ex umbris et imaginibus ad veritatem." ["Out of shadows and images into the truth."] He knew the future would reveal itself according to the measure of his present fidelity: God would not fail him.

Newman's ultimate answer was his resolution to follow his Master, to start walking on the path traced out for him, to enjoy His gifts, and to follow His call. With a conscience at peace, Newman renewed his resolution to be a faithful instrument in the hands of the Lord and to serve

---

[31] See Tristram, *With Newman at Prayer*, p. 105: In the crucible of suffering, the Newman of the future was being if not forged, at least sketched. Abandonment, the abandonment to the will of God was going to become the basis of his spirituality.

Him in the strict way of celibacy that his Master had indicated to him. The sacrifice was absolute, since he was reaching into his very depth where the will was at last autonomous, master of its choice: thus ended the battle which he had sustained against God, like Jacob long ago in the darkness of night.

Once his self-will fully submitted, his vocation was able to assert itself. God was presenting it to him as a mission to be fulfilled in the Church of England: Newman would undertake it there, not as a task chosen by him, but as a mandate received from God. The certitude that he was obeying the will of God was going to fortify his soul and protect him in all his trials, in the distrusts and jealousies. On his return to Oxford, Newman would be astonished by his own firmness and audacity. Froude had taught him previously how to dominate his personal repugnances and timidities, but in pointing out to him his mission during his illness in Sicily, God showed Newman the true meaning of all his heartrending experiences and strengthened him for the sacrifices that were to come. His striking boldness at the beginning of the Oxford Movement would be incomprehensible without "this temptation in the desert" where Newman, battling in darkness against his fever and his fears, revealed an iron-clad soul ready for all battles, prepared to encounter in them the will of the Lord.[32]

All the feelings and sentiments of Newman that came forth from his illness find themselves expressed in his famous poem, "Lead, Kindly Light." Therein is reflected a serene humility, a peaceful confidence, and an abandonment to God, all of which gives an assurance of spiritual progress and a hopeful end.

> Lead, kindly light, amid the encircling gloom,
>   Lead Thou me on!
> The night is dark, and I am far from home —
>   Lead Thou me on!
> Keep Thou my feet; I do not ask to see
> The distant scene, — one step enough for me.
>
> I was not ever thus, nor prayed that Thou
>   Shouldst lead me on.

---

[32] Thus is explained the quote of Virgil, which he adopted as a motto when the Movement started: *Exoriare Aliquis*. ("Arise avenger," Aenid IV.) The same sentiment of abandon to God and determination inspires the poem, "Discipline," in the *Lyra*, XXXII, p. 36.

I loved to choose and see my path; but now,
    Lead Thou me on!
I loved the garish day, and, spite of fears,
Pride ruled my will: remember not past years!

So long Thy power hath blessed me, sure it still
    Will lead me on,
O'er moor and fen, o'er crag and torrent, till
    The night is gone;
And with the morn those angel faces smile
Which I have loved long since, and lost awhile.[33]

---

[33] The poem entitled "The Pillar of the Cloud" is in *Verses*, p. 156. It was composed in the course of the return voyage, June 16, 1833, in the Straits of Bonifacio. See *Apologia*, p. 40.

CHAPTER VIII

THE INSTRUMENT OF GOD

O my mother! whence is this
unto thee, that thou... bearest
children, yet darest not own them?

"On the Parting of Friends" from
Sermons on Subjects of the Day, p. 407.

*U*PON HIS RETURN to England, Newman became engaged in the new work envisioned in Sicily. He knew he had a mission to fulfill in his Church and he was ready to embrace it in its entirety. There was no time for preludes and approaches; it was time for decisions and acts. The hour was grave for the Anglican Church: undermined by an evil from within, its destiny depended upon the clear-sightedness and determination of her better children. Newman knew this. With his friends, he engaged in a combat of which he did not know the outcome but which announced a trend towards reform and renewal, perhaps the last, and assuredly the most celebrated in the Church of England, the one which is known in history as the Oxford Movement.

In the 1830's, the drama for the Anglican Church was not so much that it was threatened but that it was unaware of its own peril. It seemed to have lost a clear notion of its situation with regard to the State. Multiple interferences by the Crown against the Church were, everything considered, less dangerous than the feeling of security with which it tolerated such conduct. The audacity shown by the government in its interferences in religious affairs was only a symptom of the profound apathy which pervaded the Church, to the point of forgetting her own dignity. Her own interests were disregarded because she had lost all feeling of pride. Parliament voted the Reform Bill which suppressed ten Anglican bishoprics in Ireland. Backed by the servile silence and oftentimes the complacency of ecclesiastical dignitaries, the liberals, in total quietude, were able to press for more and more audacious projects which all tended to tighten more strictly the Church to the English Crown. Arnold, the best known of the liberal leaders, went so far as to declare: "In its present situation, can any human power save the Church?"

The vast majority of Church leaders were incapable of freeing themselves from the humiliating tutelage of the State which enslaved them. Most of the bishops owed their honors to secular influences and they were more anxious to preserve their titles and prerogatives in Parliament than to fulfill their apostolic mission. Vicars in their vicarages, if they preserved in very rare instances an inclination to praiseworthy study of issues, did not allow themselves to be consumed by their zeal for the house of God. Furthermore, their theology was too inconsistent to give them the doctrinal support which would have allowed them to live a deep and true faith and to face openly the frustrations, as well as the greatness, of their pastoral ministry.

However, at the frontier of the Church, ingloriously sleepy and insensitive to the blows which were wounding her, were diverse religious initiatives, seeking to shake her spiritual torpor in advocating a return to gospel purity. As we have seen, John Wesley's methods, born from a need for reform, failed to shake up the consciences of men faithful to the Established Church but it continued to grow marginally. At the time of Newman, it survived within several sects, whereas the Evangelical current, which for a while was supposed to detach itself from Anglicanism, remained faithful to it and brought to it original and strong thinking and the spiritual vigor which could have been the basis for an authentic revival. The merit of Newman and his friends was to be perspicacious enough to denounce the evil at its roots and to engage the battle on its true terrain, which was not political but religious. It was less a question of freeing the Church than of awakening it, less of emancipating it than of shaking it up. It would be in vain to claim for the Church the inalienable rights that the State seemed to grant with one hand and take back with the other; first, one had to bring her back to a sense of her own dignity by helping her rediscover the sense of her mission. Healing would come only from within by the renewal of faith and faithful obedience to the Apostolic tradition which she had forgotten. On the continent, at the time when Lamennais, in claiming the separation of Church and State, first placed the debate on a political plane, Newman went straight to the very root of the problem, which was one of the return of the Church to the divine principles of her foundation and to the imperatives of her mission.

It was probably this radical way of looking at things which disbanded the little group that Hugh James Rose brought together in his rectory at Hadleigh several days after Keble, in his "Assizes" sermon at Oxford, had denounced the "national apostasy." Founder of the *British Magazine*, Rose, former chaplain to the Archbishop of Canterbury, was soliciting the cooperation of the most popular and most determined churchmen; therefore, he organized a round table at his home. The two Oriel tutors brought to the debate which emanated from these meetings the boldness and realism which they had learned from their contact with the "Noetics." Froude and Newman believed more in direct action on the part of individuals than in their power over institutions. Instead of starting an organization, they thought more about a campaign of harrassment in order to stimulate and stir up public opinion; they believed it was necessary to establish contacts and to surprise and almost violate sleeping consciences. Thus, they envisioned the wide diffusion of tracts destined to arouse or stir up the indifference of all those, cleric or lay people, who were expected to be interested in the affairs of the Church. Pamphlets written in a striking style, incisive and dealing with unexpected subjects, were the weapons which needed to be invented, weapons of a strike force, much greater than any platonic petitions. Referring to such an offensive and with a sense of irony, Newman said that a regular army would be less effective than a mobile and aggressive troop of sharp shooters.

The Oxford Movement owes its existence to the intrepid resolution of these two ex-tutors of Oriel. Beyond all hope, their enterprise succeeded precisely for the motives which hindered their friends at Hadleigh, who were far too wise and too reasonable. Public opinion could only be attracted and fascinated by this new, firm, direct, and uncompromising language. No doubt, certain clergymen were frightened by the vision of "bishops' careers ending with the spoliation of their benefits and martyrdom"; nevertheless, everyone understood that such utterances were less the result of impatience and challenge than of pride in their Church's tradition and a sacred passion for her future. Indeed, bishops were described as "successors of the Apostles" and this title, which was being forgotten, was in itself the justification of their grandeur and privileges.

It would take us too far afield from our purpose to follow step by step the history of the Oxford Movement since it has been so often recounted by Newman's historians and biographers. Here, we shall restrict ourselves to recalling the three great stages of this truly religious epic of the nineteenth century Church. It will help us to better situate the progress of Newmanian spirituality in the course of these decisive years.[1]

Numerous tracts mark the first years of the Movement. They reveal the determination of Newman and his friends, who breached the Establishment with the ardor of neophytes. The venerable Church of England, asleep in its traditions and its outmoded honors, was disconcerted and offended by this brutal shock, by these "outdoor games," which aroused some of her children, thus rejecting the sweet and disciplined manners she thought they had learned from her. The years 1834 and 1835 belong to the initial period of the Oxford Movement which breathes a breath of Spring, full of vigor and vitality, of zest and promises. They were filled for Newman with an intense and feverish activity: he edited numerous tracts, some of them among the most incisive; he wrote letter upon letter, traveling throughout the countryside in order to bring tracts just off the presses to the vicarages. Throughout the entire course of these years, which were only a prelude to what was coming, one can feel a hardly contained enthusiasm and a juvenile fervor.

An old friend, the venerable Pusey from Oxford, an austere and dedicated scholar who never made a decision without patiently debating the pros and cons, joined the young Tractarians as early as 1835 and did not lose any time in writing some tracts of his own, which contrasted markedly with the preceding ones in their volume and scholarly content. Newman, on the other hand, realized that no polemic could succeed without a solid doctrinal basis. In order to accomplish a real reform, a truly solid base, a dogmatic foundation was needed on which the controversy could expand. Newman sensed that the true meaning of his combat was to involve him in a confrontation with the liberal trend which was his most formidable adversary. With all its pernicious allurements, it was a threatening temptation for the Established Church.

---

[1] On the evolution of the Oxford Movement, see Appendix II, p. 223.

Liberalism, which Newman identified with the "anti-dogmatic principle," was a sort of nightmare all his life. He never ceased to denounce its sophisms which tended to submit the highest certitude of faith to the imperatives of reason and free thinking. The liberal party in England not only enlisted philosophers, whose profession was to think, but it also inspired the attitude of political men, who although they conceded to the Church its privileges and benefits, were determined to suppress any true autonomy in the exercise of its functions and, above all, to remove any claim to its doctrinal orthodoxy. They were bold enough to obtain the Crown's appointment to the highest ecclesiastical offices for men who were most committed to their ideas. For example, in 1836, Lord Melbourne offered the Chair of Regius Professor of Divinity to Dr. Hampden, whose reputation as a liberal was solidly established; some time earlier, in a cycle of conferences, he had shown the extent of his free-thinking in his treatment of the mysteries of faith. The nomination was canceled but the passionate campaign of opposition led by Newman and the Tractarians earned them the animosity of the liberals.

From that point on, war was declared between the two parties. In order to win it, more than a talent for polemics and controversy was needed from Newman and his companions. The only way to reach the vast public was to provide them with the incontestable signs of doctrinal, liturgical, and ascetical renewal which would infuse into the Church itself the clear consciousness of its own greatness, its true tradition and apostolic mission. Therefore, from 1835 to 1839, the Tractarian Movement engaged in study and theological reflection, of which Newman was the most conspicuous leader, publishing doctrinal works such as "Lectures on the Prophetical Office of the Church" and "Lectures on Justification." At the same time, his sermons at St. Mary's were drawing the largest and most enthusiastic audiences.

From 1839 on, a new and somber period of trials and difficulties began. Newman believed he had given to the Established Church an original status which was the one of "Via Media." The Anglican Church claimed her right to Apostolic succession in a special way which distinguished her from the innovations of Protestantism, born of the Reformation, and at the same time from the corruption which had weakened Roman Catholicism. Far from considering the "Via Media" as an opportunistic compromise, a sort of half-way between Protestantism and the Church of Rome, Newman saw in it that which had been recognized by the great

English theologians of the seventeenth century: the true face of Catholicism as it had been defined by the tradition of the Fathers. Newman's unique effort tended to show that the "Via Media" was the rich source towards which his Church ought to return in order to express in her acts, as well as in her life, a fidelity to her basic constitution.

In 1841, Newman published the celebrated Tract 90, that would be his last. In it, he developed the idea that the Thirty-Nine Articles, which constitute the charter of the Anglican Church, are in complete agreement with the dogmas of the Council of Trent, provided the latter are purified of all Roman accretions, which obscure and falsify their original meaning. Such an interpretation of the Thirty-Nine Articles, which too bluntly ran up against Anglican prejudices then so strongly colored by Protestantism, initiated the most vociferous reprobation. It is difficult to imagine how violent was the indignation that shook the common rooms of the University after the publication of the Tract. For many, Newman and his friends were already suspect since the publication of the preceding tracts, and above all, since the edition of the posthumous papers of Froude, who died in 1836, and about whom we shall have occasion to speak again.

The name of Newman became synonymous with that of a Romanist; he became a sign of contradiction; his disgrace was such that his name was posted on the refectory doors of the colleges! His cause was lost. In spite of the generous efforts of Keble and Pusey, Newman was definitely compromised in the eyes of the bishops. It was already the signal of death for the Movement and sanctions were taken against a certain number of Newmanians. Pusey himself was accused of Romanism for a sermon he preached on the Eucharist, in which he proclaimed his faith in the Real Presence. Newman, a prey to the most mortal agony of his conscience, retired from Oxford and took refuge in a hermitage, a few miles away from Oxford, in the little parish of Littlemore.

A long-lasting period of waiting was about to begin. It would reach its climax in October of 1845 when Newman was converted to the Church of Rome. His eight years at the helm of the Oxford Movement, starting with his return from Sicily in July of 1833 until his retirement to Littlemore in February of 1842, seemed to be so totally dominated by what was happening that one has the impression of a long interruption in his deep spiritual life. But from this point on, a blind necessity seemed to determine Newman's works and days, which drew him into the uncertainty that marked the coming days, the symbol of which was the poor cottage at

Littlemore. And yet, those eight years, so intensely dedicated to the Reform Movement, were perhaps the most decisive in terms of the blossoming of Newmanian spirituality.

To tell the truth, the religious experience of the former student of Ealing and Oriel, in spite of the painful purification of Sicily, rested more on the intuition of some principles than on the cohesion of doctrinal thinking. However, such thinking was never absent from Newman's spiritual horizon. As we have seen, the first conversion of 1816, was first of all a conversion to a personal God, present at the heart of His own revelation. But this revelation, if it is to be known in its global totality, calls for the unfolding of all the truths it contains in germ. The spiritual itinerary of Newman until now was led very much more by a profound aspiration towards sanctity and the means to reach it than it was by the fullness of theological reflection. The benefits of the years of the Movement were precisely that they compelled Newman to strive continuously to allow the basic principles of his religious life to become the foundation of an authentic spirituality. Even if this quest was imposed by the situation in which he found himself, it did not take away any of its seriousness and profundity. Quite the contrary, this situation, in obliging Newman to give himself without reservation and under constant pressure, gave his spiritual reflections the unique accent that only true experience can provide.

Only the greatest spiritual minds can transform the events of their life into intense dramas which in turn give birth to a specific and original spirituality. Indeed, this is what is revealed in Newman's life during the first years of the Oxford Movement. His personal drama was always inseparable from his acts. The fluctuations of the struggle to open up a new way for the Church and to guard her from the many stumbling blocks that were menacing her, dictated the rhythm of his own spiritual life; he led the combat with the feeling that he was at the same time safeguarding the most solid convictions of his faith and the most indisputable rights of his Church. In this effort of reflection, he experienced the fecundity of the principles which were as much the rules which governed his own life as those which inspired the reform of the Church. Since Newman's religion was dogmatic and was firmly based on the tradition of faith, the Oxford Movement was also to be a doctrinal renewal; because his belief was sacramental, the renewal was to be liturgical; finally, because Newman's faith was not separable from the demands of the Gospel, the Movement was to promote ascetic practices and a quest for sanctity. The true meaning of the Oxford Movement was to be found in an unfailing fidelity to the imperatives of the Anglo Catholic faith.[2] Such a fidelity was first lived by one man, who knew that he was gambling his own destiny on it; as a result, the final failure was not to be his but that of his Church. Indeed, her failure to pass the test to which she was being submitted did not come as much from her liberal practices as from a congenital ambiguity in the Establishment. The Church was incapable of accepting the cure of rejuvenation that the best of her children were trying to administer to her.

Likewise, it is important to place into proper perspective the attempt made by the young reformers in suggesting a spiritual and ascetical renewal. It reveals an aspect too often misunderstood about the Oxford Movement. No doubt, historians are right when they attribute to the Tractarians the merit of a return both to the dogmatic sources of faith and to a sacramental and liturgical reform whose benefits extended well beyond the years of the Movement itself. But they hardly noticed the fact that this reform embraced much more than a certain concept about the Church and went far beyond the defense of its rights. At the very foundation of Newman's thinking and that of several of his friends was a deep preoccupation with salvation: the biblical notion of man as a sinner with a nostalgia for paradise lost; the anxiety about a pardon and a spiritual liberty that man is unable to attain without the grace of Jesus Christ. Thus, the spirit which animated the leaders of the Movement and motivated their daring initiatives was stamped by an austere asceticism. There was no morbidity in that spirit but the advice that was given referred to an exacting asceticism which was designed to promote conversion and the spiritual progress of souls. Above all, they aimed at the spiritual reform of individuals by providing them with an outline for the highest ideal of perfection.[3]

This resolution was manifested persistently not only during the years of the Movement but it outlived the Movement itself. From the very

---

[2] See Appendix II, p. 223.

[3] Among the studies dedicated to the Oxford Movement, it is necessary to set apart the one of the Lutheran theologian from Sweden, Brilioth, *The Anglican Revival, Studies in the Oxford Movement* (ed. Longmans, 1925). The author has put well in relief one of the essential orientations of the Movement, which was to promote the spiritual reform of souls; but he is incorrect in interpreting Tractarian spirituality in the framework of "Conversion" and "New Birth" as it was understood by Wesley and the Evangelicals.

beginning, the tracts set the tone. They insisted as much on personal conversion as on the conversion of the Church itself.[4] Newman's sermons at St. Mary's, and those less known of Pusey, defined the conditions of the reform of souls. They speak of "conversion," but not in the Wesleyan sense of a "new birth." It is to be accomplished, not within the emotional circle of initiates and fervent believers, but in the bosom of the institutional Church and the Christian community which offers them rites and sacraments, according to a tradition which is the heritage of Apostolical Christianity. The favorite Newmanian themes are present: the unique mystery of the human condition, the duty of a clear examination of problems, the unique responsibility of the individual conscience, the privileged relationship between the self and the Creator, and the imperative need for spiritual progress. A whole spiritual vision is presented here. The real question was how to open the hearts of all to the call of the Gospel and to dispose them to enter into the narrow ways of self-abnegation and submission to God. Without an effective desire for redemption, there is no possible forgiveness of sins committed after baptism.

In parallel with the publication of the Tracts and the ministry of preaching, the leaders of the Movement made an attempt at editing masterpieces of Anglican and Catholic spirituality from the preceding centuries. Works of prayer and devotion, treatises on the spiritual life, and lives of the saints were edited, commented on, and prefaced by Newman or Pusey at a fast pace. The *Sacra Privata* of Wilson, the *Godly Meditations* of Sutton, and the *Private Prayers of Bishop Andrewes*, all of sure value to Anglican piety, were successively rediscovered. Soon, Pusey attempted to popularize truly Catholic works, such as the famous *Spiritual Combat* of Scupoli, *The Introduction to the Devout Life*, the *Letters of John of Avila*, and the *Spiritual Exercises* of Louis of Grenada. This attempt by Pusey was not entirely new: The Caroline Divines of the seventeenth century and the Methodists of the eighteenth had already adopted them on English soil and had translated several works from the Catholic patrimony. But their diffusion was neither widespread nor systematically organized.

---

[4] See Tracts 3 and 9 on liturgical prayer and the warnings given on "alterations of the liturgy." "In altering things immaterial, we tend only to elevate ourselves without satisfying a desire to correct ourselves." Tract 14, dedicated to the Ember Days, claims the necessity of prayer and of fasting, which will be stressed again in Tracts 16, 18, 21, and 32.

However, for the Tractarians, scholarly undertakings were one of the most important tasks of their reform. In fact, Pusey's ambition surpassed that of Newman: he did not hesitate to undertake the translation of large extracts from the Breviary, dismissing the objections of his companion, Newman, who rightfully feared that it amounted to "sewing a new piece of cloth on an old garment."[5]

In an irresistible fashion, the Oxford Movement began to rediscover some fundamental claims of Christian spirituality: it awakened the most generous souls to the practice of prayer and spiritual direction; it went so far as to suggest and to bring into existence the principle of community life, even without its conventual form. A series of letters at the end of 1838 revealed Newman's concern and difficulties about his project to establish a community of priests, dedicated to the service of an urban ministry. He tried to realize this project, so dear to his heart, in his little parish at Littlemore, but destiny decided otherwise. Littlemore was to become for him a shelter and a retreat and not the home for missionary training that he had hoped for. Nevertheless, it is quite significant that the idea of an apostolic community should have revealed itself at that time.[6]

As for Pusey, in his sweet obstinacy, he was trying to reestablish in England nothing less than religious communities in the most classic tradition. In 1840, he visited Ireland to see on the spot what the conditions were for a revival of congregations for women; also, he sent for the constitutions and rules of various orders from the continent. The appeal of religious life attracted his daughter, Lucy, who resolved to dedicate her life to a congregation such as her father dreamed about founding. However, she died at an early age. She was revered by Newman as a saint. Only much later was Pusey to see his desire fulfilled; communities of nuns were to bloom in the Anglican Church. Late-ripening seeds of religious life were sown by the leaders of the Oxford Movement.

Among all the works of Newman and his friends from this period, nothing reveals in a better way their original intent than the publication in 1838 of the *Remains* of Froude. By publishing the intimate papers left by the departed, Newman and Keble wished to pose the compelling question

---

[5] Liddon, *Life of Pusey*, II, p. 393 ff., Letter to E. B. Pusey, 2, Dec. 18, 1843; Cf. Ker, p. 282.

[6] *Life of Pusey*, II, p. 135. Cf. Mozley, II, pp. 351-352.

of personal sanctity before the eyes of the Anglican world. They found in Froude the embodiment of this ideal of sanctity. Froude's destiny was in itself the perfect witness of the heights of virtue and moral excellence that a human soul was able to achieve within the Anglican structure, provided such a soul took seriously the call to conversion and to the spiritual combat which led to it. The publication of Froude's *Journal* was not only a posthumous tribute of fidelity to the memory of an exceptional man; its purpose was also to provide the Church with some tangible proof of the resources of grace and sanctification within itself. Such a publication was needed to help the Church satisfy the spiritual longings of her children. The religious experience of Froude was like a call to the Church herself. It was the proof that in her bosom lived souls who took the Gospel literally and thought they could achieve an authentic state of perfection.

In the history of the Oxford Movement, the publication of the *Remains* is like a manifesto in favor of the sanctity of life. In it, Froude's soul reveals itself with total sincerity; he describes its hesitations, its state of powerlessness, its fears and anguishes, and its invocations to God. He admits how distressed his soul is; he witnesses to its refusal of evil and challenges his soul in the spiritual combat for holiness. From the first reading of the manuscript which was handed over to him by his friend's father, Newman was incapable of protecting himself from a sort of vertigo. He wrote to a confidant:

> Archdeacon Froude sent up within this last week Hurrell's private journal (1826-1827), of which I did not know the existence before, giving an account of his fasting, etc., his minute faults and temptations at the time.... These new papers have quite made my head whirl, and have put things quite in a new light.[7]

Newman's feeling of surprise is perfectly understandable when one discovers in the *Remains* some notes as revealing as the one of September 17, 1826:

---

[7] Letter of August 31, 1837, M, II, pp. 216-217. The same note in the letter to Bowden, October 6, 1837. *Ibid.*, p. 219.

I ought to fight against myself with all my strength and watch over
my thoughts on every occasion. It will be good for me to keep an
exact account of my expenses and my spending... to reserve for
myself that which is legitimate while sacrificing my own fancies
in order to be able to honor God and care for the poor.[8]

The manuscript also contains letters addressed by Froude to Keble
which reveal a conscientious self-analysis and a call for spiritual direction
from Keble.[9]

Newman was aware of the fact that Froude's *Journal* would look
unusual and strange to some Anglican readers whose perennial reserve
would be all too easily offended by such intimate revelations. In the
preface written by Newman to introduce the *Remains*, he explained his
motives in publishing the *Journal* and tried to justify them.[10] Despite these
precautions, the publication was to provoke a veritable scandal in Anglican circles; people failed to see the poignant sincerity expressed on every
page. Such an intimate confession was considered out of place and
unpleasant; people sensed a touch of Romanism throughout many of his
confidences, no matter how inspired they were by a very real need to be
united with God in a spirit of true devotion and detachment. The implicit
condemnation of the *Remains* was a way for the Anglican Church to
undermine the efforts towards a spiritual and ascetic renewal that Newman
had attempted to promote through the Oxford Movement.

---

[8] *Remains*, I, p. 11.
[9] *Ibid.*, I, p. 205 ff. See the study of Lady I. Guiney: *Hurrell Froude*, p. 43.
[10] *Remains*, I, p. VI.

CHAPTER IX

A MATURE SPIRITUALITY

Exsul factus sum in solitudine.
[I have been made an exile in solitude]

*T*HE OXFORD MOVEMENT was finally at an impasse. As early as 1839, Newman discerned that the reforms initiated by the publication of the Tracts had failed. Although the Movement was agonizing, his interior life was rich in experience and in teaching. In the sense that spirituality is defined by the possession of certain principles and by the very expression of fundamental religious attitudes, it is during the course of these years that one is able to recognize without doubt a maturing Newmanian spirituality. As we have seen, the need to deal with controversy within the Movement had stimulated a doctrinal reflection which in turn brought about a more mature way of thinking. A religious synthesis emerged: little by little, his essential spiritual convictions were forged and expanded and were given strong support and rational structure. But this rational synthesis was accompanied by an inner purification of the soul, more and more trying for Newman, to the extent that the destiny of the Movement became more uncertain and the position of the leaders more untenable. The years which preceded the conversion to Rome were assuredly the ones most loaded with anxiety and fear. Far from being useless, they represent in the evolution of Newman's spirituality that stage in his life in which he recognized and lived the faith experience in the absolute rigor of its requirements. It was the time when a firm spiritual position had to be taken. A lucid judgment of conscience, a sense of interiority, and a total surrender

115

5. The Spiritual Journey of Newman

to the will of God: such are the permanent traits of the Newmanian mystique.

Let us go back to the years of the Oxford Movement, through the various stages of the history which Newman lived intensely. His writings at the time of the first skirmishes give an unmistakable impression: a sort of feverish joy and a slightly presumptuous sense of satisfaction. He threw himself into the Movement with an energy which seemed to him to be juvenile and which surprised even himself. The first years were the ones full of hopeful combat: Newman was on the front line of battle with a hardly contained audacity and a contagious confidence. He discerned in himself at that period "a mixture... of both fierceness and of sport"[1] which gave to all his conduct a verve and freshness without precedent in the whole of his history. Thus, he wrote to Froude on September 18, 1833, after the outright success of the first tracts:

> I shall offend and hurt men I would fain be straight with. Yet what can one do? Men are made of glass: the sooner we break them and get it over the better.[2]

He was impatient and brusque with his friends, whom he found so "stupidly bashful."[3] If he flared at critics' opposition, he immediately reasserted his own boldness and self-assurance: "There is much coldness and opposition here, for this is a criticizing place; but never mind, we will beat them."[4]

This pride in what he was doing, this confidence in his success is not solely explained by his possession of a too exuberant temperament, which was for too long kept at bay. Newman's confidence came from a higher source: it transcended the sovereign pride of a man who had discovered what his mission was and who gave himself entirely to it. Much later, he was to write:

> I had the consciousness that I was employed in that work which I had been dreaming about, and which I felt to be so momentous and inspiring.[5]

---

[1] *Apologia*, p. 48.
[2] M. I., p. 403.
[3] Letter to Bowden, October 31, 1833. M. I., p. 414.
[4] *Ibid*, p. 424. Letter of November 13.
[5] *Apologia*, p. 47.

"I have acted," he was to confide to his bishop, "because others did not act, and have sacrificed a quiet which I prized."[6] This is reminiscent of St. Hilary, forced to quit the "*otium cum voluptate*" ("the idle life of unrestrained pleasure") for the arena of controversy. It is above all reminiscent of St. Paul, who did not hesitate to speak out to the Corinthians about his pride, his "kaukèma,"[7] which was nothing less than his certainty that he was being obedient to a mission. And it is, indeed, this sentiment of a compelling fidelity which gave to Newman a security in his enterprises and shielded him in a sort of rigid attitude, bordering on intransigence. He was conscious of belonging to the great lineage of the Apostles, of the Fathers of the Church who had defended the integrity of faith, of the great Anglican theologians of the seventeenth century, who had protected the Church against the dangers of heresy and enslavement:

> I reflect with some pleasure that some of our most learned men lived and acted in most troublesome times, as Usher, Hammond, Taylor, and in primitive times Clement of Alexandria, Dionysius, and Origen.[8]

It was fitting for the Vicar of St. Mary's to retain from those quickly passing years, which were so passionate and full of action, the certainty that he was fulfilling a mission as the instrument chosen for a work which surpassed him. But now, this instrument revealed a surprising rigidity. Soon, he would discover that the cause he defended would not achieve the success he expected. Yet, he never ceased to remain in the hands of God. The spirit of Newman reveals here one of his most fundamental and least contested stances: an absolute surrender to the will of the Lord.

Nevertheless, the joyous ardor of the first years of the Movement should not create any illusion. If all the action created in Newman a state of euphoria which surprised him, he refused to let himself be overwhelmed by it. He had too much control over himself to be distracted from the essential goal. He never fell into the kind of "relaxation" denounced by Pascal. His battle was the result of a conscious and voluntary resolution

---

[6] *Ibid.*, p. 80. Letter to Bagot, Bishop of Oxford, after the condemnation of Tract 90.
[7] 2 Cor 12.
[8] Letter to Froude, June 21, 1834. M. II, p. 44.

which never let him forget for a moment the need for retirement and solitude. His most personal charism was one of interiority; action itself contributed to strengthening and purifying his need for inner life. Indeed, as paradoxical as it may appear, Newman's multiple activities to serve the cause of the Movement aroused in him the need for recollection and silence. It was not for healing the secret wounds caused by his critics' lack of understanding, but in order to pass judgment upon himself, to probe his own intentions, and to ponder the seriousness of his decisions. He needed to be in the presence of God in order to evaluate better the demands of the mission entrusted to him in the same way that a prophet retreats into the desert from whence he has come in order to measure the level of his fidelity. And it was very rare that Newman, always strict in the examination of his motives, did not discern some secret weakness in his own commitment. He imputed his failures to some hidden faults for which he felt responsible before God.

Thus, in the year 1834, a painful incident led him into a sorrowful confession which revealed the depth of his moral austerity. In opposition to the current opinion of that time, which did not spare him its criticism, he refused to perform the wedding of an unbaptized woman who belonged to a dissident sect. The sacramental discipline in the Anglican Church was then very relaxed, more and more under the influence of lax theologians and liberal pastors. Newman's refusal meant the return to principles defended by the Tractarians of the Movement. He encountered hostility among his own family; even his mother did not spare him her disapproval. In a state of painful isolation, he received letters of support from Keble and Pusey. They approved of his decision without reservation. Reassured, he confessed in these very revealing terms: "I had taken my vexation as a sort of punishment for my sins, and did not expect thus to be comforted."[9]

The same admission is found several years later, after the condemnation of Tract 90, which sealed the failure of the Tractarian Movement: "I am perfectly aware at the same time that it is a rebuke and punishment for my secret pride and sloth."[10] This distraught state of a conscience obscurely loaded with guilt was to be one of the reasons which prompted

---

[9] Letter to his mother, July 8, 1834. M. II, p. 50.
[10] Letter to Rogers, March 21, 1841. M. II, p. 299.

him to solicit Keble's support and counsel.[11] Again, we find one of the prominent traits of his moral life, namely a spontaneous inclination to relate his most trying times and personal failures to an infidelity of his own conscience. It was that which the crisis in Sicily had shown: there is no interior peace without a purification which empties the conscience of all its imperfections, whether or not they are deliberate. Man is a sinner and he is not able to establish himself in grace before God without having discovered the very roots of sin. The silence and retreat of the desert is indispensable for revealing the creature to himself. In Newman, solitude was needed not only as a catharsis for quieting the passions but also as a necessary condition for living out his vocation. The words of Provost Copleston, "Never less lonely than when alone,"[12] were truer than ever.

Let us hear the explanation that he gave of himself in a letter to his sister, Jemima, several weeks after the death of their mother in May of 1836:

> While even my health lasts I wish to employ myself.... For what I know, I may in a year or two be cast aside as a broken tool having done my part. Not that I expect this, but God's ways are so wonderful.... Now I have not explained why I have said all this.... I am not more lonely than I have been a long while. God intends me to be lonely; He has so framed my mind that I am in a great measure beyond the sympathies of other people and thrown upon Himself.... God, I trust will support me in following whither He leads.[13]

Diverse circumstances, among them his family's desire to see him married, enable us to understand his firmness in the above letter. Ever since his return from Sicily, Newman was the object of more or less pressing

---

[11] Newman had always been inclined to search for his own hidden faults, unknown or secret, as the origin of his doubts and the cause of his failures. Cf. the preceding note. The same idea is found in a letter of March 15, 1845, addressed to his sister, Jemima: "...the human heart is mysterious. I may have some deep evil in me which I cannot fathom; I may have done some irreparable thing which demands punishment" (M. II, p. 412). The sermon, "Secret Faults," I Par. IV, p. 31, illustrates this tendency in Newman.

[12] *Apologia*, p. 25.

[13] M. II, p. 176. Letter from June 26, 1836.

solicitations in regard to marriage. This effort could have put an end to his celibacy, which was judged to be an inappropriate way of life for him. Before she died, Mrs. Newman expressed the wish to see him set up in his own home. She was about to see her two daughters, Jemima and Harriet, married to the Mozley brothers, who were friends of Newman. He now had to defend himself against barely veiled allusions and sometimes indiscreet attempts to influence him. All this did not prevent him from experiencing real suffering for what he was about to sacrifice. In the course of his illness in Sicily, he had already experienced the sting of this self-sacrifice.

During the years following his return from Sicily, from 1834 to 1840, it seemed that Newman accepted with great courage his resolution to renounce the world, which he had made in an earlier commitment.[14] He had no regrets or sadness whatsoever! The decision remained firm, but a series of circumstances, including a separation from his family, the deaths of his mother and his friend, Froude,[15] and the tough battles encountered in the Movement, all made him feel the weight of a solitary life more acutely and intensely. We have an echo of these trying times in a text written on March 25, 1840 at the end of a memoir about his illness in Sicily. Judging the passage too personal, Anne Mozley removed it from the publication of the *Letters and Correspondence of J.H. Newman*. After laboriously recalling various memories from his past, Newman wondered about his future:

> The thought keeps pressing on me, while I write this, what am I writing it for? I was going to say, I only have found one who even took that sort of affectionate interest in me as to be pleased with such details — and that is H. Wilberforce[16] and what shall I ever see of him? This is the sort of interest which a wife takes and none but she — it is a woman's interest — and that interest, so be it, shall never be taken in me. Never, so be it, will I be other than God has found me. All my habits for years, my tendencies are towards celibacy. I could not take that interest in this world which marriage requires. I am too disgusted with this world — And,

---

[14] See *Autobiographical Writings*, p. 203. Bouyer, p. 99.

[15] The death of Mrs. Newman was on May 17, 1836; that of Froude was on February 28th of the same year.

[16] It was the question about his friend, Henry Wilberforce.

above all, call it what one will, I have a repugnance to clergymen's marrying. I do not say it is not lawful. — I cannot deny the right — but, whether a prejudice or not, it shocks me. And therefore I willingly give up the possession of that sympathy, which I feel is not, cannot be, granted to me. Yet, not the less do I feel the need of it.[17]

Thus, did Newman consider himself a stranger in the midst of all those who loved him. He fulfilled his vocation at the price of a superior solitude which transcended the legitimate affections of the flesh and the joys of a shared love. It is precisely this theme of solitude which inspired most of the parochial sermons delivered at St. Mary's during the first years of the Movement. His preaching was marked by a serene gravity and a restrained fervor, which defines Newmanian spirituality of the invisible world, the otherworldliness of which he was the witness and prophet. He returned again and again to the necessity of resisting the seductions and ephemeral joys of the present world. Even the security and the tender affections of home life were scrutinized in these sermons. The satisfactions which they provide, however legitimate, should not deter the Christian who is invited to lift his eyes above the horizon to another universe. Abnegation should be the normal condition for anyone who does not wish to be deluded by the illusions of this present world. Here are some excerpts from the sermons preached at that period. They clearly reveal one of the most fundamental intuitions of Newmanian spirituality:

> And as to those others nearer to us, who are not to be classed with the vain world, I mean our friends and relations, whom we are right in loving, these too after all are nothing to us here... they cannot get at our souls, they cannot enter into our thoughts, or really be companions to us.[18]

> ...those who obey Him. They are sprinkled up and down the world; they are separated the one from the other, they are bid quit each other's dear society, and sent afar off to those who are differently minded.... Their choice of profession and employ-

---

[17] *Autobiog.*, p. 137.
[18] This passage was taken from I Par. II, p. 17, "The Immortality of the Soul." He delivered it on July 21, 1833.

ment is not their own... not knowing the persons to whom they unite themselves.[19]

The notion entertained by most men seems to be, that it is a pleasant thing to have a home;... that a wife and family are comforts.... All this is true... blessings from God; and it is praiseworthy and right to be domestic, and to live in orderly and honourable habits. But a man who limits his view to these thoughts, who does not look at marriage and the birth of children as something of a much higher and more heavenly nature than anything we see, who does not discern in Holy Matrimony a divine ordinance... to take interest and pleasure in our families... it is very well but it is not religion.[20]

There is no doubt that at the very time Newman became firmer in his resolve to live a solitary life, he sensed the roughness of the road with renewed intensity. It was a salient trait of Newman's character that he was never more resolute in his quest for the absolute than when he experienced the bleeding stings of renunciation in the depth of his being. A stirring in the depth of his heart was always a clear sign to him that a new height in abnegation had to be reached. Such was Newman's nature, so human and at the same time so foreign to man's usual behavior. He kept a close guard over those affections and passions which render most men vulnerable in

---

[19] III Par; XVII, pp. 628-629, "The Visible Church, an Encouragement to Faith," of September 14, 1834.

[20] III Par; XX, p. 666, "Infant Baptism," of May 34, 1835. Besides, one discovers in the *Parochial Sermons* of this period some frequent allusions to a call to solitude and to detachment from natural bonds. Thus, in the sermon, "The Good Part of Mary," (III Par; XII, December 26, 1834) the speaker evokes those "favored and honoured beyond thought if they can... put aside worldly things... and present themselves as a holy offering... to Him" (p. 688). In the one he dedicates to "A Particular Providence" (III Par; IX, p. 552, April 5, 1835), Newman develops the idea of a divine predilection for those who remain in solitude. See also: "The Ventures of Faith," (IV Par; XX, p. 914, February 21, 1836); "The Church a Home for the Lonely," (IV Par; XII, p. 842, October 22, 1837); "Solitude in the World, Condition of the Christian" (V Par; V "Equanimity," p. 995, December 22, 1839); "The Insufficiency of Friendship and of Family" (V Par; XXII, p. 1149, "The Thought of God the Stay of the Soul," June 9, 1839); "The Excellence of Celibacy in Marriage" (VI Par; XIII, p. 1285, Feb. 28, 1841); "Judaism of the Present Day."

Such a convergence in these sermons around this theme of renunciation, particularly in regard to the affections of the heart cannot be truly explained without a personal experience of detachment and constant meditation on the vocation to celibacy.

the struggles of life. But Newman's heart, no matter how wounded and bruised, emptied itself in the struggle and crossed over to the other bank.

Furthermore, his interior solitude was not only the fruit of a renunciation, which never appeared so sorrowful as in the events of 1836, but it was also the most fundamental and most decisive principle in Newmanian spirituality. This solitude was necessary for achieving a docility to God in its most radical form — that of complete abandonment. The crisis in Sicily allowed for the secret development of this sentiment which would acquire extraordinary strength due to the circumstances and events in his life.[21] As the Oxford Movement evolved, it pushed Newman towards the impasse in which he found himself after four years. At the same time, it helped strengthen his need for spiritual abandonment into the hands of God to such a degree that it totally absorbed his conscience. In order to identify the hidden steps by which Newman's soul ascended towards the absolute purification of a radical surrender, let us follow the spiritual itinerary of his life from the first years of the Movement until its end. Newman wrote:

> For years I must have had something of an habitual notion... that my mind had not found its ultimate rest, and that in some sense or other I was on a journey.[22]

As long as the goal was not reached, the soul was waiting and was available for new calls. No doubt that in the first years of the Movement, his surrender to God did not yet have the touching character of necessity which it was to take on much later. But one must note through the explosive ideas of the first tracts and the early skirmishes, a disposition in Newman which appeared again and again like a spiritual leitmotif. He was well aware that he was submitting to imperatives well beyond his understanding. He was surrendering himself to them as a simple instrument into the hand that directed him. During the vacation of 1835 while doing some research for his work, he wrote to his Aunt Elizabeth:

> And it is a very joyful thought which comes to me with a great force of confidence to believe that, in doing so, I am one of the

---

[21] See the chapter, "Illness in Sicily," about Newman's holy indifference.
[22] *Apologia*, p. 100.

instruments which our gracious Lord is employing with a purpose
of good towards us.[23]

The desire to be a simple instrument in the hands of God is
mentioned several times in his correspondence. On his birthday, he wrote
to his sister, Jemima, who had sent him the good wishes of Mrs. Newman
and Harriet:

> They will be deserved if God gives me grace to fulfil the purposes
> for which he has led me on hitherto in a wonderful way. I think
> I am conscious to myself that, whatever are my faults, I wish to
> live and die to His glory — to surrender wholly to Him as His
> instrument, to whatever work and at whatever personal sacrifice,
> though I cannot duly realize my own words when I say so.[24]

Did Newman, in writing these lines, have a presentiment that his
destiny was definitively set? They testify to a humility and an abnegation
which leaves no doubt about his integrity. He was to remember, at the time
of an approaching crisis, his vows and resolutions of 1835 and he would
discover in the most complete surrender of himself the power of his own
prayer.

God's plan was unfolding. Day after day, the generous pioneers of
July 1833 were being subjected to situations more and more trying and
desperate. Challenges were more numerous, and blame fell without
ceasing on the heads of the unhappy Tractarians.

Hesitating and intimidated, the hierarchy was reluctant to become
involved, but this reserve was in itself more a sign of reprobation than of
sympathy. The specter of Rome and the fear of conversion restrained most

---

[23] M. II, p. 116, Letter to Mrs. Elizabeth Newman: "I do verily believe that some such
movement is now going on, and that the Philistines are to be smitten, and, believing it,
I rejoice to join myself to the Army of rescue, as one of those who lapped with the
tongue when the rest bowed down to drink." This letter is one of those which best
reveals the biblical formation of Newman. This Aunt Elizabeth had contributed much
to reveal the wealth of the Scriptures to young John Henry (cf. M. II, p. 396). Very
soon, she would be closely associated with the drama of her nephew's conversion and
would share in the agonizing situation of Jemima Newman Mozley. (*Ibid.*,II, p. 399,
410 ff.)

[24] M. II, p. 152. Letter of February 21, 1836.

of those who would have followed Newman in a less radical way of thinking. When the Oxford authorities condemned Tract 90,[25] the cause was already lost. The Established Church would never endorse the principles of a reform movement which so dangerously leaned towards Romanism.

Also, it was the time which marked the end of Newman's belief in the justness of his cause. All his efforts to bring to the Anglican Church the dogmatic structures which would have justified its claim to Apostolicity remained misunderstood. Each day, he recognized the vanity of his enterprise more and more. In himself, he experienced a drama more tormenting than the one of the future of his own Church: at stake was his own spiritual destiny. Was he not responsible for the failure of the Movement, due perhaps to some hidden weakness in himself which might have overcome his own lucidity? Throughout 1840, he struggled with his conscience, which he felt needed constant examination and analysis. But in contrast with the Sicilian crisis, these interior debates, as painful as they were, left intact the power of his will.

Before taking the road which was to lead him — did he know it already? — towards conversion to the Church of Rome, Newman tried to clear a last hurdle. He needed to convince himself that the failure of the efforts he undertook to save his own Church did not come from his own mistakes. He appeared to be willing to set himself on a new direction, provided he was certain that his past was cleared from any personal fault. As he was trying to clear himself from the suspicion of having in some manner compromised his task by imposing upon it the mysterious burden of some secret faults which he might have neglected to face up to and condemn, Newman did not wish to be alone.

For this ultimate encounter with himself, Newman experienced the need for some security that comes from a witness who is also a confidant. This needed help he was to find in Keble. Between the two friends, conversations turned to a real direction of conscience.

---

[25] See above, the appearance of the celebrated Tract 90.

CHAPTER X

AN INEFFECTUAL SPIRITUAL DIRECTION

I have been as open with him
as possible.

M. II, p. 403.

THIS SEARCH FOR spiritual direction is quite surprising in Newman who, for the first and probably the last time, left to another the responsibility of bringing light and spiritual peace to his soul. He had never thought of submitting his moral life to the judgment of anyone else, whether friend or superior, who might interfere in the dialogue between his soul and God. Even after the Sicilian crisis, he had kept his secret and had not judged it necessary to open himself to anyone about the personal drama he had experienced.

It is not that the direction of conscience was new to the Anglican tradition. In the eighteenth century, the reform of Wesley gave a place of honor to the practice of some spiritual direction. Also, the example of his friend, Froude, who had for a long time looked to Keble for support and counsel to sustain his religious and moral life, was fresh in Newman's mind. But Newman had too sharp a sense of the unique dimension of his own soul to think that it could be scrutinized by someone else. Therefore, if he resolved to ask for Keble's direction, it was much more with a concern for personal justification and moral peace than to receive advice about the way to conduct his own spiritual life, which was as he said, "incommunicable."

Furthermore, he had mixed feelings about this first experience with spiritual direction. Keble, although reflecting the true spirit of the Gospel and possessing an unquestionable spiritual authority, was not a man of decision with precise and firm judgment that would have helped Newman out of the labyrinth of doubt and darkness in which he was entangled. The delicate sentiments of the poet of the *Christian Year*, when confronted with the moral consciences of other people, experienced a kind of reserve or discretion, which, when pushed to the limit, was too cautious and hesitant to help those hungry consciences to find their peace. In several instances, Newman would attempt by his courageous confessions to force Keble out of his natural discretion, but the best he could do was to elicit from him some timid suggestions. Little prepared to deal with controversial subjects, still less prepared to deal with the complexity of Newman's conscience, Keble revealed his own inadequacy.

Yet, Newman had turned spontaneously towards the Vicar of Hursley, whom he venerated as a saint. In all the affairs of the Movement, he had sought his support and approval. Without having the same jovial and playful tone towards him, which is so noticeable in his letters to Froude or Bowden, he nevertheless maintained a very great confidence in him. On several occasions when he was overwhelmed by criticism directed against the Movement, Newman submitted himself completely to Keble's judgment without any hesitation.[1]

When in 1840 a new crisis arose, one that eventually was to end in Newman's conversion to the Roman Church, it was only natural that he should consult Keble. But what Newman forcefully demanded of him

---

[1] Thus, in August of 1838, when Dr. Bagot, bishop of Oxford, expressed some serious reservations about certain expressions in some of the tracts (cf. M. II, p. 233. Letter of August 22, 1838). Then again, several months later, when his clergy were upset by certain of Newman's projects: the publication of the breviary and the foundation of a mission for priests with a view to evangelization. Keble's own brother, Thomas, pastor at Bisley, had been the most vocal among the critics. Newman then writes to his friend: "I put myself entirely into your hands. I will do whatever you suggest.... If you tell me to make any submission to anyone, I will do it. Indeed, I am determined if I can that no charge should be against me beyond that of being myself -- that is of having certain opinions and a certain way of expressing them... here too I give myself up to your judgment.... Is it to stop writing? I will stop anything you advise." The second part of the letter contains a plea: "Now this being understood, may I not fairly ask for some little confidence in me as to what under these voluntary restrictions, I do? People really should put themselves into my place and consider how the appearance of suspicion, jealousy, and discontent is likely to affect one who is most conscious that everything he does is imperfect..." (Letter of November 21, 1838, M. II, p. 240).

from that time on was much more than an expression of sympathy or encouragement for his conduct. It was not a question any more of supporting the leader of a Movement, whose ups and downs were always open to either approbation or criticism. In question was a highly personal drama of conscience. The collapse of the Movement turned into an agonizing and painful case of conscience for Newman. He was crammed with doubts about the validity of his mission in the Anglican Church which rejected it, and he was very worried about his fervent and impatient disciples who were ready upon a signal from him to throw off their Anglican allegiance.[2] Newman's convictions were more and more in disarray; the ground was collapsing under his feet. Keble, of all his friends, would be the one to point out to him a safe haven where his thoughts could take refuge while awaiting the ultimate decisions. This was his secret hope when he turned to Keble.

Newman asked Keble several questions of a very practical order. If he had lost faith in the Anglican Church, should he continue to assume the functions to which were attached certain benefices and privileges? As loyal as he was, could he retain the most enviable situation as Vicar of St. Mary's at Oxford and fellow of Oriel? Should he resign these two titles at the risk of again stirring up public opinion? Should he keep these posts, thus creating an ambiguity which would disconcert his friends and torture his own conscience?

After the censure of Tract 90, which brought the reprobation of the University and the blame of the bishops upon him, Newman wrote to John Keble because he was worried about keeping St. Mary's. Keble answered: "Try to persuade your bishop; if he does not allow it, I do not see how you are able to retain St. Mary's."[3] As if this response went too far, Keble corrected himself in the letters that followed. He hesitated and then said: "Will the resignation of your benefice be judged as a sign of secession?" Finally, it was Newman's decision to cloister himself at Littlemore which took Keble out of the impasse. He saw no objection to a prolonged stay outside of Oxford, provided that Newman continued with an active ministry in his little church outside of town.[4] But this response of Keble,

---

[2] At Littlemore, grouped around Newman, were a certain number of his Anglican followers of whom several were already near conversion.
[3] K., p. 101.
[4] *Ibid.*, p. 216.

dated March 14, 1843, eluded the real problem and did not touch any of the deep reasons for Newman's scruples.[5]

In a letter dated May 4th, Newman in very clear terms, explained to his friend the profound changes which were taking place within himself, how his prejudices with respect to Rome were crumbling; he admitted his helplessness in his attempts to reason by himself.[6] Several days later, Keble responded:

> It frightens me to think how rashly and with how small prepara-
> tion I have been dealing with these grave matters. I have all
> manner of imagination as to how my defects may have helped to
> unsettle people, and in particular to hinder you from finding
> peace.... All I want is that you should put no sort of implicit faith
> in me, but take up with what I say when you see anything in it that
> is reasonable and right.[7]

This admission of Keble's helplessness does not stop Newman, who wrote to him on May 18, 1843:

> [T]o whom can I go... but to you, who have been an instrument
> of good to so many, myself inclusive.... I feel no doubt that in
> consulting you I am doing God's will.[8]

A little later, Keble suggested that his friend suspend his theological research, which he had undertaken while at Littlemore, and he added this surprising advice which shows well his indecisive character: that Newman inquire about finding a sure confidant who would be able to help him! Then, in a long memorandum, Newman explained to Keble that he was asking him very precisely to be his adviser; he expected him to be. He went into explicit details: (1) He was keeping a detailed spiritual journal in order to communicate better to his confessor his intimate sentiments. (2) He

---

[5] In fact, Newman did not resign St. Mary's until September 1843.

[6] K., pp. 217-220. He confessed his sadness after he was abandoned by his friend, Rogers, who refused any discussion on religious subjects.

[7] *Ibid.*, pp. 224-225. Newman's term, "implicit faith," can be understood as "absolute faith."

[8] *Ibid.*, p. 225. In another letter of May 30th, Keble did not dare to press Newman to keep his parish.

asked Keble to be this confessor and to read his journal. (3) He also admitted a need for a change of occupation: "My great fault is doing things in a mere literary way from love of the work, without the thought of God's glory." (4) He was worried about his responsibilities towards his parish. He wrote: "If I were to have anything more directly practical it should be a hospital."[9]

But Keble, more hesitant than ever, declined the offer to consult his intimate journal. Impatiently, Newman answered: "As to my *Journal*, I wish you honestly to say whether you think that you will be able to advise me better by seeing it."[10]

In September, Keble tried again to avoid the responsibility:

> About my seeing your *Journal*, I know not what to say: only this: If you think it but possible that it may help me to be useful to you, do not keep it back under the notion of not paining me.[11]

Two days later, he insisted anew: "I quite thirst after some other counsellor for you. Now Pusey is better."[12] Newman, nevertheless, sent him the *Journal*:

> I think on the whole I shall send you the 10 days *Journal* I spoke to you of. Of course I cannot tell, but I don't think it will over-pain you — that is I think you may perhaps be prepared for it, on whole, if not in detail.... I have put down, not only infirmities, but temptations, even when I did not feel them to be more than external to me.[13]

As we have seen, he was tormented by the fear that an infidelity of his conscience was the source of the failure of his mission in the Church.

---

[9] *Ibid.*, p. 245. This is not the first time that Newman aspired to leave his books in order to free himself for a more direct ministry over souls. He had written to his sister, Jemima, on October 2, 1834: "I can fancy the day coming when India might be a refuge, if our game is up here." M. II, p. 60. This coming to Littlemore in March 1840 was a real discovery of a life both active and silent. See M. II, p. 269 ff.
[10] Letter, August 11th, K., p. 248 ff.
[11] *Ibid.*, p. 258. Letter of September 5th.
[12] *Ibid.*, p. 261.
[13] *Ibid.*, p. 267 ff.

The obscure and vague presentiment of a hidden fault committed by him never ceased to trouble him. And it was to clarify this point that he had turned to Keble. The *Journal* which he sent him was a vigorous and lucid account of his conscience, quite in the fashion of the merciless analyst that he was, already evident at the time of his illness in Sicily.

If we do not have in the collection of letters of direction the one which contains Keble's response, at least we know through Newman himself that his response was reassuring; it brought to his moral anguish the calm which would finally tranquilize his conscience for a time. In two of the numerous and anxious letters which he addressed to his sister, Jemima, in the course of the months preceding his conversion to Rome, Newman, alluding to his inquietude, recalled how concerned he had been in confiding himself to Keble and the assurances that he had received:

> It is the fear that there is some secret undetected fault which is the cause of my belief which keeps me where I am, waiting.... Some time ago I wrote down for Keble everything of every sort I could detect as passing in my mind in any respect wrong or leading to wrong, day by day for a certain period, and he could detect nothing bearing on this particular belief of mine. I have been as open with him as possible.[14]

Thus, in spite of his hesitations and continual drawing back, Keble provided the appeasement capable of alleviating the moral scruples of his unhappy friend. If the direction Newman was looking for did not help him out of the impasse created by the polemics in the Movement, at least it relieved the tension in his conscience. Keble did not point a way out but he comforted the traveler; if he did not appease the doubts which paralyzed Newman's journey, he neutralized the great anguish in his soul.

Somewhat reassured, Newman abandoned himself more completely to the Master of his soul and sought from Him the light that would make clear what was to be his definitive choice. In the meantime, he made a grave decision: On September 19, 1843, he resigned his curacy of St. Mary's and

---

[14] This letter is from Dec. 22, 1844 (M. I., p. 403); it was followed by one still more moving of March 15, 1845. (M. I., pp. 410-411) All the letters which precede his conversion, considering the lucidity of their analysis and their moving sincerity, constitute the richest part of the entire Newmanian correspondence.

on the 25th, he preached his last sermon at Littlemore. Henceforth, he was only a dead member of the Anglican Church. However, this decision did not resolve the entire drama. Newman continued to advance alone between two shores: the one of Rome, which always seemed to him to be hostile and withdrawn, and the other one, which was saddened by the gloomy faces of those to whom he had said good-bye.

In the months which followed, the relationship between Keble and Newman took a new turn: it was no longer the upset pastor longing for advice, hesitating to give up the Vicarage of St. Mary's and anxious not to offend his friends by too abrupt a decision. Anxiety still filled his soul; he remained concerned with the need to act without precipitation; he was anxious not to alarm his disciples; and he was afraid, above all, to hasten the conversion of impatient followers!

But his relationship with John Keble was changing: he was no longer looking for spiritual direction. He still shared with Keble his most intimate thoughts and feelings, but he no longer expected to obtain specific advice. Rather, he tried to justify his own present attitude. Newman was now more concerned with presenting his case than submitting to Keble's direction; he expected encouragement rather than a line of conduct. In giving up St. Mary's, he made an irrevocable decision: what he wanted to do now was to explain the motives for his separation from a doctrine which was no longer acceptable, and from an institution whose failure he had experienced. He also wanted to define his attitude with regard to the Roman Church from which he was still separated by a natural repulsion as well as by prejudices which he found difficult to overcome.

Always a prey to doubts which tormented him and with his heart bleeding from daily setbacks, Newman experienced in the last months of 1844 a desolation that would have thrown anyone else into a state bordering almost on despair. The affective supports which would have been able to sustain him in the dark night which he was traversing disappeared one after the other. The death of Bowden in October deprived him of a very old friend and close confidant. He was deeply hurt by the suspicions which were separating him from several of his friends and relatives and even from his own sister, Jemima, whom he believed he could rely upon. Meanwhile, his enemies organized a campaign of calumny against him, all the more cruel, since his own silence seemed to give them no reason for it. The majority of his former companions in the original Movement seemed to misinterpret his intentions and to be totally unaware of the spiritual drama which was taking place in his soul. On the contrary, they suspected that he remained too insensitive of his responsibility towards those very disciples who were feeling so disoriented and abandoned.[15] They interpreted his silence and his withdrawal as the bitter fruit of a personal deception, born from the condemnation of Tract 90 and the blame inflicted upon him by the religious authorities. Newman felt that a sort of fatality followed him and attached itself to each one of his steps. He wrote in a letter dated November 21, 1844: "I am afraid of a Nemesis."[16] And yet, in this deepest disarray which kept him feeling as if he were lying on a "death bed,"[17] he wanted to preserve the lucidity of mind without which he would have succumbed sooner or later to a move of irrevocable panic. If he was beginning to think that a change of communion was imposing itself upon him as an obligation of conscience, he had not yet reached that state of reflection and maturation where the decision imposed itself upon him. On the one hand, he was well aware that he ought not to remain and die in the bosom of the Anglican Church but on the other hand, he did not yet perceive the necessity of an immediate conversion.

In this intense interior debate, he cultivated a spiritual disposition which alone was able to help him master the calls from opposite directions and to preserve a sense of self-justification. On November 21, 1844, he wrote to Keble:

> What I try to preserve is what divines call the state of "indifferentia." Touched and grateful as one must be for the prayers of one's own friends, I have tried to make out whether there is any feeling of impatience on my mind.[18]

It is quite possible that a continuous meditation on the *Exercises of Saint Ignatius*, a book treasured by Newman at that time, as we shall soon discover in the following chapter, revealed to him the importance of the virtue of indifference. For Saint Ignatius, the most perfect detachment from all creatures is an absolute requisite for making oneself entirely

---

[15] K., p. 354. Editors' Note: Everyone took it for granted that Newman did not realize how much people depended upon him.
[16] *Ibid.*, p. 349.
[17] *Apologia*, p. 121.
[18] K., p. 351.

available to the Creator. It is precisely when he was at this crossroad, in the midst of uncertainty, that Newman rediscovered by a spontaneous inclination of his soul, the way to abandon himself to the Lord. Spiritual indifference was now for him the only state possible, crucifying but enriching, by which he remained in the hands of God, rejecting every illusion. He let himself be led, as if he wished to observe the process of spiritual maturation which was taking place in him.[19] He fully realized that a grace rich in light and promise was in him which would bloom when the time was ripe. His ultimate goal was a total detachment from emotional forces which still exercised their often blind and sterile constraints in the everyday flow of events and circumstances. In a letter to Keble several months earlier, Newman had already described his determination to aim at total indifference and the blessings he expected from it:

> I am in no distress of mind at present — that is, whatever is truth, and whatever is not, I do not feel called to do anything but go on where I am, and this must be peace and quietness — and whatever is before us, in this one may rejoice, and not take thought for the morrow.[20]

Never more than in these heartrending months had Newman perceived with absolute clarity the necessary process of emptying himself in order to be entirely enveloped by the divine will. This spiritual experience would, much later in his life, inspire the admirable texts of *Meditations and Devotions*, so full of the accents of sweetness and confidence which are the echo of a fervent submission and surrender of the soul in its dialogue with God at the very time when all human love and tenderness fail.

---

[19] This expression comes from Father Bacchus of the Oratory, who with Father Tristram, edited the *Correspondence with Keble and Others*.
[20] Letter of January 23, 1844, K., p. 300, cf. p. 322, 351.

CHAPTER XI

THE CALL TO ROME

For thou dost soothe the heart,
thou Church of Rome.

Verses, p. 153.

GROUPED AROUND Newman in the solitude of Littlemore, several of his young followers were seeking light and a model of a more austere life. A paper from 1842 contains an account of the daily schedule which was followed by these solitaries.

Rising was at five o'clock, followed by recitation of Matins and Lauds; breakfast was at half-past six and Prime was at 7:00. From 7:30 to 10:00, time was dedicated to study, interrupted for the recitation of Tierce. At 10:00, the Anglican service was held in the chapel. Study was resumed again just after lunch. Recreation took place between 2:00 and 3:00 in the afternoon. It was followed by the Anglican office. From 4:00 on, there was study, with None at 5:30. Supper was eaten at 6:00 and a short recreation terminated it. Time for study continued from 7:00 to 9:30, followed by Vespers and Compline.[1]

What strikes us about this daily schedule is its monastic-like divisions of occupations: times for work were broken up frequently by the calls to prayer. Thus, silence, prayer, and study constituted these days, which were rich and propitious for reflection.

The desire for asceticism was manifested not only in the daily activities but also by the silence which surrounded Newman and his

---

[1] K., p. 294 ff.

companions, as well as in the material conditions of their life, which were both harsh and poor. A pilgrimage to the modest Littlemore "stables" suffices to convince the visitor of the extent of Newman's detachment and that of his companions. The table was frugal, but Lenten observances were even more rigorous. Lent of 1844 was the most severe: the fast lasted until midday and there was only a light meal during the day, served either at noon or at 3:00, never including meat. Besides, we know from diverse witnesses that Newman practiced corporal mortification. Father Barberi, who received Newman's abjuration, wrote to his superior stating how deeply moved he was by the serious life of penitence which he observed at Littlemore. Furthermore, a letter written by Dalgairns, an eyewitness, revealed that one of the community members, easily identified, had inquired about a discipline and other instruments of mortification. In Newman's retreat notes, preserved among the unedited papers at the Birmingham Oratory, the echo of a persistent asceticism can also be discerned. This trait throws a certain light on Newman's spirituality at this period of his life. No doubt, these external practices of mortification were suggested by Froude's *Remains* and various works of spirituality, including Catholic editions of the saints' lives, which he had been reading at the time. But it is very significant that after his conversion, Newman did not persevere in this way.

Above all, it was the solitude that Littlemore afforded which gave Newman's soul the appeasement and serenity it needed. After working so feverishly for the Movement, he no doubt was touched by the calm of his surroundings. At last he was able to dedicate himself totally to a life away from the world, which coincided with the deepest inclination of his nature. At Littlemore, he achieved the monastic ideal practiced by the great spiritual founders, particularly Saint Benedict, of whom he always spoke with fervor.[2]

The echo of these sentiments can be found in a much earlier letter addressed to the Bishop of Oxford, in which he explained his vocation to solitude in order to answer the accusations brought against him:[3]

---

[2] See in *Historical Sketches* the chapter dedicated to the Mission of St. Benedict (t. II, p. 365 ff.).

[3] The mystery that appears to surround Newman's life at Littlemore brought upon him numerous evil-minded suspicions: one accuses him of wishing to establish a "monastery" after the manner of Rome. He confided in the *Apologia* (p. 139 ff.) how he suffered from these accusations. The Bishop of Oxford, disturbed by the rumors

With the same view of personal improvement I was led more seriously to a design which had been long on my mind. For many years, at least thirteen, I have wished to give myself to a life of greater religious regularity than I have hitherto led; but it is very unpleasant to confess such a wish even to my Bishop because it seems arrogant, and because it is committing me to a profession which may come to nothing.... And being a resolution of years, and one to which I feel God has called me, and in which I am violating no rule of the Church... I should have to answer for it, if I did not pursue it, as a good Providence made opening for it.[4]

Daily exercises of prayer and the recitation of the breviary[5] marked the life of the solitaries of Littlemore. The remaining time was spent in study. For Newman, this meant a vast theological investigation in which he sought to discover within the whole of the tradition and history of the Church the criteria for an authentic doctrinal development, which would enable him to decide for or against the apostolicity of Rome.[6]

Two retreats per year, one in Lent and one in Advent, renewed their religious fervor. The *Exercises* of Saint Ignatius were followed, with each one doing his best in the absence of a director.[7]

Little by little, Newman discovered the internal practices of Roman Catholicism by familiarizing himself with some pious booklets sent to him by an Irish priest, Dr. Russell, a professor at Maynooth Seminary, outside of Dublin. In studying these works, an inventory of which is provided in the last chapter of the *Essay on Development*, Newman wanted to determine for himself if they justified the suspicion of "Mariolatry," a frequent accusation by Protestants against Catholics. He sought to understand how the Roman communion reconciled devotion to the saints with worship to the Creator.

---

that were circulating, wrote to Newman with great tact and asked him for an explanation. See *Apologia*, p. 139 ff.; M. II, p. 350.

[4] *Apologia*, p. 140 ff.

[5] The office was recited from the Roman breviary from which were excluded the hymns to the Virgin and the invocations forbidden by the Anglican Church (K., p. 295 ff.). However, on the 2nd of March 1844, Newman confided to Keble that he saw no difficulty in reciting the breviary in its entirety. (*Ibid*; p. 306.)

[6] This study of Newman became the book of religious synthesis, *Essay on Development*, which was published soon after his conversion.

[7] K., p. 310.

Russell's books were essentially those used to nourish popular piety. They were, for the most part, of Italian origin and had scarcely any influence on Newman's spiritual life. He drew nourishment from more substantial sources, such as: *The Imitation of Christ*, the *Introduction to the Devout Life*, *Spiritual Combat*, *The Paradise of the Soul*, and *Garden of the Soul*.[8] But Russell's little booklets were significant for Newman's research. Objectively, he admitted that they were free of any suspicion of idolatry:

> About forty little books have come into my possession which are in circulation among the laity at Rome.... They may be divided into three classes: a third part consists of books on practical subjects, another third is upon the Incarnation and Passion; and of the rest, a portion is upon the Sacraments, especially the Holy Eucharist, with two or three for the use of Missions, but the greater part is about the Blessed Virgin.[9]

In no part of these booklets did he encounter any equivocation or ambiguity that would interfere "with the incommunicable glory of the Eternal."[10]

Thus, day by day, the voices that whispered to Newman's heart in the painful silence of Littlemore were revealing to him the truth about Rome. Gradually, and to the measure that he freed himself from his Anglican prejudices, the light became brighter and the call more pressing. In June of 1845, he decided to return to the lay state and to give up his Oriel fellowship, which was his last bond to the Anglican Church.

One step remained to set him free, the final abjuration and conversion. But before calling to mind this epilogue in Newman's journey, it is advisable to explain without any ambiguity the real meaning of his conversion, which was on the verge of taking place. Based on Newman's correspondence, certain commentaries have tried to explain his conver-

---

[8] On this question of the sources of his spirituality, see Tristram, *With Newman at Prayer*, p. 114 ff.

[9] *Essay on Development*, p. 431.

[10] *Ibid.*, p. 434. The expression is identical to the one found in the *Apologia*, pp. 154-55; it summarizes the entire argument on this subject which Newman would write about much later in order to respond to accusations of Mariolatry brought against him by Pusey in his celebrated *Eirenicon*.

sion as a dreaded fear of failing to achieve salvation or as a fear of sinking down into skepticism. The question is serious and deserves a thorough examination. One will pardon us for going back to the time when Newman was at the point of making his ultimate choice. Struggling after the truth with great anguish, he strove to remain in a state of peaceful abandonment to the Divine will. At the same time, he persevered in a state of holy indifference while attempting to master the contradictions which were assaulting his heart.

No matter how strong-willed the ex-leader of the Oxford Movement was in his resolution to wait and maintain silence, he could not prevent his critics from circulating suspicions and rumors about him. This long-patient waiting to which he always subjected himself before making decisions was the essence of true courage, particularly in this hour of darkness. However, while his retirement into solitude increased and protected the mystery of his destiny, it only encouraged baseless insinuations and rumors. Before his conversion to Rome, the last blow Newman faced was the onslaught of his critics without being able to justify himself against them. One had to await the success of the *Apologia* in 1864 to fully understand the true reasons for his silence and secret expectancy at Littlemore.

Scandalized by the affair of the last tract, the Anglicans interpreted Newman's retirement as some kind of defiance. In the eyes of his relatives and closest friends, his retirement appeared as a refuge and a resignation from his responsibilities. But for the young disciples who followed him and who were anxious to take the decisive step of conversion, the prolonged silence of their master seemed to arise from a sort of indecisiveness.

As he gradually sensed a web of blame and incomprehension tightening around him, Newman attempted to explain the reasons for his waiting in his correspondence. He did nothing to allay the suspicions that he was preparing for his eventual conversion; neither did he give the impression that the conversion was imminent. If he pleaded for indulgence and sympathy from his friends and confidants, he also maintained the right to safeguard his own interior freedom, anxious to obey only the claims of his own conscience. In the months prior to his conversion of 1845, Newman revealed his anguish as he considered his own eternal salvation. Whenever he recalled his conversion to Rome, he mentioned his fear of punishment and of eternal fire. Hence, the conclusion by some that

Newman's conversion was the desperate result of moral anxiety, and that his anguish about risking salvation invaded his soul so completely that it would have excluded any other feeling.

It is clear that Newman's fear of losing salvation was foremost in all the letters written by him in the course of those final months. Almost a year before his conversion, he wrote to Keble on November 21, 1844:

> My sole ascertainable reason for moving is a feeling of indefinite risk to my soul in staying.... I don't think I could die in our communion.... Then the question comes upon one, Is not death the test?[11]

On January 8, 1845, he wrote again:

> The simple question is, can I (it is personal not whether another, but can I) be saved in the English Church? Am I in safety, were I to die tonight? Is it a mortal sin in me, not joining another communion.[12]

This sentiment was joined with an anxiety that he might be tempted to fall into intellectual skepticism, so vividly perceived at the time of the Noetics of Oriel. The temptation, apparently, never totally disappeared. He confided to Henry Wilberforce on April 27, 1845:

> When a person feels that he cannot stand where he is, and has dreadful feelings lest he should be suffered to go back, if he will not go forward, such a case as Blanco White's increases those fears.[13]

Blanco White, a familiar figure around the Oriel common room, whose brilliance as a dialectician was impressive, died several years earlier in a state of unbelief after various reversals which led him from one creed to another.[14]

---

[11] K., p. 353.

[12] Letter of January 8, 1845 cited in the *Apologia*, pp. 178-79.

[13] Ward, *Life of John Henry Newman*, I, p. 81.

[14] Moreover, Newman was always pleased that he had not yielded to the temptation of skepticism in the situation where he was placed for several years. See his letter to

But let us not draw a conclusion from these letters too quickly, at the risk of attributing Newman's conversion to a matter of anxiety about his salvation. To understand the conversion, it must be placed in the framework of his previous evolution, carefully taking into account the circumstances which led Newman to this crossroad in his destiny, which someone else would have considered an impasse.

Here is a man who has seen all the promises of a genial and generous vocation in the service of his Church crumbling around him — a Church which rejected and disowned him without ever recognizing the risks he took to provide her with a new youth. He cut away all the bonds, those of honors and responsibilities, of affections and memories, which attached him to his familiar and religious world. His retreat was less a desertion than a quest for solitude. This man, who was in the fullness of his manhood, was in total possession of his intellectual and moral resources. He knew that unless he wanted to deny himself completely, he would have to open himself to a new path and pursue his personal mission. He was too aware of his vocation, which he perceived as the will of God, to believe for one minute that his failure with Anglicanism was an unforgivable shipwreck. The night he was going through was also his light; he knew that in the darkness in which he struggled, God pursued His work through him. He perceived some signs, more and more pressing in favor of the Church of Rome, for which he had previously nourished all the prejudice and bias of a loyal member of the Church of England. But he was too afraid of yielding to an illusion, without either waiting or reflecting, before seceding. He believed he should first establish himself in a state of holy indifference. Likewise, by research and study, he should inquire into the titles of apostolicity in this Church whose true visage emerged little by little from the mask which obscured his Anglican eyes. Littlemore thus offered the quiet haven which taught the soul patience and allowed for the calm and independence that stimulates theological inquiry. For Newman could not stay in a state of indecision; if he was convinced that the Church of the Apostles was not the Established Church, it had, therefore, to be the Church of Rome. And if the Church of Rome revealed itself to him with

---

Pusey, March 14, 1845: "Everyone has his temptations. I am thankful to God for having morally protected me from an intellectual doubt that would have caused me to arrive at a state of total skepticism." (Liddon, *Life of E.B. Pusey*, t. II, p. 450.)

certainty, he had to go to her. His conversion then became a responsibility of his conscience. Fidelity to his call from God, of which Newman was more conscious than anyone else, demanded his conversion as the condition for the fulfillment of his God-given destiny; without it, his life would have been an irremediable failure.

Therefore, it must be said, without any ambiguity, that Newman converted to Rome as much to remain faithful to his vocation and mission as to be assured of his salvation. The obligation he assumed was both a pledge of his submission to the will of God and the guarantee of his spiritual peace. In other words, the reward for his soul was his salvation which Newman saw as possible only through his acceptance of going a step further in his mission. At the hour of his conversion, as at all other moments in his life, his duty was never exercised in a servile obedience to a command, the refusal of which would have led only to a compromise of his salvation. M. Nédoncelle truly says:

> Fear of being unfaithful to the truth and to be a missing piece in the plan of God, explain the change in Newman and not the fear of hell.[15]

This view is confirmed by the lines which Newman addressed to Jemima Mozley on March 15, 1845:

> What means of judging can I have more than I have? What maturity of mind am I to expect? If I am right to move at all, surely it is high time not to delay about it longer. Let me give my strength to the work, not my weakness — years in which I can profit the cause which calls me, not the dregs of life.[16]

Several months later, he wrote again that among the different fears which upset him, he felt above all the one of becoming useless. By postponing a decision, was he not doing so at the risk of losing all influence?[17]

---

[15] *Apologia*, Introd. p. xiii. Translation from French edition, L. Michelin-Delimoges, Paris, Bloud and Gay, 1939.
[16] M., II, p. 411.
[17] K., p. 317, Letter of June 8, 1844.

Now, we are in a better position to understand Newman's allusions to his fear of punishment, as cited in his correspondence above, and in which certain historians wished to find the key to his conversion.

If there is no doubt that the question of his salvation is voiced in all the letters of this period which refer to his impending conversion, one should also admit that it is much more as a reference to his personal justification than a true confession of his motives and attitudes. Newman wrote to his friends, to Keble, and to his sisters. He knew that in spite of their sympathy and their desire to understand him, they were too attached to the Anglican creed to be convinced by some theological proofs. His meticulous research, accomplished through reviewing the history of dogmas and ecclesiastical tradition, provided him each day with some new reasons for detaching himself from Anglicanism and surrendering himself to Roman obedience. But his ways of reasoning did not appeal to minds unprepared to receive them and to gamble their faith on them. Argumentation was powerless over those who in all good faith stayed on the Anglican side; it was for them a rekindling or stirring up of an irritating and sterile spirit of controversy. Newman was well aware of it; that is why he refused to describe for his sister, Jemima, the tortuous steps of his itinerary. Therefore, he immediately went to the most powerful and least contestable argument, the one about his own salvation. In evoking his fear of divine punishment in the affair of his conversion, he pleaded for the peace and security of his conscience, an argument against which no one was able to raise objections. He put his cause directly before God who would be judging him and this judgment was a matter of concern only to himself. Before so powerful an argument, who could raise an objection?

Finally, we find in this attitude the earlier revelation of "Myself and my Creator." God is the sovereign master of hearts, the judge of consciences; each one is accountable only for himself before his Creator. When years later as a Catholic, Newman saw his orthodoxy and influence being misrepresented by some Roman censors, he referred again to the authority and supreme judgment of God: *Deus judicaverit.*[18]

Furthermore, in using the argument that he was concerned about his salvation to plead his cause and justify his conversion, it is possible that Newman was influenced by his meditations on the *Exercises* of Saint

---

[18] See Chapt. XV, "The Spirituality of Failure."

Ignatius, which, as we have seen, were the basis for his retreats and spiritual life at Littlemore. During this crisis in which he was struggling within himself, Newman was anxious that his decision should be the fruit of an "election," based on the form and conditions stated in the famous Ignatian *Exercises*. One knows that among the rules "concerning the second way to make a holy and saintly election or choice, the consideration of death and salvation is evoked as a criterion."[19]

Newman made several retreats in the spirit of the *Exercises*. He lived at Littlemore in a climate of very severe asceticism and silence. His theological research never ran counter to the rhythm of the meditation which ceaselessly confronted him — the grave problem of his personal destiny, which we usually call "the fundamental truths concerning salvation." Then, it is not surprising that the problem of conversion came to him not only in the theological context which was leading him in his religious evolution but also with the spiritual and moral inferences which inclined him toward his final decision.

Once again, even if Newman in his correspondence refers only to the argument about his salvation, there is no reason to conclude that his conversion might have been exclusively provoked by a fear that he might miss his personal salvation. Besides, the testimony of the *Apologia*, written some twenty years later, brings all the needed clarity about this matter; it would be fruitless to contest Newman's sincerity as if it were only the result of an abstract conception of the mind. Anglican public opinion was not mistaken in recognizing in the *Apologia* proof of the convert's good faith and sincerity.

The long waiting was quietly coming to an end. Finally, the secret of Littlemore was going to unveil itself. When a man emerges from the night, his eyes are not yet fitted to the light; he comes into a certain clarity but he does not yet discern clearly the way which he ought to go; he needs to get used to the new and brilliant landscape he discovers. Thus, the clouds of Newman's doubts dissipated around him little by little; the horizon brightened but he had not yet left the indecisive zone where light attracts the sight more than it illuminates it. He had renounced all allegiance to the Anglican Church and his eyes, henceforth, were on Rome. But before they could see the brightness of truth, more signs and calls were needed.

---

[19] See *Exercices spirituels de Saint Ignace*, ed. Doncoeur, p. 91.

Newman was particularly concerned about the problem of holiness in the Church. His last attempt while in the bosom of Anglicanism, after the failure of the *Via Media*, had been to establish firmly the Church's titles to sanctity; the result, alas, was again a failure. The spiritual blessing encountered in the Establishment was the incontestable sign of the action of the Holy Spirit on individual members but it said nothing about the sanctity of the Anglican Church taken as a whole.[20]

Newman did not deny that Rome truly possessed that which Canterbury did not, namely the holiness procured by its religious principles, its sacraments, and the action of the Holy Spirit. Nevertheless, he was inclined to think that numerous corruptions in the cult, the ways of praying, and the unfortunate collusion with secular politics took away from the Catholic Church much of its titles to a living sanctity and its concrete and influential holiness which he admired so much in the first ages of Christianity.[21] Hence, this letter to Dr. Russell in April of 1841:

> O that you would reform your worship, that you would disown the extreme honors paid to St. Mary and other Saints, your traditionary view of Indulgences, and the veneration paid in foreign countries to Images! ... And in our country your alliance with a political party... rid your religious system of those peculiarities which distinguish it from primitive Christianity.[22]

---

[20] Newman thought several titles of sanctity ought to be accorded to the Anglican Church. It was able to demonstrate its divine origin and its supernatural economy. Since 1841, however, following some unhappy decisions of the hierarchy, Newman reduced the range of his argument: sanctity or holiness of principles does not exist in the Anglican Church. However, Anglicanism was not excluded from holiness since it enjoyed the actions of the Holy Spirit and the spiritual presence of Christ. With regard to Rome, it was in a situation similar to the one of Samaria with regard to Jerusalem (*Apologia*, p. 126). This argument which grants to the spiritual presence of grace the same demonstrative force as the external criteria of sanctity was criticized by Keble. Newman had developed the argument in four of his sermons, "On Subjects of the Day" (see Keble, p. 255). Much later, Newman would return to this argument in order to criticize it (see this subject in the *Apologia*, p. 176; *Difficulties Felt by Anglicans*, chapt. III, p. 66 ff.)

[21] *Apologia*, p. 124; Cf. Ker, p. 225.

[22] Besides the complaints familiar to all Protestants with regard to the cult of the saints and other Roman devotions, we find an echo of the scandal provoked by the alliance of the Irish Catholic leader, O'Connell, with the English liberal party which favored his politics. Another letter of this period, written to the convert, Spencer, who came to

However, Newman's familiarity with works of spirituality, the attentive inquiry which he paid to all the literature sent by Russell, and several meetings with Catholic priests all contributed to opening his eyes and eliminating the last obstacles. An unpublished note in his *Intimate Journal*, dated April 1843, announced an evolution or change in the state of his mind:

> Considering the saints of all ages as a single company, the Roman Church is it not truly on their side, and not on our side? That which impresses me so much at this time is discovering the holiness of the Roman saints since our separation.[23]

This is not to say that he was in full agreement with all those on the other bank who were seeking to lend him a hand, often in an indiscreet manner. He was much more responsive to the tact of a Russell, who "left him in peace," than to the brusque approach of a convert, like Spencer, who kept prodding him.[24]

Actually, the instrument of his conversion was to be a man of God, unexpected and unknown, Father Dominic Barberi. Newman came to recognize in him the traits of Roman Catholic sanctity. He saw in Father Barberi's visits to Littlemore the providential sign that the hour of decision had come. He later wrote:

> He played a great part in my conversion and in that of others. His attitude involved him as some sort of saint. When his figure came into my view, I was deeply moved in the strangest manner. In his gestures, joy and courtesy, with all his holiness, were of them-

---

visit Oxford in 1840, conveys well the indignant feelings of Newman: "This is what especially distresses us; ...how Christians, like yourselves... should, in the present state of England, ally yourselves with the side of evil against the side of good.... Alas! all this it is that impresses us irresistibly with the notion that you are a political, not a religious party" (*Apologia*, p. 104).

[23] Cited by Tristram, *op. cit.*, p. 30.

[24] "I was very stern," he wrote in the *Apologia*, "in the case of any interference in our Oxford matters on the part of charitable Catholics, and of any attempt to do me good personally. There was nothing indeed, at the time more likely to throw me back" (p. 105).

selves an edifying sermon. There is nothing surprising that I should become his convert and penitent.[25]

Father Barberi was a Passionist, born near Viterbo, from a modest background. He taught theology at the Roman seminary of his congregation, and Newman saw in him a wise and profound religious culture. Attracted to England by a missionary spirit, he was sent there in 1844; he preached a mission at Radford, not far from Oxford. He went as far as Littlemore to see, as he said, a companion of Newman with whom he had already corresponded. Following this visit, he wrote to his superior that he had been received with great cordiality and perfect courtesy by Newman, the founder, and by his disciples. Newman himself showed a reserve about his recollections of the visit. He said that he saw the Father only "a few minutes" but he seemed, nevertheless, to have been attracted by his simplicity and self-effacement. And so it was that Newman suddenly announced to his two young friends, Saint-John and Dalgairns, who were on their way to meet Father Barberi on a rainy October night in 1845, that he was ready to pronounce his abjuration from Anglicanism and to enter the Catholic communion, "the one fold of Christ."[26]

The last summer months were decisive. Newman left unfinished his manuscript on the *Essay on Development*. He had begun it some months earlier in order to put an end to the confusion of his mind and to help him reach certitude. Now that he had found the truth, certain and all so near, he had no need of waiting; it was with a heart at peace and deeply moved that he knelt before Father Dominic and made his confession.[27]

Thus was accomplished the crucifying odyssey of one who, believing he was saving his Church, was forced to leave it. Perhaps more than an

---

[25] Young, C.P., *Father Barberi*, p. 261, cited by Tristram, *op. cit.*, p. 34.

[26] *Apologia*, p. 181.

[27] See the moving account of the conversion in Tristram: "Homage to Newman," p. 31 ff. Since the publication of these pages, Father Barberi, in religion Dominic of the Mother of God, has received the supreme honor of beatification at Rome on Sunday, October 27, 1963. Recalling the merits of this servant of God, Paul VI recalled his meeting with Newman: "He went to the one, who guided solely by love of the truth and fidelity to Christ, traced an itinerary, the most toilsome, but also the most meaningful, the most conclusive, that human thought ever travelled during the last century, one may even say during the modern era, to arrive at the fullness of wisdom and of peace." Address at the Beatification of Blessed Dominic Barberi, C.P.

abjuration, his conversion to Rome was a personal call which engaged him for the future. The holiness which Newman insisted upon as a requisite mark of the true Church remained for him now to ˋ ˋcomplish in his own life if he were to reveal the fullness of truth to those whom he left behind.

CHAPTER XII

INTERIOR PEACE

*It was truly a gift come from
the invisible world.*

Callista

NEWMAN NEVER BREATHED a word about his feelings at the moment of abjuration. He believed he had spoken sufficiently about his journey so that the conclusion remained an affair between God and himself. "Egotism is true modesty," he repeated much later in the *Grammar of Assent*, alluding to the signs which accompany every man's endeavor to reach his own religious assent. This is also true of a convert.[1]

Besides, one can easily guess that his conversion did not carry with it any emotional feelings. It was a conclusion more than a crisis. The illumination which oftentimes overcomes converts had no place in a soul who had long foreseen the coming of the light. Newman admitted it in the *Apologia*: "I was not conscious to myself, on my conversion, of any change, intellectual or moral, wrought in my mind."[2]

The only sentiments that Newman experienced in the depth of his soul were those of peace and security. And such sentiments are rooted more in the depth of silence than in emotional piety. This is what Newman

---

[1] *Grammar of Assent*, p. 384. We would be disappointed if we were trying to discover the secrets of his soul at the time of ordination. At the end of 1846 came the ordination to minor orders. Except for a few notes, Newman said nothing of the retreat he attended at Maryvale near Birmingham. These notes are, above all, examinations of conscience, conserved unpublished at the Birmingham Oratory.

[2] *Apologia*, p. 184.

described in his novel, *Loss and Gain*. It is found in the well known account
of the conversion of his hero, Charles Reding:

> He was still kneeling in the church of the Passionists before the
> Tabernacle, in possession of a deep peace and serenity of mind,
> which he had not thought possible on earth. It was more like the
> stillness which almost sensibly affects the ears when a bell that
> has long been tolling stops, or when a vessel, after much tossing
> at sea, finds itself in harbour... as if he were really beginning life
> again. But there was more than the happiness of childhood in his
> heart; he seemed to feel a rock under his feet, it was the "soliditas
> Cathedrae Petri."[3]

These last words are significant. Above all, that which Newman
experienced was the serenity of faith. The images in which he described
these blessings suggest more than an ecstatic impression; they indicate a
feeling of great peace and perfect silence. His soul was at last wide open
to the Catholic creed; the certitude of possessing the true faith filled his
heart and spirit; no emotional feeling could ever compare with the
tranquility of such a certitude. Newman had many occasions to bear
witness to this inner peace which he found in the Catholic Church, the
peace which rests entirely upon religious certitude.

At a lecture in London in 1850, he confessed: "I am in a communion
which renders its members happy, who are drawn to her."[4] In 1864, the
Apologia carried this decisive confidence: "I have been in perfect peace
and contentment; I never have had one doubt."[5]

Such assurances are beyond debate; they show well enough how the
initial impression of his conversion remained in his soul and it was not
emotional fervor. The affections were so little involved in the whole event
that Newman did not hesitate, in the days following his conversion, to

---

[3] *Loss and Gain*, Longmans, Green and Co, London, 1898, p. 430.
[4] *Difficulties Felt by Anglicans, in Catholic Teachings*, I, p. 3.
[5] *Apologia*, p. 184. Other testimonies can be found from his correspondence with his
friends and even with his Protestant friends. Letter to Lord Blanchford, Ward, I, p. 201.
Letter to Smith, January 8, 1864: "I have been in the fullest peace and enjoyment ever
since I became a Catholic and have felt a *power of truth* and divine strength in its
ordinances" (*Ibid.*, I, p. 570). The same affirmations are to be found in his last letters to
Spurrier, December 11, 1886, and to Edwards, February 24, 1887 (*Ibid.*, II, p. 526 ff.).

write to several of his friends about his total absence of natural enthusiasm
or feelings:

> Coffin (another recent convert) writes to me that he is full of peace
> and joy unknown for many years. This seems to have been the
> experience of each one of us but one, I suppose he has not faith
> enough.[6]

Why should one be disappointed by such a controlled attitude, as if
the outpourings of enthusiasm should necessarily color every conversion?
Above all, why imagine some secret vexation in the soul of the convert as
does Bremond? He compared the conversion of 1816 to the one of 1845,
discerning in the former a stirring enthusiasm which no longer existed in
the latter.[7]

These are gratuitous interpretations which risk falsifying or pervert-
ing the true significance of the religious change. Was the conversion of
1816 as Bremond claimed? It is far from being sure. The fact remains that
the solitary theologian at Littlemore was no longer the troubled and avid
adolescent of Trinity College. That which the young student had discovered earlier was the depth of faith, recognized through the imperious calls
for a certitude not centered on reason but on the God of Christian
revelation: "I fell under the influence of a definite creed, and received into
my intellect impressions of dogma."[8]

In fact, the two conversions are related, one augmenting the other
towards a greater certitude. Religious truth, freed from any emotional
feelings, is enough to establish the soul in a state of peace and serenity. In
1816, the evidence was still incomplete. Yet, it stimulated and guided
Newman in his search. But in 1845, the light was at its fullness, and truth
was grasped as a peaceful and secure possession.

Perhaps, living his first Catholic days in the austere yet familiar
surroundings of Littlemore provided Newman with the illusion that
nothing had changed. He continued to live, as before, in silence and prayer.
The course of his life was hardly interrupted by insignificant events: some

---

[6] Ward, I, pp. 107-108.
[7] Bremond, *Newman*, p. 305 ff.
[8] *Apologia*, p. 16.

trips to Oxford to attend Mass and receive communion in the little church of St. Clement's; a quick visit from Father Barberi; and the departure of the convert, Dalgairns, for the continent, where he was to prepare for the priesthood.

Monsignor Wiseman, whom Newman had visited in Rome during his voyage in 1833, had become the rector of Oscott Seminary near Birmingham and he was Coadjutor to the Vicar Apostolic of the district. He had always followed the evolution of the Tractarians with interest. Their outcome, which he had foreseen and hoped for, fulfilled his expectations. He wanted to be the protector of the little group from Littlemore, although he himself was not without some degree of indiscretion. His first encounter with Newman revealed uneasiness on both sides. Endeavoring to take the converts out of their isolation, which could have become burdensome, Monsignor Wiseman arranged their first contacts with the leading personalities of English Catholicism. He suggested that they leave their Littlemore retreat and take up residence at old Oscott, near the seminary, where they could consider their future vocations.

His disciples having preceded him, Newman was the last to leave Littlemore, a dear home, rich in memories, where he had lived out the most intense drama of his life. It was the 23rd of February 1846, a day very close to his birthday. Several letters from this period express the distress in his heart. Torn by the necessity of leaving behind all the things that signified for him his attachment to the past as well as his rupture with it, he wrote to Copeland, his former curate:

> I quite tore myself away, and could not help kissing my bed, and mantelpiece, and other parts of the house. I have been most happy there, though in a state of suspense. And there it has been that I have both been taught my way and received an answer to my prayers. Without having any plan or shadow of a view on the subject, I cannot help thinking I shall one day see Littlemore again, and see its dear inhabitants, including yourself, once again one with me in the bosom of the true fold of Christ.[9]

The new residence at old Oscott, which Newman named Maryvale, was a happy surprise, for it was a home full of peace and charm. However,

---

[9] Ward, I, p. 117.

Newman did not stay there very long. It had already been decided with Wiseman that Newman would spend some time in Rome, preparing to receive major orders. Also, through his contacts with Roman theologians, he was to prepare for a teaching mission in a school of theology, that was to be founded when he returned to England.

In September, he set off leisurely, sojourning at Langres where Dalgairns lived, and then on to Naples where he remained a whole month. He was accompanied by Ambrose St. John, who, henceforth, was to be his most intimate and affectionate confidant.

At the threshold of a future which was still unfolding, the heart of the convert was full of projects and hope. He experienced something of the expectation that filled him during the days after his illness in Sicily and before his return to Oxford. He was facing up to a destiny that would call for his best efforts. He was ready to undertake any great enterprise that was revealed to him, and he was ready to risk everything. His great hope radiated his confidence. Thus, he wrote to Miss Giberne, his friend from boyhood, who in January of 1846 became a convert:

> As you say, "one step enough for me" — let us hope and believe that the Most Merciful Hand which has led us hitherto, will guide us still — and that we shall one and all, you as well as I and my Littlemore infants, all find our vocation happily. We are called into God's church for something not for nothing surely. Let us wait and be cheerful, and be sure that good is destined for us, and that we are to be made useful.[10]

The feeling that many more beautiful years were yet to come attenuated his regrets. With the converts of Littlemore, he shared the strong desire to pursue a great design. Wiseman and the English Catholics saw in the recent conversions at Oxford the seeds of a much greater harvest that was to have included the whole Church of England. Such a dream did not seem to have been entertained by Newman. Nevertheless, in the months which followed his abjuration, he showed his optimism at such beautiful promises and he hoped for a beneficial shaking up of Anglicanism. The tone of his letters, especially when he wrote to close friends like Henry

---

[10] Letter to Miss Giberne (Ward, I, p. 127, ff.).

Wilberforce, revealed an accent of joy and triumph which contrasted with the heartbreaking confidences from the days before his conversion.[11]

In the course of these last months, everything in the heart of the convert indicated a loyal openness to a new world, a desire to enter into it and to find a place in it. Nothing justified the notion of a vanquished and wounded hero, solitary and withdrawn, resistant to the appeals of those whom, until yesterday, he distrusted too much to deliver himself to them without reservation. On the contrary, he tried to think and live as a true Catholic, attempting to measure up to his new religious world with its distinct rites and prayers, while cultivating a Catholic mentality, experiencing a dogmatic certitude, and sharing in the daily life of its worshippers. He understood well that with his conversion, nothing was finished and all was beginning. He was ready to face a new existence with new relationships, in circles which until yesterday were unknown or hostile, and a daily life with its own particular style, familiar habits, modes of thought and feeling.

Some parts of him were not quite in accord with the Catholic mentality, particularly with the mentality of English Catholicism. It was still fixed in an auto-defensive attitude, an inevitable consequence of centuries of enslavement and ostracism. The mentality in most of the Catholic circles in nineteenth century Great Britain was loaded with defiance and prejudices; it was on the fringe of a nation which had identified its destiny and history with Anglicanism. In response to a British tradition which had imposed constraints and humiliations on them, the Romanists answered by their reticence and voluntary isolation which at the time of O'Connell aligned itself with the political opposition.

Newman, who felt himself "English to the core," hardly condoned the mentality of English Catholics, who were filled with defeatism and resentment. The drive of his life as a convert was to help the Catholic conscience assert itself, to raise its head, to deliver it from its complexes, and to invite it to face up to the Anglican and national opinion proudly. Often, he was not understood by his own. The fundamental misunderstanding between Newman and his new religious family was the source of his misfortunes among Catholics. But he had not yet reached that point. Now, his main effort was to be initiated and to understand the spirit and

---

[11] See letter of June 25, 1846 and the one of August 1st (Ward, I, p. 127 ff.).

style of what he called the "Catholic system": the concrete ordinances of its faith and its prayer, and its faithful attachment to its religious traditions. Newman explored these practices and devotions with the open and attentive eyes of a neophyte. Considering his sharp, critical powers, he could not have failed to recognize the narrow-mindedness and strangeness of some of the practices and prayers, especially those he viewed while traveling in Italy. But for the present, the convert appeared to see nothing. Only much later was he able to sort out the distinction between religious principles of faith and culture, and the way these principles are translated into practices which are at times questionable. At the time of the controversy surrounding the definition of the dogma of the Immaculate Conception, Pusey challenged the religious value of Catholic devotions, particularly Marian devotions. Newman responded:

> A convert comes to learn not to pick and choose. He comes with simplicity and confidence and not with the idea of weighing and of measuring each act and each practice which he meets in those to whom he is united.[12]

Also, he added: "Converts come, not to criticize but to learn."[13] Thus, he fully entered into the Catholic spirit, adopting for himself a rule of life and practices which he intended never to criticize. In a letter to William S. Ward, he wrote: "Are we able to submit ourselves, according to the demands of our conscience as our conscience tells us to do, to the mind of the church as well as to her voice."[14]

His stay in Italy taught him the rich diversity of its popular devotions. He was disconcerted but yet thrilled by the churches in Milan, Rome, and Naples. Amused, he allowed himself to be conquered by the noisy and colorful fervor of the crowds which filled the churches. Newman's letters to Henry Wilberforce, his trustworthy friend, were full of astonishment and admiration. On arriving at Milan, Newman greeted the city of St. Ambrose and was deeply moved by its numerous memories of a Christianity where the authority of the Church was once proclaimed and where

---

[12] "Letter to Pusey, A Response to *Eirenicon*."
[13] Cited by Ward, I, p. 134.
[14] Ibid., p. 134.

the conversion of St. Augustine took place. This enchantment redoubled after attending a service at the Cathedral:

> It has moved me more than St. Peter's did — but then I studiously abstained from all its services when I was at Rome, and now of course I have gone wherever they were going on and have entered into them. And as I have said for months past that I never knew what worship was, as an objective fact, till I entered the Catholic Church and was partaker in its offices of devotion, so now I say the same on the view of its Cathedral assemblages. I have expressed myself so badly that I doubt if you will understand me, but a Catholic Cathedral is a sort of world, everyone going about his own business, a religious one; groups of worshippers, and solitary ones —kneeling, standing — some at shrines, some at altars — hearing Mass and communicating; currents of worshippers intercepting and passing each other —altar after altar lit up for worship, like stars in the firmament — or the bells giving notice of what is going on in parts you do not see, and all the while the canons in the choir going through matins and lauds, and at the end of it the incense rolling up from the high altar, and all this in one of the most wonderful buildings in the world and every day — lastly all without show or effort — but what everyone is used to — everyone at his own work, and leaving everyone else to his.[15]

In Rome, he repeated the pilgrimage made at an earlier visit. He wrote about his impressions after a visit to the catacomb of Saint Agnes. However, his viewpoint was entirely changed since 1833, when he found the Eternal City only an occasion for scandal and indignation. Then, he wrote: "O Rome! That thou were not Rome."[16] The Neapolitan devotion, which formerly filled him with utter disgust, now found him indulgent; he even wrote in support of the cult of Saint Januarius and of the holy House of Loretto.

Thus, Newman gradually entered into a religious world whose principles and fundamental doctrines he undoubtedly knew but whose practices and devotions had not yet been revealed to him. After several months in Italy, his impressions were far from disappointing: a faith was

---

[15] Letter to Wilberforce, September 24, 1846. Ward, I, p. 140.
[16] Letter written to Rickards in March of 1833, when he was on his first trip.

unveiled before his eyes which was living and popular, serious and child-like.

Doubtlessly, the hour had not yet come when he could distinguish between religiosity and authentic piety in the "Catholic system." He was still hesitant about separating the essential from the accessory and to keep for himself what was most conducive for his own prayer life. Only much later, did he express his opinion on this matter. Then, released from the burden of an excessive piety, his spiritual life blossomed freely, as seen in his *Meditations and Devotions*. But for a convert of such recent vintage, his exposure to the world of Catholicism was indispensable. If he had not at first accepted the totality of the Catholic cult and practices, Newman would not have been able to avoid the scruples which always tormented him when he had to make choices and preferences.

Besides, all this exposure taught him an essential lesson: the central place of the Eucharist in the religious life and sentiments of Catholic people. The various manifestations of personal Catholic piety can over-flow and be multiform but they find their ultimate center in the fervor and unity of a Eucharistic faith. Devotional experiences are always bound to the Sacrifice of the Mass and the Real Presence.

We see here the major pole towards which Newman's spirituality was henceforth oriented. What is new and significant is not so much the fact that Newman understood the dogma of the Eucharist more clearly, but that he found in it a universal prayer and a bond of unity for all the faithful. This contemplation never left him feeling alone. The invisible world peopled with presences, angels, and saints, was never absent from his prayer life.[17]

During his entire life as a Protestant, we cannot find a decisive page which shows such unity of faith taking place in the community of the faithful. Newman needed the doctrine of the Eucharist and of the Real Presence to discover this fundamental aspect of the Christian faith. In the two novels written by Newman to occupy some leisure time while he was in Rome, we find an enthusiastic echo of this discovery. How can we fail to recognize the Eucharistic fervor of our convert in the confidences of his hero, Charles Reding, in *Loss and Gain*?[18]

---

[17] III, Par. XVII, The Visible Church, etc.

[18] *Loss and Gain*, p. 430. Compare the description of the Eucharistic worship in *Callista*. Introduction by Alfred Duggan, Burns and Oates, London, 1962, pp. 188-189.

After his conversion, a more tangible bond appeared to bind him and fill him with joy. In the Eucharist, he discovered a new intimacy, and his soul, so thirsty for the mystery of God, enjoyed a higher peace in the realization of the presence of his Master. Wilberforce was again the confidant of these emotions:

> I am writing next room to the Chapel. It is such an incomprehensible blessing to have Christ's bodily presence in one's house, within one's walls, as swallows up all other privileges and destroys or should destroy every pain. I know that He is close by — to be able again and again through the day to go to Him, and be sure my dearest W., when I am there in His Presence you are not forgotten.[19]

Thus, the Eucharist contributed to increasing Newman's faith in God's Providence, which surrounded and guided him. His conversion to Catholicism revealed a God very near and intimate to him and made him feel most pressingly, "The Shadow of the Providential Hand."[20]

---

[19] Ward, I, p. 118.
[20] Cf. *Verses*, poem CXI: "Semita Justorum," p. 187.

Chapter XIII

THE ORATORY

'Tis an old man of sweet aspect,
I love him more, I more admire.

Verses, p. 296.

*F*ᴏʀ ᴛʜᴇ ᴄᴏɴᴠᴇʀᴛs ᴏғ 1845 and for Newman in particular, the choice of a state of life was as important as the kind of ministry they were to engage in. They looked to the future not only to plan for their apostolate but to determine the structure or form of living that would be most suitable to their new way of life. They were in the Roman Church, so to speak, as souls without roots, transplanted to a new terrain and estranged from all the traditions that had formerly molded their spirit and their way of thinking. Their conversion to Rome had not altered the typically English traits which they had inherited from their original milieu and which had been refined by the University and Oxonian tradition: a certain reserve of judgment and prudence of sentiment which were the first principles of life in the "common rooms," a keen awareness of culture and an innate taste for humanism which was manifested by a respect for all persons, and a refusal of any constraints.

The long years spent at Littlemore, cut off from the world, only confirmed them in their habit of patient reflection and collective wisdom. Their vocation was to the cenacle more than to the tribune. At Littlemore, Newman discovered the twofold prize of a retreat dedicated to study and a life lived in community. If he believed he was called to an intellectual apostolate, he only envisioned this mission within the supporting structure of a regular and permanent lifestyle. Within such a framework, he felt he would be able to respond to a spiritual call while guarding the originality of his earlier formation. Thus, he wrote to Dalgairns: "So then I go on to think and to trust my past life may form a sort of outline and a ground of future usefulness."[1]

At Littlemore, he was irresistibly nostalgic about his past way of life. In spite of many doubts of conscience, he experienced hours of deep calm and reflection there; he found security in submitting himself to a rule of life with the spiritual support of a fraternal community. After his conversion, he did not want to lose these precious advantages. Yet, he knew that the Roman Church was able to preserve and renew them by offering a state of life less improvised than the one designed by them at Littlemore. In the Catholic Church, thanks to the tradition of religious orders and institutions, the ancient discipline of such religious founders as Saint Benedict and Saint Augustine had been preserved. The only question for Newman and the other converts was to make the right choice of religious institute.

However, Newman radically excluded one element of religious life. He knew he could not assume the responsibilities of the vows without doing violence to himself nor could he submit to an order that was bound too strictly by its constitution. Was this repugnance an old vestige of the Protestant prejudice which had led him to write previously: "I have thought vows (e.g., celibacy) are evidences of want of trust"?[2] Or is it rather an instinctive reserve against all forms of absolute abnegation? He never explained this very well. But he did confess that he would have had great difficulty joining a religious order without having personally received a clear call to poverty; thus, he confided to Dalgairns, who was then considering becoming a Dominican: "So I, at my time of life shall never feel able to give up property and take new habits."[3] In a May 1847 document, written in the course of a retreat at Rome, he wrote these lines revealing the state of his soul:

> So far as I know I do not desire anything of this world; I do not desire riches, power or fame, but on the other hand, I do not like poverty, troubles, restrictions, inconveniences.[4]

---

[1] Letter of December 31, 1846, Ward, I, p. 170.
[2] Letter to R. H. Froude, January 9, 1830. M. I., pp. 193-194.
[3] Letter of December 31, 1846. Ward, I, p. 170.
[4] *Autobiog.*, p. 245 ff.

Thus, he rejected strict institutes which prevented him from being himself, which went against his deepest tendencies, and which might have caused him to make too sharp a break with his past. He was neither to be a Dominican nor a Jesuit. His intuition carried him much further in his search for an institute of priests with sufficient flexibility to allow his own vocation to develop as well as those of his disciples.

Very early on, Wiseman discerned Newman's aspirations. At the same time that he unveiled his project for the foundation of a seminary or a school of theology for the formation of young clerics, Wiseman launched the convert on a path which proved to be a good one, the one of the Oratory. He first spoke about it only a few months after Newman's conversion.[5] The idea took root in the soul of Newman, who wrote to Dalgairns from Milan on October 18, 1846: "I do not think we have got a bit further than this in our reflections and conclusions, to think that Dr. Wiseman was right in saying that we ought to be Oratorians."[6]

His vocation became clearer when he arrived in Rome on October 25th. His whole correspondence in the year 1847 revealed first his patient research, then his wish to set up an Oratorian foundation in England. Manifestly, Newman was conquered by the spirit of this institute, of which he knew little, and even more by the strange and striking figure of the founder, Saint Philip Neri. In opting for the Oratory in preference to all other congregations, he gave himself up to a religious tradition which did not stifle his spirituality but allowed it to grow in a way that conformed to his tastes and provided a balanced way which most faithfully expressed his own ideal of truth and of Evangelical simplicity.

Differing from each other by their constitutions, religious orders and institutes offer contrasts and nuances of coloration derived from the personality and spiritual qualities of each founder. The contagious influence and the style of perfection which each founder designs far outlast his death and live on in the family of his disciples.

Assuredly, the structure of the Oratorian life was especially well suited to please him: the flexibility of its constitution, the autonomy of each

---

[5] See letter of Newman to his follower, Faber, of February 1846, cited by Father Tristram in "With Newman at Prayer," *Centenary Essays*, p. 119.

[6] Ward, I, p. 143. Dalgairns would end by joining Newman in England and would become one of the first Oratorians.

of the houses, and the absence of vows were the things that attracted him.[7] But these were only the external reasons which determined Newman's decision to become an Oratorian. He also discovered in the Oratory the assurance of being able to safeguard his identity without betraying his own spiritual convictions, which was of supreme importance in his eyes.

Furthermore, he soon discovered that the Oratory was not only an institute of astonishing flexibility but it had a spirituality all its own. The spirituality as exemplified by Saint Philip Neri attracted Newman and brought out the very best in his prayer life and spiritual convictions.

In order to better understand Newman's spiritual journey, it is helpful to study Newman's life in Rome, to draw a profile of Saint Philip's spiritual vision, and to show how Newman was able to recognize himself in this saint.

The spirit of Saint Philip is defined first of all by the absence of conventions and of preconceived conditions. There are no prefabricated categories. No formalism. There is, however a simple and loving way of praying. It consists of a very personal and almost ingenuous way of placing oneself before God and remaining in His presence to speak with Him and confide in Him. It is a prayer filled with twists and turns in which the soul abandons itself, easily breathing forth its sighs of complaint or regret, its joys and its desires. The Oratorian tradition was not given to principles or definitions and had no well established identity. Taking the best wherever it found it, it had no technique of its own. Too respectful of the liberty of the Spirit which leads souls, it instinctively refused to impose any kind of method on its members. Philip Neri was suspicious of any kind of discipline except the one based on interior detachment. Thus, he had outlawed all pretensions and affectations among his brothers around him in the convent of San Girolamo, not only in their various styles of prayer and personal relations with God but in their personal relationships with one another.

Paradoxically, without willing it, Saint Philip had created a spirituality of his own. Cordiality, tenderness, simplicity, and abandonment,

---

[7] "The first religious lived in communities, independent one from the other and not united under a common direction; established in a particular place, these houses had no other obligations; vows were not a necessary element." "The Mission of Saint Philip," *Sermons on Various Occasions*, XII, p. 225; Cf. *Historical Sketches*, III, p. 88.

which he sought to attain, were maintained and perpetuated in a very original tradition which Newman could not experience without being infinitely touched. In a century favoring humanism, this concept of religious life tended to sustain the importance of individual rights and the sovereign liberty of the person.

According to Cardinal Baudrillart, the spirit of Saint Philip Neri consists of the following: putting one at ease, never constraining, allowing each one within certain limits to manifest the originality of his thinking and character, taking pleasure as much in diversity as in unity, and in showing an infinite respect for the originality of souls.[8]

In the Oratorian tradition, no one goes to God by force; the Spirit is the only law and the Spirit works from within, drawing souls in the way that is proper to each. The unique requirement is a total detachment from oneself, which opens the door to a complete submission to the will of God. An innate sense of the person, a respect for liberty, and a faith based more on a submission to the Divine Master than on a conformity to laws or methods are fundamental aspects of the spirit of Saint Philip. Views so much in accord with his own invited Newman to attach himself to the teachings and example of Saint Philip as a most attentive and fervent disciple.

Bremond, although a bit casual in his treatment of Newman, may be right in noting that "the neophyte has Anglicized and Newmanized his model."[9] Doubtless, it is true that Newman slightly retouched his portrait of Saint Philip, giving him traits which he wished to find in his ideal saint. But one must admit that the model lends himself admirably to these retouches. Can one criticize the intuitive genius of Newman for having favored the traits which charmed him most in the portrait of such an attractive and open figure as the one of the founder of the Oratory?

Does not the merit of all great artists lie in their ability to express the likeness of their subjects by emphasizing the most revealing traits of their personalities? Ultimately, Newman's sketch of Philip Neri was not very different from the one Goethe portrayed in his *Travels in Italy*.[10] This is

---

[8] Msgr. Baudrillart, preface for Ponnelle-Bordet, *Saint Philippe Neri et la Société romaine de son temps*, Paris, 1928, in Chapter IX, in which are described the various traits which characterize the Oratory. The text has been freely translated.
[9] *Op. cit.*, p. 309.
[10] Goethe, *Voyage en Italie*, Chapt. IX, p. 364 ff., trans., Porchet.

evidence enough that Newman did not betray his master in the numerous pages where he sought to describe his visage. He saw clearly that with very simple means, Philip Neri had rediscovered the familiar and human spirit of the Gospel. The apostle of sixteenth century Rome had purged prayer of all affectation by not tolerating clichés or constraints.

By releasing souls from the rigors of a too rigid adherence to rule, Philip Neri lessened the danger of creating a scrupulosity among his disciples. He also cut off the route to ambitions and excesses which came from an authority poorly exercised. Newman explained:

> Putting aside forms as far as it was right to do so, and letting influence take the place of rule, and charity stand instead of authority, they drew souls to them by their interior beauty, and held them captive by the regenerate affections of human nature.[11]

In Newman's view of common life, the bonds of charity, as expressed by mutual respect and concern for one another, which meant a disposition to serve, led to a greater perfection than did the most rigorous obedience. He was grateful to Saint Philip for having recalled the preeminence of charity and of having drawn disciples solely by his spiritual influence. Thus, he inaugurated a religious tradition unique among many others, which allowed the most original and spontaneous vocations to develop within the discipline of a common life, without any other constraints than the one of fraternal love. However, Philip Neri did not reach such a simple way of life without practicing a rigorous asceticism, which was well understood by Newman.

In several passages in his Catholic sermons, while speaking about self-denial, Newman recalled the figure of the Saint, so inspiring in his voluntary self-effacement. Philip's prayer was not only a candid confession of his helplessness but also a serene admission of his faults and weaknesses. Newman liked to recall how impressed he was in the face of such disarming humility.[12] He also noted Philip's willingness to forget self, his abnegation in all things, and the extraordinary influence that such an example had on his disciples:

---

[11] *Var. Occ.*, VIII, p. 119.
[12] *Mixed Sermons*, VII: "Perseverance in Grace," p. 139; cf. *Var. Occ.*, p. 96.

He did not ask to be opposed, to be maligned, to be persecuted, but simply to be overlooked, to be despised. Neglect was the badge which he desired for himself and for his own. "To despise the whole world," he said, "to despise no member of it, to despise oneself, *to despise being despised.*" [13]

Such a desire found deep resonance in Newman's conscience. He always had a taste for solitude and retreat. This desire for isolation, at least during the years of his youth, was above all the expression of his interior and personal searching. His preoccupation with exploring his own depth was also marked by a more or less conscious refusal to adhere to all social conventions. Perhaps, he feared the distractions and frivolous thoughts which never fail to increase the agitations and the clamor of the world within us when they are welcomed. His encounter with Philip Neri opened up another perspective to the Newmanian solitude: voluntary self-efface-ment and abnegation. The way of silence became the humility of the cross. At the worst times of trial, not long in coming, the convert found peace in going back to the meditation of Saint Philip on self-oblivion. In fact, his admiration did not stop here. Perfect simplicity and spiritual asceticism had given to Saint Philip's holiness a sort of beauty, a mysterious prestige, which seemed to transform and beautify all that which he touched. The radiance of his sanctity seemed to reach, purify, and expand the noblest and most generous aspirations of his disciples. At a disturbing period in history,[14] when the Lord seemed to be asleep in the depth of the bark of Peter,[15] when the forces of "good and evil were affronting each other, when sacred privileges and corruption"[16] were colliding with each other head on in the most terrible way, it was a real temptation for the Church to cut itself off from the emerging patterns of a civilization still in quest of itself.

Newman understood that the mission of Saint Philip was to prevent

---

[13] "The Mission of St. Philip," *Var. Occ.*, VII, p. 231. In several of his writings, which differ in object and tone, Newman recalled the example of St. Philip. See *Historical Sketches*, III, p. 130. *Private Journal*, Ward, I, p. 578. *Idea of a University*, p. 234 ff. Newman used a life of Saint Philip by Bacci. For a more detailed study, see the book already cited of Ponnelle-Bordet.

[14] "It was a time of sifting and peril." "The Mission," *ibid.*, p. 201.

[15] *Ibid.*, p. 302. Newman refers again here to a comparison made by Baronius.

[16] *Ibid.*, p. 209. In the first part of the sermon, Newman gives a picture of the Church at the time of St. Philip Neri (born in 1515 before the Counter-Reformation).

this rupture between the Church and his century. Philip was one of the witnesses of Christian humanism which became so famous during the succeeding century. The mission of some saints is to separate the world from the revealed truth; others to bring society together. Saint Philip Neri's mission was of this kind.[17] His spiritual influence, made up of an exquisite simplicity and a joyous optimism, embraced humanistic trends. His sanctity created a new miracle; it showed that if it is possible to give up human glory, it is also possible to transcend it.[18] Without trying, Philip Neri became the mediator who reconciled nature and grace, faith and reason.[19]

Such sanctity deeply affected the sensitive former fellow of Oriel. Its simplicity, spontaneity, and joyfulness seemed to spring from Philip's heart as much as from his confident faith. The convert found again in Philip Neri that strange marvel that he so much admired in Keble: the gifts of nature flowering in grace. Holiness revealed itself anew as the supreme poetry of the heart. From this point on, a bond of fidelity was established between Newman and Saint Philip. Far from weakening the personal character of Newman's spirituality, his devotion to Saint Philip increased it even more and brought forth the most profound personal traits of his interior life.

Bremond may have a point, after all, in suspecting that Newman recreated the portrait of Philip Neri in his own image. But the attraction exercised by the model on his disciple is unquestionable and so is its decisive influence on Newmanian spirituality. Surely, Philip brought no new method of prayer to him, nor did he reveal any new horizons. Neri, as we said, did not create any system; he was not a theorist of spiritual ways. His genius was elsewhere. We know that Newman's spiritual principles were quite well drawn up as far back as the conversion of 1845. His years at Littlemore pointed out the way. At every step of the road, the traveler verified the weight and measured the extent of his deepest convictions. It

---

[17] *Ibid.*, p. 222.

[18] The purpose of his life: to seek to subdue the world, with its variety of colors and shapes, to unite it with the divine service. *Ibid.*, p. 222; the same concept is in the *Idea of a University*, p. 239: "He preferred to yield to the stream, and direct the current, which he could not stop, of science, literature, art, and fashion and to sweeten and to sanctify what God had made very good and man had spoilt."

[19] *Var. Occ.*, "The Mission of Saint Philip." Newman contrasts the mission of Philip with that of Savonarola: "the slowest way was the surest, and the most quiet the most effectual" (p. 232).

was never a question of adding or going back on his basic spiritual convictions. As he took his next steps in the new world he had just entered, he needed to adopt a firmer, more precise, and more spontaneous "style" than in the past. In short, to use a distinction which he himself made in his sermon on Saint Philip, Newman knew perfectly well what he ought to be and what he ought to do; but he did not know exactly how he was expected to do it.[20] This is just what he discovered at Saint Philip Neri's school.

The first lesson he learned is that he ought to be himself; he ought not to deny, under the pretext of his conversion to Rome, the religious intuitions which grew deep in him during his long years of reflection and prayer. In the long inner struggle which he experienced, he discovered his true destiny, and he deepened his relationship with God. Then came the evidence which dictated his choice: faith determined his vocation as well as his behavior. In his prayer life, he was not interested in any ready made recipes like the ones imposed by Reverend Mayers, which guided him toward Evangelicalism. Oftentimes, during the days which followed his conversion to Rome, the temptation to take on a new style of prayer was very great. This happened during Newman's stay at Maryvale and during the first months in Italy when, preparing for ordination, he denounced his dryness and his fear of a lack of faith. The long confession which he wrote at the Roman convent of Saint Eusebius in the course of his retreat in April of 1847, reveals such feelings as these: he spoke about his fear of not being open enough to various methods of praying and of his difficulty in undertaking the spiritual battle.[21] This occurred again when Faber, Dalgairns, and several other young companions, with more generosity than judgment, were overcome by the opulent richness of the popular devotions they observed in the streets of Rome. They would not have labeled themselves "good Catholics" unless they had shared the colorful devotions of Italian piety. Although not inclined to be emotional, Newman nevertheless ran the risk of being caught up in that contagious kind of piety. Yet, he was unable to explain, even to himself, the reasons for his reserve, nor to justify it to the eyes of these young "zelanti." For them, adopting the popular devotions expressive of Roman piety gave the illusory impression of a greater loyalty to the Church.

---

[20] *Op. cit.*, p. 228.
[21] See Chapter XVII, "The Prayer of Newman."

The Oratory and Saint Philip turned him away from this direction that held no promise for him and taught him how to remain himself. In contact with the saint, Newman started to go to God again with simplicity, away from distractions. Saint Philip, so respectful of the unique character of each soul, reminded Newman that truth is to be found only in confident, humble, and spontaneous prayer. Also, he showed him that even a sophisticated convert from Oxford could find his place in the Communion of Saints, keeping his own system without adopting an unnatural style of prayer. Only an open and sincere heart was necessary. It was a lesson that Newman was to remember all his life. Later, he attested to the fact that devotion is not necessarily faith. Piety can be expressed in ways which are uncontrollable, because popular piety has its own laws. It has a disconcerting facility for appropriating even the most sacred things. True piety need not be expressed in too extreme or too noisy a way. Newman gave us a good example of true piety in *Meditations and Devotions*, his spiritual masterpiece. These meditations are so pure, so discreet, so full of fervor and yet so measured that everyone can feel at ease with them.

Saint Philip's influence on Newman's prayer not only kept it away from questionable modes of expression not made for him, but it enriched it with a touch of tenderness and a sense of abandonment. In his book, Bremond remarks that the former fellow of Oriel had too much of a tendency to shut himself off in his dialogue with God. Overanxious to be in the presence of his Creator, Newman displayed in his prayers a certain note of austerity and tension.

This tension, resulting from the conflicting emotions of awe and fear, is too closely interwoven in his meditations to allow for the spontaneous bursts of the heart and affections. Fear and love meet here together without doubt, but a reading of the Sermons at St. Mary's, particularly the last ones so intensely religious, reveals that fear most often takes the form of love. The term reverence appears again and again as a leitmotif and gives a tone to the preaching filled with the awe of a creature on his knees.[22]

Thanks to Saint Philip Neri, Newman's reserve, born from his Anglican education, was soon overcome. Biographers of Saint Philip noticed the place he gave to effusions of the heart in his spiritual life and

---

[22] See in particular V Par., II, "Reverence: A Belief in God's Presence"; V Par., V, "Equanimity." The same accent on reserve is in the religious poems in the series, *Reverence*.

also to the climate of confidence which he created in his instructions at San Girolamo.[23] With Philip's help, his disciples discovered the depths of Divine Love, once their consciences were free from the guilt of sin. He invited them to express themselves with confidence and joy. His prayers always took a very affective turn, familiar and touching. He was never conventional nor pompous in the exhortations he addressed to the members of his Oratory. They were only the outpourings of a heart trying to communicate with other hearts in order to lead them in the same path of fervor and abandonment to God. Thus, prayer became a very simple and spontaneous dialogue with God; the rhythm was rapid, broken only by emotions overflowing the soul.

Newman did not model his prayer on that of the Saint from the first day but only after a long period of familiarity with him. Day after day, the convert felt the spirit of Saint Philip Neri growing within him. His meditations became warmer and more peaceful; the tone of tenderness and respect they reveal give to his prayer an undefinable and unique accent:

IN THY SIGHT

O my God, I confess and bewail my extreme weakness.
O my dear Lord, give me a generous faith.
In asking for fervor, I ask for all that I can
need, and all that Thou canst give....
Nothing would be a trouble to me,
nothing a difficulty, had I but fervor of soul.[24]

Later, when the years of distress, oblivion, and misunderstanding would give Newman the bitter feeling of not being appreciated and of being useless, he would again look to Saint Philip. He would turn to his patron to learn from him the hard truth of detachment and abnegation:

---

[23] One of the first disciples, Simon Graziani, reported some of these talks between the Saint and his penitents: "The father prayed, and one saw in him an intense fervor of spirit, the entire body shaking and it looked like he was trembling while speaking with God, and yet while prayer lasted one hour, we found the time short and we could have stayed there all night, so much did we experience delight. And he said: 'Here is the milk which Our Lord gives to those who begin to serve Him.' He held his lamp very low in a way that one could hardly see him." Text cited by Ponnelle-Bordet, *op. cit.*, p. 124.

[24] *Med. and Dev.*, pp. 68 and 99.

I am tempted to look back. Not so O Lord, with Thy grace, not so! What I had meant to say then, to ask of Thee then I ask of Thee now. What a shame that I should fear to ask it. I have asked it often in times past, I think long before I was a Catholic! Yes, I have referred to it above, as in my words of thirty years ago, "Deny me wealth, etc." It has been my lifelong prayer and Thou has granted it, that I should be set aside in this world. Now then let me make it once again. O Lord, bless what I write and prosper it — let it do much good, let it have much success; but let no praise come to me on that account in my lifetime. Let me go on living, let me die, as I have hitherto lived. Long before I knew about Saint Philip, I wished, "*nesciri*" ["to be unknown"]. Let me more and more learn from Thy grace "*sperni*" ["to be despised"]: "*Spernere me sperni*" ["And to despise being despised"].[25]

Newman's daily cross as a Catholic included his acceptance of the fact that his intellectual gifts were restricted and that he had to submit to an isolated and idle existence at a time when he had expected to be available for an intellectual ministry, which was his specific vocation. The example of Saint Philip helped him to carry his cross which tore out of him on certain days some heartrending cries. Saint Philip inspired him to fight against the deep resentment that such trying times could have instilled in a heart so wounded.

Some biographers have suggested that the Oratory was an unhappy choice for Newman. They said that in opting for this institute, Newman had condemned himself to limiting his possibilities for influence as he had isolated himself from those very enterprises which needed his presence and genius. This is an unfounded hypothesis. No matter what position he would have held in the Catholic Church of England, the convert would have been misunderstood. At the risk of sacrificing the best of the gifts he brought to English Catholics, he could not find among them a mission truly commensurate with his talents and his worth. He could not have played a role without breaking down certain barriers. So, more than that of an animator or innovator, the mission of Newman was one of a prophet. And a prophet, more or less misunderstood for his message, creates scandal. He was a victim to the opposition and a symbol of defiance to those unable to

---

[25] *Autobiog.*, note of Jan. 8, 1860, p. 252; cf. Trevor, *Light in Winter*, p. 216.

rally to his side without renouncing their own prejudices and inhibitions. Indeed, it was an uncomfortable position, yet it was the sole one he could assume if his mission as a prophet were to be effective. Clouds gathered around him; repeated failures obscured his sense of direction; his soul was shaken by repeated jolts; and he did not see the horizon which the light of his message was bringing into view.

As a matter of fact, the Oratory was the most marvelously adaptable form of religious life for Newman. Without even knowing it, in submitting himself to the teachings of Saint Philip, Newman provided himself with the most favorable conditions for the accomplishment of a mission which, let us say it once more, in English Catholicism during the nineteenth century, could only be that of a precursor, with all the rebuffs that usually involves. Discovering in Saint Philip the living model of an asceticism based entirely on self-effacement and obscurity, Newman found in him the moral support and comfort he needed at the time of his severest trials. It was a new bond which simplified the religious life of the convert; it was no longer a question of following the call for a stronger moral integrity in the pursuit of perfection. Henceforth, he would be free to follow a type of sanctity that was best attuned to his own vocation in the Catholic Church.

Perhaps, this profound communion with Saint Philip's spirit best defines the religious profession of Newman. It was no longer a question of discipline and prolonged fasting, not even of vows in the strict sense. The conscience of the convert was henceforth bound to live faithfully in the spirit of obscurity and humility, which was the one of the founder. Vainglory, which Newman had always shunned as a moral imperfection, he now reproved as an attack on his interior consecration and an infidelity to Philip, "father of an unworthy son."[26] Indeed, it is the very meaning of this prayer which came forth from his heart:

> Thou hast given me Saint Philip, that great creation of Thy grace, for my master and patron —and I have committed myself to him — and he has done great things for me, and has in many ways fulfilled towards me all that I can fairly reckon he had promised.[27]

---

[26] "The Father of an unworthy son," in a letter of 1864.
[27] *Med. and Dev.*, p. 68.

Thus, we can conclude that Newman's determination to become an Oratorian was neither accidental nor improvised. As soon as he recognized the visage of Saint Philip and discovered his spirit, he felt himself drawn into his spiritual orbit.

Certain hesitations noticeable during the first months of his Roman sojourns disappeared little by little. As early as January 1847, he wrote to Dalgairns of his determination to study the rule of Saint Philip. He confessed his desire of adopting it as being suitable for converts in view of his intention to establish a foundation in England.[28]

The assurances of Theiner, superior of the Italian Oratory, and the encouragement of Pope Pius IX himself, ended Newman's last reservations. His entrance into the Institute was decided. Pius IX assigned the monastery of Santa Croce as the place for a four-month novitiate. It was in this house, with its flexible rule of life, that Newman and his faithful friend, Saint-John, gathered with their companions. Preparation for major orders had been completed before this novitiate period.[29]

Looking towards the future, Newman was already thinking about his return to England and the foundation of an Oratory. In July of 1847, he visited with Wiseman at Santa Croce. They exchanged views on the subject while the papal brief was being drawn up.

In August, a trip to Naples brought Newman in contact with an Oratorian Community whose members he found to be young, vibrant, and pleasant.[30] On returning to Rome, he occupied his last months there with writing his novel, *Loss and Gain*, and making useful contacts for his future projects, but he was ever attentive to prayer and meditation. Thus, he wrote to Wilberforce: "Lead thou me on! In the present situation, it is quite as appropriate as ever, for what I shall be called to do when I get back, or how I shall be used, is quite a mystery to me."[31]

Having paid his respects to Pius IX, Newman left Rome on December 6th and returned to England by way of Munich and Ostend. He was reunited at Maryvale with his novitiate companions who had preceded him, and the English Oratory was solemnly inaugurated on February 2, 1848. A new life was beginning.

---

[28] Letter of January 12, 1847, W. I, p. 170.
[29] Cardinal Franzoni conferred Orders at the end of May 1847.
[30] Ward, p. 188.
[31] *Ibid.*, Letter of August 11, 1847, p. 161.

CHAPTER XIV

GREAT TRIALS

While in faith they love those
who are called by Christ's name
... they cannot but see much in many of them
to hurt and offend them.

III Par. XVII, p. 630.

*T*HE LITTLE COMMUNITY at Maryvale, made up of the original disciples including Ambrose Saint-John, Dalgairns, and Coffin, very quickly grew in size with the arrival of Faber and several young converts who came with him.

Among Newman's followers, Frederick William Faber, descendant of a Calvinistic family from France, most misinterpreted the deep sensitivity of his master and yet was the least capable of resisting the attraction of his influence. From the very beginning, the Catholic faith was without problems for this neophyte. Forgetting the road he travelled in order to discover the true faith, Faber was astonished that the whole world did not partake of his convictions. He tried to communicate his views with the disarming candor of those who believe they will be understood as soon as they open their mouths or take up their pens. Having preceded Newman in his conversion to Catholicism, he had already rallied around himself a small school of disciples who were called "Wilfridians." He led them to Newman to increase the numbers in the Oratorian community but their coming together made both men unhappy. Faber was as powerless to free himself from the psychological ascendancy exercised on him by Newman as he was insensitive to Newman's intuitions and ways of expressing his genius. Newman was too reserved to impose himself bluntly on anyone and he was too sensitive not to suffer from an ambiguous situation in which neither he nor Faber dared to be entirely himself.

The first occasion of conflict, veiled and therefore more trying than an opposition clearly declared, occurred over the publication of the *Lives of the Saints* that Faber had undertaken with a disconcerting naiveté. This edition aimed at revealing to the English people the treasures of hagiography that were buried in historic sanctuaries and other holy places on the Continent. Faber and his friends worked with a zeal totally deprived of a critical sense and with all the fervor of young zealots who expected to convert the whole world, and England as well, by unearthing the oddest ancient practices of popular piety. They mixed legends, folklore, and history together. The spirit with which they had undertaken this work often revealed a harsh resentment towards their own past. They had left the Anglican Church and henceforth considered it with a sort of sacred horror. Faber wished to dedicate his life "to a crusade against the detestable and diabolical heresy of Protestantism." This aggressiveness, encouraged by his friends, made him seek in Catholicism whatever was able to shock and scandalize the Anglican conscience, such as ostentatious devotions and the cult of the saints in the Neapolitan manner. His superficial theology, based more on sentiment than reason, did not agree much with scientific principles and the proceedings of methodical research. To all this, he added an incontestable courage, an obvious good intention, and a generous and meritorious desire to serve the Church. At first, Newman could only bow before such good will and so much naiveté. For a while, he allowed himself to be overcome by the enthusiastic enterprise of Faber and his *"giovanni,"* as he called them. Thus, Newman agreed to sponsor the risky first edition of the *Lives of the Saints*. However, he was not long in realizing that they had taken the wrong direction, and were in danger of being trapped in a dead end, so he quickly disassociated himself from the enterprise. It increased a feeling of uneasiness within the Oratorian community at a time, in 1848, when they had to move twice before settling at last in the very heart of Birmingham on Alcester Street.

Faber, to whom Newman had given charge of the novices, soon emigrated to London with Dalgairns and several other companions. There, he founded a second Oratory, and succeeded in obtaining its direction. This separation was not considered a break but it was scarcely better than one. The initial incomprehension between Newman and Faber's group, although expressed only in innuendos, persisted even after the inauguration of the London house. It was to be the poisoned source of intrigue and conflicting views from which Newman would suffer at the very heart of his own religious family. Although less visible and public than the ones he would endure from the Catholic hierarchy, this painful situation was felt more cruelly by the convert for he did not find in the community of his brothers the support and consolation he needed during the bitter failures which piled up on him in the course of the two decades following his return to England.

Indeed, the Catholic life of Newman offers the disconcerting spectacle of a man who never knew any success. He seemed always to be running after his destiny. At the very moment he became involved in a new field of action and settled into it, the ground gave way beneath him and the project was withdrawn until a new one came which was every bit as deceiving as the preceding one. There is something extraordinarily poignant in such an existence which seemed to draw down upon itself, by some sort of mysterious fate, the least foreseeable setbacks and frustrations which were so very painful to his ego.

This surprises the historian who asks how such repeated failures can be explained. We are no longer speaking of the *Lives of the Saints*; that was not Newman's undertaking and it was doomed to failure. Let us also set aside certain mishaps that occurred during the first years of his Catholic life: for example, the unfortunate eulogy he gave in Rome on the occasion of the death of Miss O'Brien, which was judged so inappropriate in tone and content that the Pope himself was alarmed at it.[1] Such again was the series of sermons he preached in London during Lent of 1848 before a sparse audience, ill-prepared to appreciate his message. These are faux pas which were less attributable to Newman than to the men who were eager to make a public display of him.[2]

---

[1] Miss O'Brien Talbot was the niece of Lady Shrewsbury, a famous Catholic and a friend of Newman. Although not yet a deacon, Newman was solicited to preach the funeral eulogy for the departed; ceding to pressure, he preached his sermon in the Church of Saint Isidore, before an audience composed of both Protestants and Catholics. They found his sermon to be inopportune and blamed the firmness with which he insisted upon the necessity of conversion.

[2] It was Wiseman, having recently become the Vicar Apostolic of London, who compelled Newman, along with several other Oratorians, to secure the series of Lenten Sermons in the Catholic churches of the capital.

Other more serious disappointments awaited him in the two decades to follow. He was undoubtedly thinking of this sort of nemesis, which seems to have weighed so heavily upon him, crushing his projects, when he wrote: "As a Protestant, I felt my religion dreary, but not my life — but as a Catholic, my life was dreary, not my religion."[3]

Besides, his sufferings did not come only from the disappointment of repeated failures. These could be explained by circumstances; certain undertakings were too hasty and some projects too ambitious. But underlying the failures, Newman discovered other causes: the carelessness, the ill-will, and distrust of those who invited him to act, yet who hesitated to commit themselves; then, dropping their support, they were ready to make him responsible for actions they did not anticipate or did not want to undertake. The lowest type of calumnies and criticisms were often made by the very persons who should have supported and defended him. One can easily conceive that it was a cross for Newman to carry out his destiny as a Catholic. While vividly conscious that he had a mission to fulfill in the Catholic Church in England, he nevertheless found himself scoffed at and contradicted at every turn. Feelings such as these, much more than the succession of his failures, made up his calvary.

Some good souls, too inclined without doubt to confuse sanctity with indifference or stoicism, were scandalized at the spectacle of Newman groaning and agonizing at this period, as he appeared to do in several of his letters and intimate papers, as if a follower of the Gospel did not have to experience in his heart and soul something of the ultimate distress which Christ himself endured in His agony. The tragedy here would have been if such misfortunes engendered a spirit of despair or revolt against God but not if they troubled his conscience and deprived it of its human support, throwing it into God's hands as its supreme recourse. Newman does not lose any of his greatness in our eyes because he has given us this image of himself chiselled by suffering and pain. What finally emerges from all the evidence of his first twenty years of life as a Catholic is his invincible conviction that he remains firmly in the hand of God.

Again, one can recognize here, amid the harshest and most depressing human circumstances, a note of confidence and abandonment to the will of God, which is decidedly the key to Newmanian spirituality. When

---

[3] *Autobiog.*, entry of January 21, 1863, p. 254.

he is called to start a work which is interrupted because the road is closed and leads nowhere, he retreats to his solitude, as a recluse, behind the walls of the Oratory but he always finds a way out. God is the sovereign judge. His justice is not the justice of men, even if they are men of the Church. Like Job, when he appeals for a Divine decision, Newman hands himself over to his God: *"Deus judicaverit."*

At this stage in Newman's life, it is useful to follow the vicissitudes of the drama which he lived through in the midst of his own. They appear to be like the confrontations of a man with his fate, like the combat of a solitary individual exposed to the blind tyranny of events.

At the end of 1850, a lamentable affair began in which Newman found himself almost unknowingly implicated. An Italian defrocked priest, named Achilli, with neither morals nor money, came to London in order to excite public opinion against imaginary tortures inflicted upon him by the Roman Church Courts; he presented himself as a victim of the Inquisition! Wiseman had previously denounced such behavior. In a lecture to Protestants, Newman, in stinging terms, exposed the imposture of this miserable man. But the man sued Newman for defamation of character; a lawsuit was started. Since Newman's case against Achilli was based on the factual information reported in Wiseman's previously published article, he asked Wiseman for the necessary pieces of evidence. However, he waited for them in vain. Therefore, Newman had to search out and bring from abroad the actual victims of Achilli's seductions to support his allegations. Nevertheless, he lost the case and had to pay a heavy fine and court costs. Fortunately, subscriptions from all over the world poured in to help defray the heavy financial liabilities which Newman incurred because of the negligence, if not unpardonable behavior, of Wiseman.

While the Achilli affair was still in progress, Newman was called by the bishops of Ireland to found a Catholic University in Dublin. Seemingly, this was a marvelous and unexpected occasion for the former tutor of Oriel to play a role once more in a university and to undertake a task of the first magnitude, commensurate with his genius. But from the very beginning, there was poor communication and planning. The Irish bishops were looking at this foundation only as a means of countering the recent creation of Queen's Colleges. They distrusted the presumed neutrality of the colleges and they dreaded the idea of having young Catholics share an education with Protestants. Therefore, their new project was by nature essentially defensive. Before deciding anything, they asked Newman to begin a series of lectures whose purpose was to denounce the dangers of a mixed education. Such a narrow-minded point of view was hardly reconcilable with Newman's thinking. As a humanist, he believed that the role of a university was to give Catholics, those of England as well as those of Ireland, the proper tools to form and cultivate a broadminded elite, fully open to the problems of the times, ready to be integrated into national life, to play a public role and exercise a definite influence.

In spite of conflicting opinions and reticence among the bishops, some of whom made it clear that they did not believe in the possibility of any success for the enterprise, Newman put himself to work and multiplied his efforts to launch the university. Dr. Cullen, who became Archbishop of Dublin in 1853, seemed to distance himself from the project after having encouraged Newman to accept it. It cannot be said that one is lacking in objectivity if one maintains that Cullen, by his own actions, torpedoed the project which he fathered. Indeed, it is he who, in Rome, opposed Wiseman's suggestion that Newman be elevated to the episcopate. Newman, already Rector of the University of Dublin, was being greeted from all sides with the title "Right Reverend," the one used to address a bishop. Wiseman once again gave up his initiative on Newman's behalf, leaving Newman with the hurt that comes from being passed over.

Soon, the situation at Dublin became impossible for Newman even though he had succeeded in advancing the work of the University and in building a church. Circumstances were such that he resolved to resign his functions and he returned to his community. Newman felt that his presence in Birmingham was essential. During Newman's absence, Dalgairns, then a member of the Birmingham house, played a role unworthy of the confidence placed in him by his superior.

In 1858, it was Wiseman and the English bishops who asked Newman to undertake a new and difficult task, well suited to obliterate the disappointments of Dublin. They wanted a new translation of the Bible for the use of Catholics, who only had at their disposal the Douai version, which had some texts of debatable fidelity to the original source and others which were apparently outdated. Newman assembled a team of collaborators for the work. He already wrote the preface before he learned that some bishops in America had already undertaken a similar English version of the Scriptures. No one had informed Newman about this and Wiseman, true to himself, dropped the whole idea, which in turn forced the unfortunate Newman to extricate himself from the project as expeditiously as possible.

Like the former undertakings, the failure of the English version of the Bible was due, above all, to the negligence, fickleness, or shortsightedness of those who, having authority in the Church, thought it was a good idea to entrust Newman with responsibilities commensurate with his talents but then did not give him the proper support and means for action. Nevertheless, they were conscious of his genius and were inclined to give him their trust; always preserving their right, however, to dodge when their own interests were at stake or when the carrying out of the work already started demanded too much from them.

In conclusion, it was more a lack of vision and resolve on the part of the bishops and, above all, of Cardinal Wiseman, than any lack of confidence or real sympathy for Newman himself. Although hurt by such pusillanimity, Newman was not put on the black list and did not feel he was in any way compromised. But the year 1859 marked a turning point for Newman. Henceforth, he would know a regime of suspicion and intrigue which would hurt him infinitely more than the failures of the Dublin period.

Half way into the nineteenth century, the pontificate of Pius IX, which stressed the integrity of Christian doctrine, was on the defensive in the face of a growing liberalism. Liberalism was reaching into all domains: faith versus reason; anthropology; the sacred sciences; and biblical exegesis. The Roman Curia was more and more powerful at the very moment that a last battle was being fought in defense of the Papal States. The wind of ultramontanism blew over England as well as over the Continent. The men who seemed to resist it were quickly considered suspect. Many misguided zealots thought they were serving the interests of the Church by denouncing those Catholics who, with regard to the problems of the times, were much more inclined to accept a lucid dialogue than to resort to polemics and the inquisition. Newman was truly one of those who wished at any cost to maintain an open debate with the philosophical and scientific thinking of his times. He was one of the first to recognize and to fear the danger to the faith from a liberalism which completely ignored the dogmatic certitudes of the Christian revelation. He was also among the first to suspect that this same liberalism, so anti-dogmatic and pro-science, was only a mask behind a way of thinking still at too early a stage of development not to appear presumptuous and aggressive. Putting aside the excesses and prejudices that characterized some aspects of the liberal spirit, Newman nevertheless had the presentiment that a new humanism was being born and that the Church needed men in positions to understand it and be determined to appropriate some of the incontestable values contained in it.

Maintaining a clear-sighted attitude in the face of controversy and in confronting the critical issues of the day seemed to Newman to be more apostolic and effective than for the Church to entrench itself in an attitude of defiance and denial. One can easily understand why Newman, so far ahead of his times, would collide with those in England who were blind to the issues of their day and were seeking, like Ward and Manning, the remedy to this anarchy of ideas in a submission to a dogmatism all too unyielding. What is more difficult to understand is how these men could ruin the reputation of someone who had been their former leader by using the worst procedures of intrigue and, with their own bias, by reporting on Newman's activities to Rome.

The chapter of religious history which such men wrote during the last half of the nineteenth century is a curious prelude to the one which followed the modernist crisis at the beginning of the twentieth, in which some men of uncontainable doctrinal integrity were denounced and calumniated in a spirit of bad faith. The marvel in all of this was that Newman did not succumb to the passionate campaign of those who seemed dead set against him but, instead, found in those overwhelming trials the source of his own greatness and spiritual influence.

It was in seeking to save the *Rambler*, a review which was placed in an unfortunate position because of the imprudence of its successive editors, that Newman provided his adversaries with the chance to strike and discredit him in Rome. The *Rambler* claimed to be a review for liberal Catholics concerned with the problems and issues of the times, and it wished for the Church an *aggiornamento* such as that which a recent pope declared to be an essential and permanent condition in order to maintain the life of the Church. But the publishers of this English review worked with more enthusiasm than prudence. They too easily pronounced final judgments on extremely delicate questions, such as the issue concerning the reform of seminary education. Moreover, they adopted an irritating style, which very soon tried the patience of the bishops. Already in several instances, Newman attempted to use persuasion with those responsible for the policy of the *Rambler*, with whom he was in sympathy, with the hope of leading them to more balanced and judicious stances. But it was all in vain; in June of 1858, the bishops were ready to censure the *Rambler* if the review persisted in its original orientation. Newman was asked to intervene to secure the resignation of the editor. He did not have any idea that he himself would be asked to replace him. He was convinced by those in charge that he was the only one capable of salvaging the review. After much hesitation and prayers and with the approval of his bishop, he accepted.

However, the bishops envisioned for him a role which he found difficult to fulfill. They wished purely and simply that the *Rambler* completely change its title and its orientation, henceforth avoiding all current controversial questions bearing on faith and theology. Newman, on the contrary, thought that the way to revive the *Rambler* was to appeal to the educated audience it never had previously reached. In salvaging the *Rambler*, he saw the perfect occasion to provide a forum for a Catholic reflection which had not yet found its expression, in the balanced and generous style that was expected of it. Enjoying an unequalled intellectual prestige, Newman was in a position to offer the Catholic Church in his country and in his times a unique occasion to renew the dialogue between faith and science and to force Catholic opinion not to satisfy itself with assurances or prejudices which were close to amounting to naive credulity or ignorance.

The project was audacious and Newman was aware of the risks involved. His contribution to the review in 1859 consisted of two articles on the role of the laity in the Church. Leaning on historical facts and the tradition of the Church, he demonstrated that it had never denied the faithful their right to express their thoughts on problems touching on the practical discipline of the Church's life or to express their views on matters concerning faith and morals. Filled with all the necessary nuances and supported by the most solid arguments of history, these two articles of Newman appear today to be of an orthodoxy so indisputable that one remains perplexed at the scandal they caused. Persuaded by Ward and Manning, then provost of the chapter at Westminster, several bishops denounced Newman with the utmost vigor. The article, "On Consulting the Laity in Matters of Doctrine," was sent to Rome where some zealots rushed to discredit the author in the eyes of the Curia. As soon as he learned about the danger he was in, Newman, to avoid the suspicions of the Propaganda, the congregation entrusted with safeguarding the faith, hastened to send to Wiseman, then in Rome, a memorandum asking about any explicit passages in his article that might be considered contrary to the Church's teaching in order that he might explain them satisfactorily. But the Cardinal, whose negligence with regard to his protege is beyond understanding and is unexplainable, did not lift a finger to clear Newman's name. The Propaganda had no other alternative but to show its mistrust of what appeared to them as a silent and unhappy Newman whom they felt had not responded to their inquiry.

Thus, his attempt to keep the *Rambler* afloat resulted in his disgrace. He would not be long in measuring the consequences of this disgrace in a new episode, which had to do with the Oxford Oratory, and which was, without doubt, the most humiliating for him personally.

The need for educational reform was becoming a crucial question in England, and Catholic circles did not miss a chance to stir it up. The problem of education for Catholics at the university level was an extremely divisive issue. The ultramontane party strongly condemned the entrance of Catholic students in state-run universities, opened to them since 1854 (Oxford in 1854 and Cambridge in 1855). Newman and the best informed minds did not see any grave danger to the faith of young people in going to state universities, provided they received support from nearby Catholic structures. Newman, who had been thinking of establishing an Oratory at Oxford, had looked ahead to the future when he arranged to buy some land. Bishop Ullathorne, his bishop, had already offered him the pastorate of the Catholic parish at Oxford. Newman hesitated a long time before accepting the offer. Indeed, a new cabal was already starting against him. In December of 1864, a meeting of the English bishops voted for a resolution which, without formally condemning Catholic students from attending Oxford and Cambridge, nevertheless warned against it in very strong terms. The request for the foundation of an Oratory at Oxford was carried to Rome where it took an unexpected turn. It conceded the foundation of an Oratory at Oxford but decided that Newman should be *"blande and suaviterque"* [blandly and sweetly] prevented from appearing in the city where his presence was unwelcome! Newman at first was unaware of this stipulation. Finally exasperated by so many lies and innuendos circulating about him, he decided to send two of his closest confidants to Rome to obtain some clarification on the issue.

His astonishment was great on learning that Rome's suspicions about him were motivated, above all, by the silence they thought he had maintained when he was asked to explain the *Rambler* articles. At the time of the affair, he thought he had done everything to give them some assurances and to dissipate any suspicions about his orthodoxy. However, Propaganda had received nothing from Newman because the officials then in Rome had not delivered Newman's response to them. Barnabo, Cardinal Prefect of the Congregation, carefully manipulated by the intrigues of some people like the turbulent and agitated prelate, Talbot, was under the impression that Newman, with all his novel ideas, was really a sort of dreamer who did not deserve the trust of the Church. Barnabo had maintained this prejudice since the *Rambler* affair.

The impasse about Oxford put the final touch on the series of projects which forced the convert to leave his retreat in order to actively participate in the life of English Catholicism. It should not be forgotten that Newman was as much a man of action as he was a man of thought. His role as undisputed leader during the early years of the Oxford Movement, and the multiple steps he took in order to put the University of Dublin on its feet despite a thousand obstacles, are sufficient examples to show that Newman had all the necessary gifts to initiate and conduct with success the affairs and government of men. The great disappointment in his Catholic life was to look like an underemployed, even a useless tool in a Church which never knew how to use him according to his talents. It is not that he was lacking in courage and good will; he answered all requests from ecclesiastical authorities and accepted and assumed all roles proposed to him with the same loyal and generous heart with which he pursued his own personal projects. Nevertheless, one remains under the irresistible feeling that by giving him these various tasks, the Catholic hierarchy was seeking more to keep him busy than to truly entrust him with their confidence. The history of a man who seems always to be running after his destiny, without ever attaining it, is always worthy of pity. But what can we say when such a man is Newman! It is hard to prevent a feeling of irritation and regret at the spectacle of all those occasions lost for the Catholic Church in England and for the whole of the Catholic Church during the second half of the nineteenth century.

The development of science and scientific inquiry, and the blossoming of a humanism, still surprised by its own audacity, made it necessary for the Church to revise its attitudes and its style, particularly in the field of education and religious culture. Newman would have been the genial explorer for these new ways which would one day have to be invented,

after decades of research and much hesitation, if the Christian faith were
to maintain a true dialogue with the modern mind.

True, Newman's disgrace ended with the triumph of a justice he
never expected when, in 1878, Leo XIII conferred upon him the honors of
the Cardinalate. But this ultimate recognition honored him more for his
genius and his thought than for his works. In the eighteen sixties, nothing
seemed to indicate the possibility of such a restoration of his good name.
After 1864, when he was crushed under the weight of incomprehension,
deception, intrigues, and calumnies, he stopped thinking about the possibility of any new positive action and confined himself to the Oratory at
Edgbaston, henceforth dedicating his life to prayer, silence, and meditation.

CHAPTER XV

THE SPIRITUALITY OF FAILURE

I ask not to see,
— I ask not to know,
— I ask simply to be used.

Med. and Dev., p. 7

IN SPITE OF HIMSELF, Newman was forced to return to the isolation which he had once known at Littlemore. From the cloud of silence which enveloped the convert's existence in the days ahead, the portrait of a profoundly spiritual man, possessing a deep and original wisdom, slowly emerged. This portrait ultimately revealed to the Church an authentic master of the spiritual life.

In 1864, English Catholicism lost in Newman an apostle who could have developed new approaches and made possible a reconciliation between the Church and modern humanism. Yet, the retreat of their most lucid and devoted priest later gave English Catholics a chance to recognize the spiritual genius they were waiting for.

Withdrawn into himself, Newman felt the weight of total abandonment by his fellowmen. Such rejection, which would normally lead to despair and dejection, brought forth in Newman a spiritual lucidity that enabled him to detect a loving Providence in all his trials. He learned to accept them faithfully in a spirit of loving submission to God, by which he joined the family of the spiritual masters of all time. As a matter of fact, at the end of 1864, having given up all illusions about exercising a role in the public life of the Church and despairing of ever seeing the hierarchy open to his projects, Newman wrote to a confidant:

It is still the Blessed Will of God to send me baulks. On the whole,
I suppose looking through my life as a course, He is using me, but
really viewed in its separate parts, it is but a life of failure.[1]

Newman's willing acceptance of his isolation and trials is likewise
seen in one of his earlier sermons preached at St. Mary's: "When received
in the faithful heart, the cross remains there. It abides as a living principle,
but deep and hidden from observation."[2]

There is no dearth of material for the study of Newman's spiritual
journey after 1859. Without doubt, this period is the most decisive and
crucial in the development of his spiritual life. Most of the information is
supplied by Newman himself in his intimate notes, prayers, and letters
which were extensively quoted by Wilfred Ward. All these sources are of
extreme value to us because Newman was completely open in the spontaneous outpouring of his heart to correspondents and to God in prayer. And
none of these outbursts can leave us indifferent to his plight.

The very diversity of the documents requires a great deal of circumspection if we are to draw from them the proper implications and conclusions. Two different dialogues, one with men and the other with God,
appear to be the things which led Newman to abandon his solitude. These
dialogues do not bear any more resemblance to each other than do the
confessions at the time of his conversion, which were also addressed either
to God or man. The confessions he addressed to persons made of flesh and
blood, whom he wanted to reassure or convince, do not resemble the
intimate confessions which he made in the presence of God alone.[3] The
agonies of the same ordeal provoked different reactions from Newman,
depending upon whether he was opening his heart *in writing* to his
correspondents or *in prayer* to God. Thus, these same documents lend
themselves to different interpretations, depending upon their destination
— God or man.

In particular, one series of texts is of major importance for us. It is

---

[1] W. II, p. 67. Letter to Sister Imelda Poole. This nun belonged to the Dominican
Convent at Stone. These sisters provided Newman with prayers and great sympathy at
the time of his worries during the Achilli trial.
[2] VI Par., VII: "The Cross of Christ, the Measure of the World," p. 1229.
[3] See text in Chapter XI, The Call to Rome, "God and Myself."

a collection of intimate papers grouped under the title, *Private Journal*.[4] This collection includes twelve confessions, of unequal length, written at regular intervals between December 15, 1859 and September 10, 1876. They are expressions of Newman's need for reflection and are a personal apologia. Newman distanced himself from the events in his life; he defended his failures and misfortunes, asserted the purity of his motives, and pleaded not guilty.

Written in a moment of utter confusion, the *Journal* expresses the succession of sentiments which haunted his conscience during the course of those trying years: the bitter feeling of growing old, of dragging along, and of living a useless life; the distress of knowing himself to be misunderstood and set aside; the disenchantment of a heart wounded by dashed hopes; the bitterness which comes from distrust; and the constant suffering from continual intrigues.

Judging too hastily, the reader may be tempted to stop here, misunderstanding totally the meaning of these outcries, coming so unexpectedly from a man who was generally so much in control of himself. True, certain of his confessions in his *Private Journal* are ruthless in their severity and clarity: sometimes, the tone reaches to such a pitch that his complaint becomes sarcastic.[5] Even the memories of a period of sweet feelings and consolations, as in the days following his conversion, are mixed with somber remarks which are the effect of a too long contained indignation. Newman's piercing judgment denounced injustice and exposed the duplicity of all those who, refusing to give him their confidence, preferred to use the language of ambiguity and double dealing. He made veiled

---

[4] Ward, in the long two volume *Life of Cardinal Newman*, provides generous extracts from his *Private Journal*; some notes are found there *in extenso* (Notes I, IV, V, VII, X, XI, and XII). Ward did not believe it to be opportune to deliver the other notes to the public in their entirety; he justly feared that the public might misunderstand the tone of bitterness which oftentimes pervades them and that some of the allusions may be too direct or too personal. Thureau-Dangin published many excerpts of the *Private Journal* in his book, *Newman Catholique*. Father Bouyer, in his biography, refers to all of the notes. Father Henry Tristram has published these notes in their entirety in *John Henry Newman: Autobiographical Writings*, Sheed and Ward: New York, 1957.

[5] See in particular the entry of January 21, 1863, which recalls not only the slanders surrounding the *Rambler* affair but also many indiscretions and insensitivities Newman experienced in Catholic circles after his conversion. (*Autobiographical Writings*, p. 255 ff.)

accusations on almost every line and the talented polemicist that he was, he wrote with a sharp and formidable pen when he so wished.

Is not such overflowing bitterness as we find in the *Private Journal* a sign of lack of self-control and serenity? Newman seems to have been caught in the act. In expressing his complaints too sharply, was he not finding in them a sort of sweet revenge? Was not the flame burning within him kept so hot that he found in it some secret source of consolation? Without even knowing it, did he not show a face which was, as it has been said, the face of a resentful man? Wasn't the conversion to Catholicism of the Oxford leader the direct result of a resentment born in his mind out of a continual disappointment with his attempts at reform within the Anglican Church? Would his life in the Roman Church become the source of a more subtle and less apparent resentment, yet just as revealing of Newman's true nature and spirit?[6]

If such interpretations of his character have been made possible, it is because Newman's own autobiographical writings have put his critics on the wrong track. He was not afraid of a total openness and of facing up to the naked truth in a lucid examination of his conscience. In confessing the great trials which oppressed him, he sought neither to inspire pity for himself nor to justify himself before those whom he trusted would ultimately learn the real truth. If he wrote about his sufferings and trials, it was to bring more clearly before his eyes the ways he was being called to use such incidents in the fulfillment of his personal destiny. This required him to be open and always available to the call of God. His intimate notes have no other meaning than that of being a purification or a catharsis for his conscience which was fully confident it could detect the signposts that pointed him onward in his religious journey. Therefore, events in his life were mentioned in his *Journal* only to the degree that they offered his conscience a field for personal exploration and examen.

Newman's conscience considered the variety and complexity of many mixed feelings, including those which depicted his distress or his disenchantment. It expressed the remarkable lucidity of his views about himself, thus placing him in a state of absolute truth before his Sovereign Judge. But it would be the most serious misconception to claim that

---

[6] This is the thesis sustained by Cross, *John Henry Newman*, "Tractarian Series," Allan, 1933.

Newman's revelations of himself reveal a morbid pleasure in exposing his most secret feelings of distress and despondency. Furthermore, he was not deceived by the fact that, one day or another, he might have been betrayed by his own weaknesses; he confessed that he found certain of his early notes "affected, unreal, egotistical and petty."[7] He had no delusion about the ambiguity of keeping personal notes, never denying what he once preached in an Oxford sermon:

> Moreover, as to religious journals useful as they often are, at the same time I believe persons find great difficulty, while recording their feelings, in banishing the thought that one day those good feelings will be known to the world, and are thus insensibly led to modify and prepose their language.... Another mischief arising from this self-contemplation is the peculiar kind of selfishness... which it will be found to foster.[8]

If Newman was not convinced that he should give up confiding in his *Journal,* nor that he should have destroyed his notes, it is because he thought they were useful to him in identifying the steps in his spiritual journey. If we respect this intention, we can make use of these incomparable documents of spiritual autobiography.

Upon reading Newman's intimate notes of this period, one's first impression is of a certain feeling of depression, similar to what one would experience while observing a man who seems powerless to surmount the mishaps in his life and who is unable to shake off the obstacles on his road. Like a leitmotif, Newman's awareness that his life was passing fill the pages: Years full of the promises of life belong to a past which is gone forever; the weight of age is inexorably felt; his strength is diminishing and his vitality is lessening. He feels the first signs that he is entering "the autumn of his life."[9] The graceful spontaneity of his youthful years is now gone:

> And I repeat because I think, as death comes on, his cold breath is felt on the soul as on the body, and that viewed naturally my

---

[7] Note of October 30, 1870. *Autobiog.,* p. 268.
[8] II Par., XV, "Self-Contemplation," p. 329.
[9] This expression is in a letter to H. Wilberforce, W. I, p. 302.

soul is half-dead now, whereas then it was in the freshness and fervor of youth.[10]

But if Newman was not able to see the years passing by without sadness, it was not only because he was aging but because he was filled with regrets created by missed opportunities. In the past, he played a major role. His mission was clear and exciting; he knew he was the instrument of God in the service of an unquestioned cause. Alas! with the passing of years, those promises were all gone. And the sentiments of being useless pervaded his conscience. He was too lucid to keep any illusions regarding his future usefulness and yet too motivated to silently resign himself to a state of what he considered to be idleness. Thus, at the end of his sojourn in Ireland, he wrote to Ambrose Saint-John:

> To the rising generation, to the sons of those who knew me, or read what I wrote 15 or 20 years ago, I am a mere page in history. I do not live to them, they know nothing of me; they have heard my name, but have no association with it.... It was at Oxford, and by my Parochial Sermons, that I had influence, — all that is past.[11]

And a little later, he confided to Wilberforce: "But at present I shall lie fallow."[12] It is above all in the notes from the *Private Journal* that he expressed his regrets for not being able to fulfill his mission in the Church: his memories of days gone by filled his analysis; he was constantly tempted to compare the rich years of the past with the sterile and vain labor of the present:

> I am nobody, I have no friend at Rome, I have laboured... to be misrepresented, backbitten, and scorned. I have laboured in Ireland, with a door ever shut in my face. I seem to have had many failures and what I did well was not understood.[13]

Might not the cruel misunderstandings that plagued him since his conversion incite him to turn in upon himself and to look backwards? "I

---

[10] *Autobiog.*, p. 250.
[11] Ward, I, p. 387.
[12] *Ibid.*, p. 573.
[13] *Autobiog.*, p. 251.

am tempted to look back. Not so, O Lord, with Thy grace not so!"[14]

Some time later, the same inquietude was expressed in the most somber note of all those in his *Private Journal*; it is dated January 21, 1863:

> This morning, when I woke, the feeling that I was cumbering the ground came on me, so strongly, that I could not get myself to go to my shower-bath. What is the good of trying to preserve or increase strength, when nothing comes of it? What is the good of living for nothing? ... Of course one's earlier years are (humanly speaking) best — and again, events are softened by distance — And I look back on my years at Oxford and Littlemore with tenderness... it was the time in which I had a remarkable mission, and since I made great sacrifices, to which God called me, He has rewarded me in ten thousand ways. O how many! but he has marked my course with almost unintermittent mortifications. Few indeed successes has it been His blessed will to give me through life... since I have been a Catholic, I seem to myself to have nothing but failures personally.[15]

After enumerating once more the list of lost causes, he continued:

> I do not wonder at trials; trials are our lot here; but what saddens me, is that, as far as one can see, I have done so little, amid all my trials. My course has been dreary because to look back on it, it is so much of a failure.[16]

Recalling once more the suspicions and mistrust around him, he continued:

> Now I say again, I am noticing all this opposition and distrust, not on their own account, for St. Philip had them abundantly, but because they have (to all appearances) succeeded in destroying my influence and my usefulness.... I am passé, in decay; I am untrustworthy; I am strange, odd; I have my own ways and cannot get on with others.[17]

---

[14] *Ibid.*, p. 252.
[15] *Ibid.*, pp. 254-255.
[16] *Ibid.*, p. 256.
[17] *Autobiog.*, pp. 256-257.

During the most crucifying hours of his state of utter confusion, Newman molded his prayer. Along with his pain, he also experienced the temptation of withdrawing into a state of sheer desolation but he knew that these very failures and disappointments were for him both a risk and a challenge. He wrote: "I have all my life been speaking about suffering for the truth — now it has come upon me."[18] And again:

> For twenty years I have been writing in verse and prose about suffering for the Truth's sake, and I have no right to complain if, after having almost courted the world's injustice, I suffer it.[19]

Failure constitutes the test of spiritual sincerity. It can never be desired for itself. I do not know of any state of sorrow or pain that is foreign to true asceticism, but because failure is the test of truth, it forces the conscience to break away from all illusions and false securities and recognize itself in its most absolute authenticity.

Even when a spotlight is thrown on one's interior life, there still remains a real danger for one to become closed and hardened. Newman knew this risk too well to indulge in this dangerous form of introspection which finally makes one a prey to sterile regrets and resentments. It was on his knees that he wrote. God is always a party to the debate, and the most sorrowful notes in the *Journal* always end in prayers of praise:

> O my dear Lord.... Time and place are not hindrances to Thee. Thou canst give me grace according to my day.... Thy hand is not straitened that it cannot save. It is plain that what I feel Thy servants have from the earliest times felt before me: Job, Moses, and Habacuc felt as I feel thousands of years ago, and I am able to plead with Thee in their never-dying words. O my God, not as a matter of sentiment, not as a matter of literary exhibition, do I put this down. Oh, rid me of this frightful cowardice, for this is at the bottom of all my ills. When I was young, I was bold because I was ignorant — now I have lost my boldness, because I have advanced [sic] in experience. I am able to count the cost, better than I did, of being brave for Thy sake, and therefore I shrink from sacrifices.[20]

---

[18] Ward, I, p. 286. Letter to Sister Imelda Poole, November 25, 1851.
[19] Ward, I, p. 294. Letter of June 27, 1852 to Mother Margaret Hallahan.
[20] Note in *Journal*, December 15, 1859; *Autobiog.*, pp. 25-251.

This surrender to God is never more necessary than when a clear and upright conscience is tempted to withdraw while under pressure of suffering and distress. The most subtle temptation in time of failure (as Pascal previously noted) is in shutting oneself off in an attitude of abnegation which is in some way a form of pride and personal self-sufficiency. Thus, the renunciation is the result of vexation rather than a submission of the heart. Newman knew about such a danger. There is no doubt that he resolutely engaged in a battle within himself in order not to give in to such a threat. Victory is possible only if the soul is capable of crossing over the threshold by submitting to the purification process, a necessary condition for a victorious combat. It is not enough to be open and sincere within oneself; it is necessary that this sincerity subordinate itself and submit to a much higher design: a total surrender into the hands of God is now required.

Such is the dialectic movement of the Newmanian conscience revealed by the notes of his *Private Journal*. The only reason for the conscience to look upon itself is to expose itself to the sight of God, the final judge. Lucidity is not sought after for itself. It is always directed toward self abandonment in God. We find here the familiar approach of both the psalmist and Job, who were tempted constantly to remain stuck in the impasse of their failure and confusion but always moved by a spiritual drive to remit into the hands of God their justification and their destiny.

On several occasions in his *Private Journal*, Newman justly evoked the image of Job. The analogy of his situation with that of his biblical hero is so striking that he went so far as to borrow some of his complaints from him.[21] Newman was as convinced of his own righteousness as Job was. He had no doubt about the justice of his cause and his confidence in his Judge. In the face of the powerful conspiracy of those dead set against him, the Oratorian raised his voice in a cry, both of distress and confidence, exactly like the man from the land of Uz, when betrayed by his friends: *Viderit Deus*. [But God shall see to it.] This embittered cry is an audacious complaint, which is audacious only because he was convinced of the truth of his cause. Finally, it is to Job himself that God rendered justice, not to his friends.

---

[21] *Autobiog.*, p. 262. See the beginning of the note, October 30, 1867. Cf. letter to Cardinal Barnabo, March 21, 1867 in *Letters and Diaries* Vol. XIII, p. 94.

The whole of the confessions in the *Private Journal* continue the call of Job. God is the sure and secret confidant that Newman invoked. To this God, he recounted familiarly all the disappointments, misunderstandings, and failures which had thrown a gloom over his heart: trials so cruel that they emaciated his face; suspicions and distrusts which wounded his heart; shocks to a conscience too easily moved by past memories; and finally, the excessive reactions arising from a sensitivity which was very difficult to control.

In particular, he elaborated with great firmness on what he sensed to be his mission in the Church; how he envisioned his influence and role which, in spite of the obstacles, he was confident might one day be useful to the Church. After having vigorously denounced the tendency, so frequent in men of the Church, to please their hierarchical superiors through compliance, he outlined what he believed to be his own vocation:

> At Propaganda, conversions and nothing else, are proof of doing anything.... This is what was expected of me. But I am altogether different — my objects, my theory of acting, my powers, go in a different direction; and one not understood or contemplated at Rome or elsewhere.... For me conversions were not the first thing; but the edification of Catholics... when I have given as my true opinion, that I am afraid to make hasty converts of educated men, lest they should not count the cost and should have difficulties after they have entered the Church, I do but imply the same thing; that the Church must be prepared for converts, as well as converts prepared for the Church. Now from first to last, education in the large sense of the word, has been my line.[22]

Newman's confidence in persevering in his vocation, despite the intrigues and accusations surrounding him, finally gave him the serenity to rise above such criticism:

> Though I still feel keenly the way in which I am kept doing nothing; I am not so much pained at it —because I am (I feel) indirectly doing a work, and because its success has put me in spirits to look out for other means of doing good.[23]

---

[22] *Ibid.*, pp. 257-259. Note of January 21, 1863.
[23] *Ibid.*, p. 261. Note of February 22, 1865.

Henceforth, Newman did not lose time and energy in justifying himself. As he told one of his correspondents, he counted on time to be God's great justifier:

> I consider that Time is the great remedy and Avenger of all wrongs, as far as this world goes. If only we are patient, God works for us. He works for those who do not work for themselves.[24]

Finally, it was Newman's religious strength that provided the only explanation of the notes entered into his *Journal*. Even the most bitter of its pages do not fool anyone. The *Journal* has to be seen as a whole with its accents of simplicity and confidence; it can only belong to a disciple of St. Philip Neri. In spite of so many sufferings, one can always find a great desire for humility, for a life lived in silence, and for self-effacement:

> We are in God's hands and must be content to do our work day by day, as He puts it before us, without attempting to understand or anticipate His purpose, and thanking Him for the great mercies He has bestowed on us and is bestowing.[25]

The entry for June 25, 1869 begins and ends on the same subdued tone of discreet and peaceful prayer, expressing the theme, so dear to Newman, of the unique character of his own personal destiny:

> The Providence of God has been wonderful with me all through my life.... I suppose every one has a great deal to say about the Providence of God over him.... Yet I cannot but repeat words which I think I used in a memorandum book of 1820, that among the ordinary mass of men, no one has sinned so much, no one has been so mercifully treated, as I have; no one has such cause for humiliation, such cause for thanksgiving.[26]

The *Private Journal*, with all its pages of complaints, is not, in and of itself, the decisive document, although several historians have at-

---

[24] W. II, p. 129. Letter to Emily Bowles, January 8, 1867.
[25] *Autobiog.*, p. 266. Note of January 29, 1868.
[26] *Ibid.*, pp. 267-268. Note of June 25, 1869.

tempted to use it in order to depict Newman as a man filled with bitterness and regrets. Without doubt, this mistake comes from the fact that Newman noted every possible feeling about himself "as a sort of relief to my mind."[27] Confession is always deliverance. But there is more to these entries. They reveal Newman's ultimate motivation in his spiritual combat.

Trying to maintain one's peace of soul is never so demanding as during times of distress and dejection. It is not a question of battling enemies from outside but against the shadows within the depths of one's heart. Newman was too conscious of this menace not to unmask it at the very same time that he analyzed his feelings. The *Journal* is both a confession and a prayer. It is the genius of Newman that he was able to raise this knowledge of his own failures, with all their dramatic repercussions in the depth of his own human affections, to the highest spiritual level. In the last resort, a sense of the Divine Presence illuminated his conscience. It always knew that it was being led by this Pillar of Cloud, which had been revealed to him once at the end of his illness in Sicily. The prayer of Newman took flight to his true home, the invisible world, where the brilliance and clarity of the sweet and peaceful light dissipates all the anxieties born in a conscience distraught by frequent failures. A poem, entitled "The Two Worlds," composed during those years of trial, expresses this flight of his soul well beyond the reach of his wounds and sufferings:

The Two Worlds

Unveil, O Lord, and on us shine
   In glory and in grace;
This gaudy world grows pale before
   The beauty of Thy face.

Till Thou art seen, it seems to be
   A sort of fairy ground,
Where suns unsetting light the sky,
   And flowers and fruit abound.

But when Thy keener, purer beam
   Is pour'd upon our sight,

---

[27] *Ibid.*, p. 262, note of October 30, 1867.

It loses all its power to charm,
   And what was day is night.

Its noblest toils are then the scourge
   Which made Thy blood to flow;
Its joys are but the treacherous thorns
   Which circled round Thy brow.

And thus, when we renounce for Thee
   Its restless aims and fears,
The tender memories of the past,
   The hopes of coming years,

Poor is our sacrifice, whose eyes
   Are lighted from above;
We offer what we cannot keep,
   What we have ceased to love.[28]

---

[28] W. I, p. 592. In *Verses*, p. 319. This poem is dated from 1862.

Chapter XVI

THE ROUTINE OF EACH DAY

In nidulo meo.
[In my nest]
W. II, p. 313.

THE SUBURB OF EDGBASTON, where the Oratorian community has resided since 1852, still appears today as a green and silent oasis in Birmingham. It is only when one has left the heart of this great city, often oppressed by the heavy clouds which darken the Midland sky, that one experiences the peace that is to be found behind the red brick walls, the residence on Hagley Road, which served as Newman's retreat during the last forty years of his long life. Bordering as it does on the major artery which joins Birmingham to the surrounding cities and towns, the Oratory serves as a bridgehead between the populous districts of the city on the one side, with their crowded alleys and lanes full of noise and traffic, and a vast park on the other, with quiet rows of cottages and greenery. It is in this provincial and familiar setting that Newman found the retreat which he had always wanted. His letter to a correspondent testifies to this:

> Sometimes I seem to myself inconsistent, in professing to love retirement, yet seeming impatient at doing so little; yet I trust I am not so in any serious way.... And when I came here, where I have been for 14 years, I deliberately gave myself to a life of obscurity, which in my heart I love best. And so it has been and so it is now that the routine work of each day is in fact more than enough for my thoughts and my time. I have no leisure.[1]

---

[1] W. I, p. 589. Letter of May 29, 1863 to Miss Bowles.

The former student of Trinity, so attentive to the silent language of stones and things, always felt a secret bond with the privileged places associated with the accomplishment of his own destiny, and this was the case of the Birmingham Oratory. It was the work of his own hands. Its silence was for him a rampart against the offenses of the world. The sweetness and intimacy of the place, the calm and peaceful life which reigned there, seemed to be the symbol of the Providence which tirelessly guided him. He felt this Providence in the library where he assembled his precious collection of patristic and theological works, or in the church which he built in the Palladian style, for which he had an affectionate interest. Here, Newman found the atmosphere of silence and retreat which evoked for him the invisible world of angels and saints, toward which he knew he was being led. Angels are among us.

Except for six years in Dublin and occasional trips imposed by circumstances, the Oratory was the only place in which he lived during the course of his long Catholic career. It was the little nest of his sheltered life where he jealously protected himself against the possibility of any change of residence. Thus, in 1864, he wrote to a friend who was anxious to see him enter a field of action less cut off from the world:

> I assure you it would be a strong arm, stronger than any which I can fancy, that would be able to pull me out of my "nest," to use the Oratorian word, — and I am too old for it now — I could not be picked out of it without being broken to pieces in the process.[2]

Besides, his physical constitution suffered badly from change of location and even short trips. He had suffered during the days of his novitiate in Rome. Much later, when he returned to the Eternal City to be elevated to the cardinalate, he felt so physically weak that he hastened his return and only regained his strength when home in England. His love for the Isles was in his bones and in his very blood. For example, when he was offered the red hat, the fear that his life might change spoiled his joy. The prospect that he might end his days in Rome, far from his beloved English Oratory, was too hard on him. Upset, he confided to his bishop, with accents which reveal how alarmed he was:

---

[2] W. II, p. 313.

For I am, indeed old and distrustful of myself; I have lived now thirty years in *"nidulo meo"* in my much loved Oratory, sheltered and happy, and would therefore entreat his Holiness not to take me from St. Philip, my Father and Patron... in consideration of my feeble health, my nearly eighty years, the retired course of my life from my youth, my ignorance of foreign language, and my lack of experience in business, to let me die where I have so long lived.[3]

Nevertheless, he knew how to silence his own repugnance when events imposed upon him the need to travel. The preceding chapters have shown how much he remained totally available to calls from the hierarchy. Sometimes friendship or dear remembrances compelled him to make brief trips from which he returned with an uplifted heart: "I have not been in a friend's house these twenty years,"[4] he wrote to his former disciple, Rogers, on December 24, 1864. This letter was a break in a long silence, which was self imposed. But it was not that Newman was either forgetful or ungrateful. Now that time had passed and suspicions no longer touched him, Newman was less hesitant about renewing relationships with friends of former times. Thus, he accepted invitations to London from Rogers, who became Lord Blachford, and from Richard Church, who became Dean of St. Paul's in London. Some months later in September of 1865, he paid a last visit to Keble, his companion in the Tractarian battles, who had grown old in the peace of his village of Hursley. So intense was the emotion of the two men that they faced each other in total silence for a long time.[5] Still later in 1884, he journeyed to Oxford to assist his old friend, Mark Pattison, on his death bed, in an attempt to remove his doubts and bring peace to his conscience.

In order to appreciate fully what these bonds of friendship meant to the heart of the Oratorian, let us reflect on these lines, the first that he had written to Keble, after a silence of more than eighteen years:

Never have I doubted for one moment your affection for me, never have I been hurt at your silence. I interpreted it easily, —

---

[3] *Ibid.*, II, p. 439. Letter to Bishop Ullathorne, February 2, 1879.
[4] *Ibid.*, II, p. 74.
[5] W. II, p. 92 ff. See the account which Newman gives.

it was not the silence of others.... You are always with me, a
thought of reverence and love, and there is nothing I love better
than you and Isaac and Copeland, and many others I could name,
except Him Whom I ought to love best of all and supremely. May
He Himself, who is the Over-Abundant Compensation for all
losses, give me His own Presence, and then I shall want nothing
and desire nothing, but none but He can make up for the loss of
those old familiar faces which haunt me continually.[6]

In his prayers, Newman joined again with his old companions and
revived the invisible ties of friendship that time had erased. He was always
ecstatic about the benefits of friendship, his friends from the past as well
as those from the present time; he sometimes blamed himself for not
having responded to them generously enough.

Outside of these few short trips, the heavy veil of silence which
covered his life at the Oratory isolated him anew. His daily horarium was
indeed filled. We know this from the memoirs of Father Neville, his
confidant during the very last years. It is not quite the austere rule of
Littlemore; the Divine Office no longer interrupted the rhythm of daily
tasks several times a day. The rule at Edgbaston maintained the flexibility
of the Oratorian houses; their community life was not of necessity the same
as a convent in a religious order and was not opposed to the relative
independence of each one of its members. Newman, who always lived in
solitude, found at the Oratory the best climate to accomplish what he
wished most. He was alone but not lonely on his return to Edgbaston after
receiving the honor of the cardinalate.

The first hours of the day at the Oratory were reserved for religious
exercises: meditation, followed by Mass and the recitation of the Office.
The morning was spent on multiple tasks: personal studies, correspondence, and classifying papers. The life of Newman cannot be understood
without keeping in mind those long hours consecrated each day to
reflection and research. Victim of a sort of scruple that appears paradoxical
only to those who think they have earned peace once they have finished
their work, Newman always blamed himself for losing time. He lived with
an obsession for time lost. In his *Private Journal*, he took a precise count

---

[6] W. I, p. 591. Letter of August 5, 1863.

of his literary works in order to persuade himself that he had not squandered his life. The thought that he had not written any new works since his conversion to Catholicism haunted him.[7]

However, it is hard to imagine Newman being inactive in the course of the long mornings of study at Edgbaston. One picture shows him at his desk totally absorbed with his task of writing, reminiscent of Holbein's portrait of Erasmus. This was the way his life was spent for almost forty years. Numerous works required his attention: updating his own writings; scholarly research; and new publications. To a large extent, while his life as an Oratorian appeared to be unproductive, it can readily be identified with many publications. During the twenty some odd years of his retreat at Edgbaston, masterpieces of religious thought were produced which continued and expanded the writings from his Anglican period. *The Idea of a University*, written in 1852, outlined in a prophetic manner the foundations of a Christian humanism for the modern world. In 1864, it is the remarkable *Apologia Pro Vita Sua*, an answer to the sarcasms of a pamphleteer, which turned Protestant opinion around and awakened English Catholicism. In 1866, in response to Pusey's attack on Catholic veneration of Mary, Newman wrote his famous *Response to Eirenicon*, a masterpiece of modern Marian literature. In 1869, the *Grammar of Assent*, the fruit of patient reflection, opened a new way of approaching the problem of faith and reason. In addition to these works, often written under the tremendous pressure of a particular event — for example, three weeks of intense and passionate labor were sufficient to give birth to the *Apologia* — Newman kept busy updating the past editions of his books and classifying his notes and papers. On top of all this, he responded promptly to the numerous letters which he received.

Correspondence was for him an obligation and a relaxation. He saw it as a means of spreading his ideas, of fulfilling a mission among some anxious and concerned friends, and of strengthening the bonds of friendship and sympathy. An often tired hand filled pages with the same cursive, tight handwriting, with rapid and firm strokes, which kept its elegance and distinctiveness. Precise and methodical, Newman spent several hours a day on his correspondence. Often, he complained of a numbness in his

---

[7] *Autobiog.*, October 14, 1874, p. 271; W. II, p. 399. This obsession bothered him until the end of his life; W. II, p. 530.

fingers but he overcame it by the sheer effort of his will and it quickly became a routine. He wrote: "I am like an old horse... who stumbles at first, but once he gets into his trot he goes as well as ever."[8] His genius expressed itself straightforwardly in his letters and his life was reflected in them as in a mirror. Each one of his letters was written to hearten a confidant, to respond to an avowed or suspected need, or to express a regret, a desire, or a joy which touched the heart.

Newman, the Apologist, appears here as Newman the familiar friend; the least banal and the most important of his missives are perhaps to be found among the short quick notes suggested to him by some trivial incident. He told a friend:

> I have a pen which writes so badly that it reacts upon my composition and my spelling. How odd this is! but it is true. I think best when I write. I cannot in the same way think while I speak. Some men are brilliant in conversation, others in public speaking, — others find their minds act best when they have a pen in their hands. But then, if it is a bad pen? a steel pen? that is my case now, and thus I find my pen won't work, much as I wish it.[9]

The following delightful witticism he addressed to his dear friend, Saint-John, who had sprained his wrist and was spending some days vacationing in Switzerland:

> I rejoice... to find that you write so well —but don't presume. You won't be content without some new accident. You forget you are an old man. In one year — (from your volatility, most unsuitable at your time of life) you have broken your ribs and smashed your wrist. This is the only difficulty I have in your going to Lucerne. You will be clambering a mountain, bursting your lungs, cracking your chest, twisting your ankles, and squashing your face — and your nieces will have to pick you up. If you will not do this, I shall rejoice at your going to Lucerne.[10]

His works were generally interrupted in the early afternoon by a

---

[8] W. II, p. 315; Cf. *Ibid.*, p. 527. Letter to his cousin, Emmeline Deane.
[9] W. II, p. 315.
[10] *Ibid.*, p. 320.

walk which was part of Newman's daily ritual. Walking had always been for him the best exercise; alone or accompanied, he strolled through the small woods and little hills in the outskirts of Edgbaston.

At six o'clock, the community reassembled for dinner and the superior took his turn at serving table. After the reading, it was in the Oratorian tradition to invite a debate among the Fathers on dogmatic or moral subjects; casuistic cases of conscience usually found Newman severe in resolving them.

This repast was followed by a time of relaxation in the Victorian drawing room where coffee was served; Newman chatted about anything and everything, recalling his past memories and keeping informed about current events.

In 1864, Rogers and Church offered their former mentor a violin. He played Beethoven and Mozart sonatas with the emotion of his youth and found new joy in their execution. His artistic nature found pleasure in these subtle distractions which continued in their own way the musical tradition of St. Philip Neri. When in need of a change, he retired to the house at Rednal, several miles outside the city, which was purchased by the Oratorians. There, he enjoyed complete rest, taking an interest in the smallest details of gardening.

The death of several friends often cast a shadow on these later years. Keble died in 1866, some time after the visit Newman made to him at Hursley; in 1873, it was Henry Wilberforce, and in 1884, Mark Pattison. With them were gone numerous memories from the Oxford days and of times past. Also, death struck the members of his community, particularly the first companions of the foundation: Fathers Gordon and Caswell and his most intimate and devoted confidant, Ambrose Saint-John, who died in 1875. Miss Giberne, a religious sister, confidant and friend, died in 1885.

This succession of deaths and the resulting solitude seemed only to confirm Newman in the conviction that he was meant to live alone. He wrote to a Dominican nun in her convent at Stone:

> You refer to St. John's age. Yes I often think, can it be God's will that as the beloved disciple outlived all his brethren, I too am to have a portion of that special cross of his.[11]

---

[11] Letter of December 27, 1875, *Ibid.*, II, p. 414. Cf. IV Par., XX, p. 920.

His reflections on death became much more frequent with the numerous deaths which marked his last years. In the midst of his personal papers, there are some notes with various dates where meditations on the ultimate meaning of life are most accentuated.[12] The desire for the supreme vision is expressed in this letter: "But so many of us are getting old, that one is tempted to ask O Lord, how long? How long are we to enjoy that calm and happy time which thou has granted us so long?[13]

Finally, it is the thought of self-abandonment which ends this letter:

> I am in His Hands — And I can but repeat what I found among dear Father Ambrose's morning prayers, "Do with me what Thou wilt; I shall ever be in peace if I live and die in Thy love."[14]

The prospect of death does not interfere with the lucidity of his judgment about the events taking place in the course of time and with the evolution of ideas. He judged events both with wisdom and uncertainty, finding prophetically in them the forthcoming signs of a new humanistic culture more and more detached from God. Almost an octogenarian, he wrote to a lady correspondent:

> But my apprehensions are not new, but above 50 years standing. I have all that time thought that a time of widespread infidelity was coming, and through all those years the waters have in fact been rising as a deluge. I look for the time after my life, when only the tops of the mountains will be seen like islands in the waste of waters.[15]

This image should haunt the old; then, he wrote again:

> When I see an intelligent and thoughtful young man, I tremble as in an agony and fear while thinking of the future. How will he be able to resist the deluge of reason which is growing up against Christianity?[16]

---

[12] The notes found in *Meditations and Devotions*, p. 263 ff., carry three dates 1864, 1876, and 1881. *The Dream of Gerontius,* a long meditation on death and the mysteries of the world beyond is from January 1865.

[13] W. II, p. 388. Letter to Sr. Mary Gabriel, Easter of 1872.

[14] *Ibid.*, letter of December 27, 1875.

[15] *Ibid.*, letter of Mrs. Maskell, January 6, 1877.

[16] *Ibid.*

Newman did everything in his power until the very last years to work against the threat coming from the scientific rationalism which he thought would annihilate the traditional faith of the younger generation. In his book written in 1868, entitled the *Grammar of Assent*, he attempted to reconcile adherence to faith with legitimate claims from reason. This work, the fruit of patient and laborious thinking, had finally unraveled a multitude of thoughts that Newman had been nurturing for a long time. His demonstration seemed to be decisive to many; William Ward himself, in an article in the "Dublin Review," was all praise for his former master, whom he had hurt and betrayed often in the past.

Many letters written around this period are also centered on the problems of faith. In them, Newman was often seeking new ways to reach a more balanced approach in the dialogue between religious thought and the advances of modern science or he was attempting to dissipate the religious doubts or objections of certain of his correspondents.

Here are a few pages from a long letter to a friend, in which Newman tried to help him put aside some doubts and to situate the role of reason in its true place with regard to religious certitude:

> You must begin all thought about religion by mastering what is the fact, that anyhow the question has an inherent ineradicable difficulty in it.... It will come up in one shape or other.... There is a difficulty in believing nothing; an intellectual difficulty. There is a difficulty in doubting; a difficulty in determining there is no truth; in saying that there is truth but that no one can find it out; ... in saying that there is no God; that there is a God but that He has not revealed Himself except in the way of nature; and there is doubtless a difficulty in Christianity. The question is, whether on the whole our reason does not tell us that it is a duty to accept the arguments commonly urged for its truth as sufficient, and a duty in consequence to believe heartily in Scripture and the Church.
>
> Another thought which I wish to put before you is, whether our nature does not tell us that there is something which has more intimate relations with the question of religion than intellectual exercises have, and that is our conscience... the idea of duty, and the terrible anguish of conscience, and the irrepressible distress and confusion of face which the transgression of what we believe to be our duty, causes us, all this an intimation, a clear evidence,

that there is something nearer to religion than intellect; ... We
have to ascertain the starting points for arriving at religious
truth.... To gain religious starting points... we must... interrogate
our hearts, and (since it is a personal individual matter) our own
hearts, — interrogate our own conscience, interrogate, I will say,
the God who dwells there.[17]

Thus, the weight of years did nothing to remove the firmness with
which he had, all his life, denounced the deceits of liberalism. Liberalism
had become scientism and the recent scientific progress was undermining
the very foundations of faith at the same time that biblical exegesis claimed
that it was tolling the death knell of revealed truth. Newman, almost eighty
years old, strongly resisted this new wave of thinking. At a time when
many Catholics did not see any other alternative but to absolutely refuse
to accept a dialogue or to maintain their arbitrary self-constructed systems,
Newman suggested solutions which appeared too bold to some only
because they treated the questions of the day in the context they were
asked. Newman invited theologians not to wall themselves off in their own
narrow-minded systems but to give a new vigor to their ways of thinking,
face to face with the new culture. In particular, he was most anxious to see
Catholics undertake exegetical research that would be capable of dissipating the difficulties raised by the liberal criticism. Having become a
Cardinal, he was emboldened in his projects and spoke of nothing less than
a trip to Rome in order to better inform Leo XIII on this question, so dear
to his heart.

A Catholic biblical exegesis, renewed in its methodology and its
principles of interpretation of the inspired text, seemed to Newman to be
the key to solving the problems raised by the liberal criticism of the day.
Illness alone prevented him from leaving for Rome. But who knows if a
meeting of those two great minds, Leo XIII and Newman, so different in
their origins, so close by culture, equally open to the humanism of the
times, both anxious to establish bridgeheads which could lead eventually
to a Christian synthesis, would not have ended up in the creation of some

---

[17] W. II, p. 330. Letter of June 25, 1869. Is this correspondent William Froude, brother of
Hurrell, with whom Newman had some exchanges? See the book edited by Harper,
Cardinal Newman and William Froude, A Correspondence, 1933.

institute or research center that would have at least allowed the Church to lessen the danger of the approaching modernist crisis?

However, Newman was not going to die without knowing the joys of an ultimate recognition. At a time when he did not expect anything anymore, a series of events reminded him that in spite of his retreat and silence, he remained the most famous Catholic in England, whose name could not be ignored without injustice.

In 1877, his old college, Trinity, conferred upon him the title of Honorary Fellow. Newman returned to see again the familiar surroundings where he had spent his days as a youth. He had submitted his acceptance of the honor to his bishop, Ullathorne, evoking memories of the past in the most moving terms:

> Trinity has been the one and only seat of my affections at Oxford, and to see once more, before I am taken away, what I never thought I should see again, the place where I began the battle of life, with my good Angel by my side, is a prospect almost too much for me to bear.[18]

A few months later, he received the unexpected and unforeseeable news of his elevation to the cardinalate, so moving and thrilling because it was a sensational reparation. Wishing to emphasize the orientation which his pontificate was going to take in the selection of his first Cardinal, Leo XIII gave the "red hat" to the old forsaken priest of Edgbaston. Official and ultimate consecration, even if late, brought serenity to Newman in the last years of his life. It helped him to enter into his own immortality as a solitary and prophetic genius, whom the Christians of his times had so poorly understood, but who would be a guide and a witness for future generations. From that time on, Newman never left his Oratorian retreat. He wrote to his nephew at that time: "Looking beyond this life, my first prayer, aim, and hope is that I may see God."[19]

During these years, he became more impatient at waiting for the "beatific vision," the prospect of which made it even more painful and hard

---

[18] *Ibid.*, letter from December 18, 1877.
[19] *Ibid.*, letter of February 26, 1880 to the son of Mrs. Mozley, his sister who had just died.

for him to bear the trials of this earth. He took refuge in prayer to appease his desire for heaven. A most intimate union was increasingly developing between the Cardinal and his Creator. The final impression he gave to those who witnessed the last stages of his prodigious career was that of a man of prayer; a man penetrated by the sense of God and accustomed to recognizing His presence; and closer than ever to the luminous cloud which always preceded him and attracted him all his life.

Strictly punctual about attending all community spiritual exercises, he even anticipated the sound of the bell which announced the prayer service. Father Neville recalled his attitude during prayer. Nothing conventional nor rigid, he respected the rules: kneeling, getting up. Before the Blessed Sacrament, he generally prayed on his knees, his hand supporting his head, in a spirit of intense recollection. All of his gestures were involved in the silent prayer which he addressed to his Lord. Moreover, he was very attentive to following the rubrics in all the liturgical functions at the altar; it was simply for him the sign of the profound respect that every priest ought to bring to the celebration of the Sacrifice of the Mass. Sometimes, he did not hesitate to make some well intentioned remarks when he observed some carelessness in this regard in one or another of his brothers of the Oratory.

Devotion to the Eucharist was the center of his prayer life. This was, as we know, one of the first discoveries he made at the time of his conversion. The presence of the Lord, in the Sacred Host, was his greatest support in times of trial. He used to pass entire hours before the tabernacle in fervent colloquies.[20]

Again, Father Neville tells us that Newman was very assiduous in his devotion to the Sacred Heart; he spoke of it with love, adding that this devotion had the most powerful attraction for him personally. Very near his own room was a little chapel dedicated to the Sacred Heart which had been built with his own money. It overlooked the Oratory Church, and it

---

[20] W. I, p. 118. One of the first letters written after his conversion expresses this new fervor in his devotion to the Blessed Sacrament. The same in a note in his *Private Journal* of January 8, 1860: "It has made me feel that in the Blessed Sacrament is my great consolation, and that while I have Him who lives in the Church, the separate members of the Church, my Superiors, though they may claim my obedience, have no claim on my admiration." *Autobiographical Writings*, pp. 251-252; Cf. W. I, p. 577.

provided a solitary and silent retreat within the large Oratory house, already so peaceful.

We know also how he spoke of the Mass and how he celebrated it. This "marvelous solemnity" never lost for him its prodigious attraction. The Mass was an action, "the Action" par excellence, where words followed every gesture of the sacrifice; each one of them performed with swiftness and precision. He wrote:

> Words are necessary.... They hurry on as if impatient to fulfil their mission. Quickly they go, the whole is quick... for they are awful words of sacrifice, they are a work too great to delay upon.[21]

Some witnesses have noted the utmost refinement of his gestures at the altar and his way of whispering with his lips, as he pronounced the sacred words.

After having been made a Cardinal, he celebrated Mass in a more familiar setting, on the altar dedicated to St. Francis de Sales, established in a corner of his own room, surrounded on the side walls with numerous memorial cards from his life-long departed friends. In 1889 at Christmastide, he stopped celebrating Mass because of his poor eyesight and physical weakness which did not allow him the mobility needed to say Mass. Nevertheless, he learned by heart the Mass of the Holy Virgin and the Mass for the Dead and he kept repeating the one or the other to himself with the secret hope that one day, he would again be able to say Mass.

During his last days, he also had to put aside the recitation of the breviary, to which he was very attached and which perhaps he never said without thinking about the one who those many years before had made it known to him, Richard Hurrell Froude. He replaced it with the Rosary, which he recited daily, finding in it a new source of fervor and grace. However, his fingers could not assist him any longer and he had to give up this last devotion, seeking refuge more and more in continuous prayer.

---

[21] *Loss and Gain*, pp. 327-328.

CHAPTER XVII

NEWMAN AT PRAYER

I am asking for the gift of prayer, because it will be so sweet.

Med. and Dev., p. 99

ONE WOULD LOVE to know more about the secrets of Newman's interior life and prayer. Ever since the days of Littlemore, when he became acquainted with the *Spiritual Exercises* of Saint Ignatius, the convert had taken up the practice of mental prayer, as outlined by the solitary of Manresa in his "Rules and Annotations." But Newman quickly disengaged himself from too definite a method of prayer and from prayer presented in too rigid a form.

Bremond ventured to say that his hero prayed laboriously, a pen in hand, attentive to detecting in his soul the touches of divine grace. According to him, it was for Newman an indispensable means for battling against the spiritual dryness which invaded him and brought his soul, so unprepared for mystical experience, to the verge of despair. Father Tristram easily deflates this legend, probably grown out of some superficial remarks by Father Neville.[1]

What is true is that Newman, after his mental exercise of prayers, wrote down his most impressive thoughts. He left a copybook with the notes of his first retreat at Littlemore, in which we find his written personal comments following each of the spiritual exercises. In this, he was only following the counsels of St. Ignatius and other spiritual writers. His style

---

[1] See Father Tristram's study: "With Newman at Prayer," in the collection, *Newman Centenary Essays*, p. 116.

is elliptical, voluntarily concise and rapid. He noted his difficulties at collecting his thoughts, and his state of spiritual dryness and absence of fervor, but he also marked out the spiritual fruits which he tasted and the transports he occasionally experienced.

It is probable that in his subsequent meditations, Newman went back to this practice, reminiscent of the heroic times when he went into retreat without any director; perhaps he never really abandoned it entirely; it corresponded so well to his austere and lucid disposition of mind. He accused himself too much of lack of fervor and lack of faith for not submitting himself to this meritorious practice, which also had the advantage of taking certain of his scruples away.

These notes taken by Newman during the exercises were used again by him later. Putting aside too personal a comment, Newman was able to recapture the tempo of his meditations and express them in a more suggestive way. His *Meditations and Devotions*, in particular the section, "Meditations On Christian Doctrine," appear to have been composed in this manner. Gravitating around a central theme, the meditation develops into brief but fervent sentences. There are very intimate conversations with the Lord, like the breath of his own soul, captured in some privileged moments, which express what Father Tristram justly calls the "quintessence" of Newmanian spirituality.[2]

However, such notes remain only an external expression of prayer itself. It is the tempo of the prayer with its transports and its own spiritual pace that we wish to know more about. Does the evidence that Newman himself offers us concerning his prayer allow us to determine its true characteristics? Is it possible for us to trace with some precision the rhythm and nature of Newmanian prayer? The particular question which comes to mind is: can we know if a mystical element is included in the spirituality we are studying? No matter what Newman himself has told us about his life of prayer; do we have the right to exclude all mystical experience? In a sermon from his Anglican period, Newman said: "Before being a privilege, prayer is an obligation for Christians."[3]

---

[2] *Ibid.*, pp. 116-123.
[3] "But, in what I shall now say concerning prayer, I shall not consider it as a privilege, but as a duty; for till we have some experiences of the duties of religion, we are incapable of entering duly into the privilege." I Par., XIX, "Times of Private Prayer," p. 156. Idem, IV Par., XV, "Moral Effects of Communion with God," p. 869.

Effort and self-denial are the preconditions of prayer, and we know that he submitted himself to them. However, he did not seem to have experienced the favors and consolations which are the privilege of certain souls, at least not frequently. In several instances, Newman had to admit his own difficulties and even his distress. His retreat notes are full of such laments. And how significant! The most revealing document for our subject is the "Confession at St. Eusebius."[4] It was written in Latin on seven pages of a copybook, from April 8 to April 17, 1847 at the convent of St. Eusebius in Rome, several weeks before his ordination to major orders. They contain the most rigorous analysis that Newman would ever make on his interior life. Certain admissions, motivated by circumstances, show well enough that the soul is in a period of expectancy and uncertainty in the days following his conversion when he was on the brink of having to make a decisive choice. But the interesting part of this confession is not limited to the events in his life which have provoked it. His total spiritual experience is revealed here in this text of astonishing depth. The soul of Newman surrenders itself with its insights, its withdrawals, its impulses, and its doubts.

The dominant impression that emerges appears to be the maturity of a religious conscience which has reached an adult stage of development. The vision of the convert lingers for one last time on the past in order to contrast it with the present. The soul perceives a sort of collapse of a whole side of itself; it no longer has the enthusiasm and the spontaneity of former days.[5] Something is gone forever. It is aware that a stage of its history is now passed and that it can never go back to it. In this sort of strict spiritual accounting, Newman's soul appears to have submitted to a certain moral and spiritual discipline which was the result of many habits and many experiences; it is to juvenile enthusiasm what adulthood is to youth. As Saint Paul said: "When I was a child I spoke as a child."[6]

Conversion, indeed, brought a radical change in Newman's life.

---

[4] *Autobiog.*, "Confession at St. Eusebius," pp. 239-248.
[5] *Ibid.*, pp. 247-248. "When I was growing up, and as a young man, I had confidence and hope in God, i.e., I committed myself without anxiety to His Providence.... And now the cheerfulness I used to have has almost vanished. And I feel acutely that I am no longer young, but that my best years are spent, and I am sad at the thought of the years that have gone by, and I see myself to be fit for nothing, a useless log."
[6] 1 Cor 13:11.

Henceforth, a certain sense of stability fixed his soul in a clearly defined situation in which his destiny was able to fulfill itself. Corresponding to this stage in his destiny, there was also the stage in his interior life. It is not that his soul had reached perfection or terminated its journey but it was to develop and achieve its perfection within a new framework.

In particular, Newman's soul seemed to have lost all its fervor which so far had protected his spiritual life and assured it of its rhythm. Newman no longer felt the consolation of a heart that was satisfied with its renouncements and sacrifices. How much easier was the practice of virtue when the soul was transported by the powerful tides of promises not yet fulfilled. It was a time of spiritual progress with a touch of fervor and heroism.[7] But those days were gone. The ardent youth carried away by faith and love had been replaced by an inglorious and uneventful maturity. The soul believed it was dragging along the painful road of mediocrity. It had not given up its responsibilities nor betrayed its promises, but in its fidelity, it risked hardening itself in a narrow conformity.[8] There are none of those desires or longings which warm the heart and console it in failures! The soul knew only how to control its forces; the will remained entirely submitted to God to fulfill its duty, but it no longer had the zeal to carefully carry out every detail.

This lack of spiritual energy had a direct impact on the disposition of his spirit, which became afraid of initiatives, was withdrawn, and cared only for peaceful reflection and for the calm possession of truth which satisfied it.[9]

---

[7] *Autobiog.*, p. 247. The quote continues: "I had the greatest faith in the efficacy of prayer, in all adversity I used to say calmly that He would deliver me and mine in His own good time. I encouraged others, and was active and joyful." *Ibid.*, p. 247: In contrast with the piety of childhood, the present difficulty stands out: "Further, I have not that practical, lively and present faith against the persistent working and wiles of the evil spirit in my heart, which I ought to have."

[8] *Ibid.* "Although I have the fixed habit of referring all things to the will of God; and a desire to do His will, and although in practice I really observe this principle in greater matters, yet I do not in practice seek His will in lesser things. And even in those greater matters, although I have often prayed earnestly to do His will, yet my actions have proceeded rather from a conscientiousness which forbade me to act otherwise, from a sense of correctness, from perceiving what became me, in doing which I should be consistent, than from faith and charity."

[9] *Ibid.*, p. 246. "In almost everything I like my own way of acting; I do not want to change the place or business in which I find myself, to undertake the affairs of others,

Prayer seemed most affected by such coldness. It was like a paralysis which seemed to prevent any elevation of the soul. Yet, it was still attracted by the invisible world where Newman's awareness of God's Presence was most felt.[10] But this Presence was experienced less by the heart than it was acknowledged by faith.

Prayer had become a labor, clouded over by listlessness, languor, and powerlessness. It was invaded by all sorts of distractions and the soul no longer succeeded in overcoming them. It had the impression of crawling and dragging itself at a time when it wished so much to fly. Such aridity hurt the soul and it did not know how to overcome it. This feeling of spiritual dryness provoked laments and scruples in Newman:

> But further still; it is difficult to explain and stranger even to myself, but I have this peculiarity, that in the movement of my affections, whether sacred or human, my physical strength cannot go beyond certain limits. I am always languid in the contemplation of divine things, like a man walking with his feet bound together. I am held as it were by a fetter, by a sort of physical law, so I cannot be forcible in preaching and speaking, nor fervent in praying and meditating. This besides, I can never keep my mind fixed and intent on the subject proposed for meditation, nor on the words of the daily office. My mind wanders unceasingly; my head aches if I endeavor to concentrate upon a single subject.[11]

This last text leaves no doubt concerning the profound difficulties which Newman experienced in prayer. His analysis, it is well to recall, pertained not only to the days following his conversion but defined a law that is constant in Newmanian prayer. It should not be forgotten that at the period when Newman was writing his "Confession," his spirituality was

---

since I prefer to remain at home. I am querulous, timid, lazy, suspicious; I crawl along the ground; feeble, downcast and despondent." In the same sense, he confessed a little earlier: "I like tranquility, security, a life among friends, and among books, untroubled by business."

[10] *Ibid.*, p. 247. After having recalled the old danger of intellectualism back to the time of his first years of study, he remarks: "I have not lost either my intimate sense of the Divine Presence in every place, nor the good conscience and the peace of mind that flows therefrom.... That subtle and delicate vigour of faith has become dulled in me, and remains so to this day."

[11] *Ibid.*, pp. 247-248. This text ends the "Confession at St. Eusebius."

already determined; he had enough experience of the ways of prayer to be able to discern its different characters and most intimate contours. If after his conversion he confessed his powerlessness, it was only because he had experienced such a humiliating state for a long time, perhaps forever.

This difficult situation arose from two basic dispositions: one was the absence of fervor; the other was the lack of concentration in meditation. Such difficulties, which might generate a habitual state of indifference, were caused much more by Newman's own character than his own will. By nature, Newman rebelled against any stimulation of a sentimental nature so the absence of fervor would not have alarmed him, but another problem came on top of the first one: the lack of concentration of his mind in prayer. Here, above all, was the source of his anxieties.

Some other confessions show us that this painful state did not stop with the feelings of his own powerlessness. His feeling of being unable to pray came from a much deeper source and produced a true feeling of desolation in his soul. This special difficulty in prayer is easy to identify in several of the letters Newman addressed to some of his most distressed and anxious friends. These letters of spiritual direction show that their author is not unaware of some of the difficulties and anxieties which he sought to allay. Thus, he wrote to a correspondent, Miss Holmes:

> As time goes, you will know yourself better and better. Time does that for us, not only by the increase of experience, but by the withdrawal of those natural assistances to devotion and self-surrender which youth furnishes.... Then the soul is left to the lassitude, torpor, dejection and coldness which is its real state, with no natural impulses, affections, or imaginations to rouse it, and things which in youth seemed easy then become difficult.... Then it understands at length its own nothingness; not that it has less grace than it had, but it has nothing but grace to aid it.[12]

The difficulties revealed in this letter are of another nature than the ones found in the "Confession at St. Eusebius." In the "Confession at St. Eusebius," we learn of a sadness which filled a soul eager to rise above its languor and to put aside its distractions. Newman tells us that this desolation is different. It resides in the feeling of a certain sense of

---

[12] W. II, p. 326 ff. Letter of July 1850. See other letters, *Ibid.*

dereliction which deprives the soul not so much of its emotional support, but of its appreciation of God's free gift of grace. The soul then finds itself established in a state of pure faith, with a disposition of humility and a sense of utter abandonment.

This state, which Newman's soul experienced for many years, is well known among spiritual writers who designate it under the name of "aridity." It consists of a feeling of being deprived of all light of a supernatural order which thus marks the entrance of a soul into the "dark night of senses," of which St. John of the Cross speaks in his second book, *The Ascent to Mount Carmel*. It is precisely this kind of "aridity" which seems to characterize the prayer of Newman. And we have no indication that he was able to move from that stage and reach a higher level of mystical experience.

However, such a state, in spite of the aridity into which the human faculties are enveloped, is not a state which entirely binds the soul; it can be reconciled with another disposition by which the soul is invaded and reassured by the peaceful certitude of the Presence of God. St. John of the Cross has shown clearly how this calm possession of God can be found in the "night of the senses" despite the soul's state of desolation and dryness.[13]

This spiritual experience produced by a "consciousness of God that is pervasive and affectionate" we find in the soul of Newman at the same moment when it complains of its powerlessness. This recourse to pure faith is noticeable in his letter to Miss Holmes. But already in the "Confession at St. Eusebius," the convert had very firmly recognized in himself the persistent sense of the Presence of God. Recalling those distant times when he first experienced his doubts, he wrote:

> I lost my natural and inborn faith, so that now I am much afraid of the priesthood, lest I should behave without due reverence in something so sacred; then too I have lost my simple confidence

---

[13] *Ascent of Mount Carmel*, II, Chapter XIII, p. 258. St. John of the Cross, that great Spiritual Doctor of the Church, examines here the signs of infused prayer: "The third sign, which is the most certain of all, occurs when the soul is pleased to dwell alone in the depth of its being, to lovingly give its attention to God, without occupying itself with any particular consideration.... It is then that the soul is penetrated with a knowledge of God, broad and affectionate without conceiving anything in particular."

in the word of God.... But I have not lost either my intimate sense
of the Divine Presence in every place, nor the good conscience,
and the peace of mind that flows therefrom, but I no longer
thought, or at any rate much less than formerly, that the habit of
prayer was not only a prescribed duty but also a great talent and
privilege, by which we can do all things. That subtle and delicate
vigour of faith has become dulled in me, and remains so to this
day.[14]

A sentiment such as this authorizes us to speak about a mystical
element in the spirituality of the Cardinal. Newman did not likely experience the supreme joys of a soul who sees itself elevated to the highest state
of the spiritual life, but that is not to say that he never found himself on his
way to Pure Love. It is arbitrary to reduce, as it is done too often, mystical
life to a certain exceptional type of religious experience. This betrays a lack
of understanding of a religious phenomenon which is quite common
among souls who are honestly in search of God. Indeed there are souls
who, without experiencing the highest graces of a transforming union,
have nonetheless, at particular times, been penetrated by a deep inner
feeling and have been inspired by motions of Divine grace, neither
announced nor called for. Such motions do not exclude at all a state of
spiritual desolation, but the interior peace which accompanies them or
follows them leaves no doubt about their nature and origin.

Such appears to us to be the mystical gift in Newman's soul. He
probably never asked himself the question of whether he had such a gift.
Obviously, he never spoke about it. He would have been too fearful of
deceiving himself, or of appearing presumptuous. But his testimony does
not absolutely prevent us from attributing a character of authentic mysticism to his prayer.

It remains that such a grace was to be very exceptional in his life. It
prevented neither one of the difficulties mentioned above. Yet, Newman
had a profound peace and found a new burst of confidence and abandonment to the will of God, which helped him to rise above his most secret and
silent difficulties.

We should not be surprised then to find in his *Meditations and
Devotions* a frequent echo of these sufferings. Newman expressed his

---

[14] *Ibid.*, p. 247. "Confession at St. Eusebius."

miseries more than he exalted the spiritual gifts he received. It is our task to detect the profound rhythm which animated his prayer and to recognize its source. He asked his dear Lord for the gift which would sweeten his prayer. It was both his weakness and his grandeur. He admitted that his prayer dragged itself along pitifully, without any fervor or enthusiasm. This man, who had such a sharp consciousness of the realities of the world beyond, was stopped at the very threshold of that world of which he was a witness among men. Between knowledge and prayer, there is an abyss and Newman was unable to fill that gap without help from on high. As the years went by and the invisible world somehow became more real to his spirit, he more and more felt an intense need of entering into its mystery through his prayer. Already, some friendly voices called him and the luminous clouds came closer; already, his eyes were eager for the vision and his heart was anticipating the supreme encounter. But such a desire is vain without the grace of God. It belongs to the Creator to make Himself known and to give Himself. Newman knew he was powerless without Divine assistance. It is the reason why the prayer wherein he found his refuge is above all a confession of humility; he confessed his difficulties and his dryness. After having once recognized in his prayer this source, so truly mystical, it is much easier to appreciate the real worth of certain of his complaints in his meditation. Far from seeing in them a hopeless complacency and lack of fervor, we recognize an admission of weakness and powerlessness and both a call and recourse to the grace of God. Finally, in this authentic spiritual soul, the last word belongs to humility and surrender to God. This is the true meaning of his prayer in *Meditations and Devotions*:

> Take me out of the languor, the irritability, the sensitiveness, the incapability, the anarchy, in which my soul lies, and fill it with Thy fullness. In asking for fervour, I am asking for effectual strength, consistency, and perseverance. I am asking for the gift of prayer, because it will be so sweet; ... In asking for fervour, I am asking for that which, while it implies all gifts, is that which I signally fail. Nothing would be a trouble to me, nothing a difficulty, had I but fervour of soul.[15]

---

[15] *Med. and Dev.*, p. 99.

This admirable prayer extends over two pages. Nowhere else do we discover Newman so intimate and so simple; at the same time, we see the profound distress which discouraged him at certain times.

God awaited Newman's act of supreme humiliation of the self which recognized its own nothingness. *The soul understands at length its own nothingness.* It was the ultimate surrender of the soul finally purified. The grace of the Savior Lord, which illuminated and comforted him revealed to him the fulfillment of his destiny and vocation. The "narrow way" led to clarity and this "kindly light" transfigured the pilgrim's way during which he never committed a sin against it. *Angels are among us.* Never has the tremor coming from the invisible world been more intense than on that evening of August 11, 1890 when the soul of the great Newman was delivered into the hands of his Creator at the end of his earthly pilgrimage.

CHAPTER XVIII

CONCLUSION

Ex umbris et imaginibus ad veritatem.
[From shadows and fantasies to truth]

*I*T IS IMPOSSIBLE TO understand anything of Newman's history if the spiritual drama that he lived is not given primary importance. This drama goes far beyond the crisis of the conversion of 1816 or the other crisis of 1845. It filled the whole of his life since the day when the soul of the young boy acquired "his first religious convictions" until the day when his soul arrived at "a conscious communion with the Invisible."[1]

His birth and education had given this son of a city banker a delicate and upright conscience, aiming at an uncommon ideal of rectitude and integrity. However, his childhood, which was entirely confined within the narrow limits of moral duty, hardly showed any religious inclination. In reading the Bible and learning the Anglican catechism, John Henry was obviously submitting to good family tradition more than he was establishing a personal relationship of faith and love of God. Moreover, his spirit was of such a nature that it was quite unprotected against both the doubts of philosophers and the fantasies of superstition: the adolescent read Hume and Voltaire, but was afraid of the night and its mysteries. And then, one very special day, the grace of conversion illumined this undecided soul. His conscience, which had been limited to a strict moralism, discovered a new horizon whose dimension he was unable to size up. It was no longer

---

[1] It is the wish expressed by the hero of the celebrated *Dream of Gerontius*, written by Newman in 1865.

just a matter of faithful obedience to a strict moral code but a loving submission to an interior Master. Henceforth, he turned less to moral values as a guide to rule his conduct than to listening to the One in Whom the supreme harmony of moral values is achieved.

Thus, the conversion of 1816, in spite of persistent traces of Evangelicalism, freed Newman from sheer moralism in order to introduce him into a more religious way of life. This new approach brought the young Anglican of yesterday, through a uniform yet "gentle pressure,"[2] to a very pure and detached spiritual life which found in the invisible world the object of its contemplation, and in the practice of abandonment its most effective tool.

The interior evolution of Newman's soul was contained between these two boundaries: the moral austerity which characterized his youth and the self-surrender to God in his Oratorian years. We have sought to reconstitute the main lines of this evolution which led him from the haze of English Puritanism to the appeasing light of the spirituality of St. Philip Neri. There is nothing arbitrary in this evolution; it follows a law of continuity which we have to spell out distinctly.

Let us be clear on this point. If one considers only the religious changes revealed in Newman's autobiography, one is tempted to see in those changes a sort of instability, as if Newman were unable to remain for any length of time in a single place. His spiritual nature, rejecting any set of rules or any systematic doctrine, would have little by little bypassed all religious systems, forgetting what he owed to them and denying his own origins. Resenting the frustration of a conscience in waiting, Newman would have finally come to despise the very values which had temporarily attracted him. Thus, the successive conversions of Newman would be seen as resulting from strong affective undercurrents, entirely dominated by a complex instinct that the modern psychologists have denounced under the name of resentment.[3]

---

[2] In the *Dream of Gerontius*.

[3] It is Max Scheler who developed this theme of "resentment" already sketched out in the religious critique of Nietzsche. It is not Scheler, however, who applied this thesis of resentment to Newman; he was his admirer and disciple. We have only to group here diverse interpretations of Newman's spiritual doctrine which blend this theme of resentment. For a study of Scheler's philosophy, see *Mélanges Théologiques* of R.P. de Montcheuil, S.J., "Ressentiment dans la vie morale et religieuse," pp. 187-225.

Thus, to the legend about the "solitary soul at Edgbaston," another would be added which would make of him "a man of resentment." Were not his character and life the best proofs to support such an hypothesis? His strong emotions represented an enormous potential for the hidden buildup of unconscious anger. His complex sensitivity was always torn between the attraction of a religious ideal and the seduction of human affections.

The element of chance in his life allowed him to encounter some very distinctive types of religious personalities, from the obscure and poor Mayers to the successful and obstructive Manning. A variety of calls and influences surged and contradicted themselves in this life which knew so many disappointments. In brief, weren't all the required conditions present to make of Newman the perfect victim of religious "resentment"? If he abandoned the deism he discovered in his early readings, wasn't it because of his irritation with a certain form of rationalism which eliminated a sense of moral responsibility? If much later he rejected Evangelicalism, wasn't it due to his inability to experience the passionate fervor of a true conversion? If his fidelity to Anglicanism collapsed, wasn't it because the leader of the Oxford Movement failed in his attempt to reform the Established Church? And finally as a Catholic, if he did not leave the Church of his choice, wasn't it because he was unable to deny it without simultaneously denying his own spiritual destiny?[4]

There is no point in pausing here for a lengthy discussion of Newman's religious evolution. If the hypothesis were true, that Newman was a man of resentment, the Cardinal would not have been haunted by the invisible world, which we have recognized on every page of his history. Unhappy and unstable, say his critics, he would have been resigned to the failures in his life among the ruins of various Christian confessions, and he would have been equally incapable of satisfying in any way his desires and of fulfilling his spiritual ambitions.

Absolutely nothing in the life and writings of John Henry Newman authorizes us to label him "a man of resentment." Indeed, he possessed a

---

[4] In hardly veiled terms, here is what the Anglican author, Cross, insinuates in an effort to explain the conversion of 1845: "Incapable of finding victory where he sought it, he contented himself with a pseudo-victory" (Cross, *John Henry Newman*). As for Faber, the author of the *Oxford Apostles*, he interprets Newman's religious changes like an historian influenced by psychoanalytical theories, as if the study of the religious personality were only limited to the reading of the subconscious!

certain sensitivity which often submitted with difficulty to external constraints and which provoked painful reactions within him that were difficult to control: there is the dramatic confession in Sicily in which he expressed a distress that is so baffling to us; there are the letters to Keble, where the analysis of his conscience often becomes irritating by an excess of precision and rigor; and there is, above all, his *Private Journal*, an account of his most somber days out of which flow, like burning lava, complaints and sighs. But would Newman's genius have been greater had he not known the ups and downs of such a delicate and sensitive nature? Should his influence be less effective because he did not find the proper balance in his earliest years and experienced moments of distress and confusion?

We ought to accept Newman as he is, with his joys and his painful questions. He was too sincere to give an image of himself which was not his. In fact, spiritual masters of his caliber do not have to look for excuses and apologies. They only have to be. They express themselves the way they are in order to open the door to those who from far behind take up their message and follow their lessons. Cardinal Newman was a man with the highest spiritual ambition, which is sanctity. That holiness which he was seeking to realize in himself, he was anxious to discover in the religious confessions offered to him, not only in their doctrines but among the men and women who espoused them. His soul, so thirsty for an absolute truth, was attracted by the various creeds offered to him. At first, he wanted to persuade himself that they were true. "Beggars are not choosers," he wrote at the close of a debate about the sincerity of his conversion. He had begged for perfection in each of his conversions. Thus, he was exposed to deep disappointments when doctrines were weak and men mediocre. The real drama inherent in his life, as in the lives of exceptional characters, was to resign himself to accept the wounds unavoidably caused by outmoded institutions and the mediocrity of men. The unity of Newman's life was not altered by the disappointments and trials he had to surmount. The conviction that he had a mission to fulfill assured Newman of continuity in his destiny. Against such a conviction, adversities are nothing. They can only stimulate and confirm the conscience in its own fidelity.

This fidelity to a mission received from God is never seen in timorous spirits. In overanxious souls, the gift is paralyzed by anxiety which prevents the soul from clearly seeing the mission it had accepted. When a religious life limits itself to a strict obedience to the law, the moral conscience is reassured but it never reaches the point where it forgets itself and opens itself freely to a more intimate association with God. Indeed, the studious pupil of Ealing, who expressed a preference for virtue and an aversion for piety, knew about such a risk before his conversion. But the conversion of 1816 came right on time to upset all of this unformulated Kantism. To the young adolescent, it revealed the presence of a living God who called him, who invited him to know Him and to love Him, and who revealed to him his mission. Henceforth, it was with a heart filled with generosity that the young convert was able to determine the conditions of his fidelity to God: *"Ama et fac quod vis."* [Love and do what you will.]

In order to succeed in the mission to which he knew himself called, Newman had to accept the demands of a fidelity which called for a greater detachment of the self. The greatest detachment of all, the most necessary and the most crucifying, is the denial of self. The great laws of Newmanian "surrender" are these: no self-complacency ever; allow God to work within the self at the same time that He specifies the way to follow; master one's own heart and empty it of every desire and ambition to be totally available; be indifferent to the judgment of men to be attentive to the judgment of God; always preserve peace, in spite of agitations of a heart which groans under the blow of events; do not fear the long delays imposed by the Lord, and stay without moving for a long time on a road where there is only silence and desolation; and move ahead only when called, without any certainty that the signs are clearly understood. Thus, filial abandonment is the key to the spirituality of Cardinal Newman.

What validates such a spirituality is that it is experienced in a life before it is defined as a rule of life. Events themselves led Newman to understand fully that man is not able to be open to God totally without renouncing himself. His illness in Sicily had been the first providential occasion which enabled him to grasp all that was at stake in this spiritual combat. But subsequently, he had to accomplish the slow and laborious denial of self, day after day. Never was such evidence clearer than during the years preceding his conversion of 1845. Never was it more cruel save perhaps during the course of those years in the eighteen sixties, which were years of dereliction and detachment for him. All of Newman's thought draws its truth and its comprehensiveness from the depth of his own spiritual experience. If Newman is a philosopher and a theologian, an orator and a historian, it is only because he is first a spiritual man, a man of God, for whom the only thing that matters is dialogue with the Creator.

If the message remains so genuine, it is because, like St. Augustine, he expresses the eternal truth of man through the singularity of his own personal destiny.

In a sermon of 1831, the preacher at St. Mary's in Oxford recalled the mysterious influence which is exercised by lives hidden and buried in God:

> For they (faithful servants) had lived in contemplation and prayer, while others praise the goodly stones and buildings of the external Temple, have heard from Him in secret how the end shall be. Thus they live and when they die, the world knows nothing of its loss, and soon lets slip what it might have retained of their history; but the Church of Christ does what she can gathering together relics, and honouring their name, even when their works cannot be found.[5]

Newman could not be more to the point. Did he ever think that his own words might apply to himself? He did not fall into a sacrilegious oblivion. His memory and his works have not followed him into the grave. The cult which has surrounded his memory has given to him this survival which is all the more remarkable since the Oratorian of Birmingham was an exception among the men of his own time.

Our generation seems to be unappreciative with regard to the contributions of some of the most prominent teachers and popular witnesses of the religious history of the nineteenth century. Probably because they were too involved in the battles and controversies of a Church too often forced into a defensive position, their doctrine remained too dependent on the passing events of their day. Who still dares to feed himself spiritually on the eloquence of a Lacordaire or on the sibylline prophecies of some popular person of that age? But the religious heritage of Newman remains intact. His message is still applicable today. Why? Because he had enough vision to bypass the events of his own time in order to point out the way in which the Church of today would recognize itself.

The efforts made by Christian institutions during the last three or

---

[5] II Par., I, p. 11, "The World's Benefactors." Newman develops here the theme of sanctity as hidden from the eyes of the world.

four decades to renew Christian life have been tremendous. There is not one single area in which Newman did not act as a precursor and a guide.

We wish only to emphasize here that the Newmanian spirit of self surrender to God has much to offer the men and women of our time. Newman, as a witness to the realities of the invisible world, as a person totally committed to prayer and an interior life, and as a voice encouraging Christians to accept risks, can teach us the true meaning of life and of human efforts. Our century has increased beyond reasonable proportions man's temptation to annex and master the whole universe.

Newman challenges the selfish conquests of reason and science. He reminds all of us that science is vain and that the triumph of technology is an illusion if human beings are not haunted by preoccupations of a much higher order. Reason and will are doomed to failure if people, in their impatience to break free from their bonds, are not willing to open themselves to certitudes other than those of their own calculations and enterprises. Prometheus remains chained even when he believes himself to have broken the ring of his servitude. *"Ex umbris et imaginibus ad veritatem"* [From shadows and fantasies to truth]. This inscription which Newman wished to have engraved in the little cloister yard at Edgbaston reminds us that there is never any other issue for man than that of preparing for his encounter with God; he never stops discovering Him; he is made in His own image and likeness and he belongs forever to His kingdom.

EVANGELICALISM

Origin and Development

In the religious history of England during the eighteenth century, the Evangelical movement spread in its own way only to be absorbed by the much more powerful Methodists. The origin of Evangelicalism can be found in the need for reform felt by several members of the Anglican clergy, anxious to put an end to the moral and religious crisis which was affecting persons from every class of society during the course of the century. The first Evangelicals: Hervey, Grishaw, Beveridge, and the well-known John Newton aspired to recover the spirit of the Gospel. Their preaching was directed, above all, to the poorer classes living on the outskirts of the overpopulated cities who were just beginning to feel the effects of the industrial revolution. But these scattered little groups were quickly dominated everywhere by the contagious preaching of John Wesley, the passionate advocate of "new birth." They soon modeled themselves closely on Wesley and his disciples, called Methodists. However, they differed from the Methodists on two essential points.

On the one hand, the Evangelicals had a repugnance with regard to maintaining the too extreme thesis of Whitefield, the most fanatical of the Wesleyans, who taught a staunch Calvinism. For example, they rejected the unmerciful logic of Calvin in his doctrine of predestination.

On the other hand, they denied themselves any right of jurisdiction in every territory where they had not received a mandate from the authority of the Anglican hierarchy. It is known that Wesley considered the "whole world" as his parish and did not hesitate to bypass bishops' jurisdictions to interfere in the life of their dioceses. It was precisely such an attitude of non-conformism which determined the rupture of the reformer from the Established Church and finalized the separation of the Methodists. On the contrary, the Evangelicals wished to affirm their respect for the various jurisdictions within the Church. Their loyalty to their bishops was never in question.

With the death of Wesley (1791), though, and above all with the consummation of the schism between Methodism and the Anglican Church, Evangelicalism reasserted its autonomy and evolved according to its own laws, clearly distinct from the prevalent Arminian current which continued Wesley's doctrines, and from the *Confession of Lady Huntingdon*, which reflected a faithful attachment to Whitefield's theories.[1]

A Religious Profile of Evangelicalism

Various streams of thought at the heart of Evangelicalism make it difficult to identify its nature clearly. As the name itself indicates, the claim of the first Evangelicals was to recover the purity of Christian life by a return to the spirit of the Gospel. In fact, their religion identifies itself with a very pragmatic moralism in which three dominant traits can be recognized.

First, a doctrinal ambiguity. The Evangelical never knew how to choose between conflicting theses at the heart of Methodism, oscillating between the extremism of Whitefield and the more pragmatic doctrine of John Wesley. From the first, rigid Calvinism was directly conducive to antinomianism, a doctrine according to which the elect, assured of salvation, are freed from any moral obligation and from the practice of good works. Faith alone is necessary to salvation. By contrast, Wesley repudiated a system which could prevent the soul from abandoning itself to the love of God in a true conversion. His thought was closer to the Arminian doctrine which insists on the necessity of good works: after the "new birth," the convert ought to manifest the truth of his conversion through the austerity of his life and the practice of good works.

---

[1] On this history of Evangelicalism, see Wakeman: *History of the Church of England*, p. 437 ff.; Elie Halévy: *Histoire du peuple Anglais au XIX siècle*, t. I, p. 409; the article on Evangelicals, in the *Dictionary of the Church of England*, p. 331.

Between these two conflicting tendencies, the Evangelicals never knew what to choose for themselves. Their teaching encouraged both, without seeking to resolve the contradiction.

Romaine, whom Newman read,[2] was inclined to accept Calvin's doctrine of predestination; Thomas Scott, suspicious of antinomianism, was even accused of professing the heretical doctrine of the Arminians. All Evangelicals, nevertheless, admitted the two major theses in the system of Calvin: the radical corruption of human nature and the unique value of the merits of Christ. In practice, their preaching stressed the sweet assurance of God's love, which finds itself expressed in the Cross of Christ. These verses of Toplady (1778) are an example: "Nothing in my hand I bring, Simply to Thy cross I cling."

This sort of doctrinal syncretism which allowed the Evangelicals to subscribe to the Thirty-Nine Articles of the Anglican Church was crowned by an austere moralism. In this, they followed John Wesley, who was anxious to lead his followers to conversion and moral progress. Newman has emphasized in the *Apologia*[3] the influence of Thomas Scott, whose maxims were so familiar to him: "Holiness rather than peace"; "Growth is the sign of life."

Evangelicalism had trained generations of pious souls eager to pursue perfection. The first preachers became known for the sanctity of their life, a reputation which was carried on by several writers of the next generation. Passionately zealous, they multiplied conversions and were responsible for moral reforms which reached into their parishes, families, and even the social order.

The foundation of the Clapham sect clearly reveals at the beginning of the nineteenth century, the attraction of an Evangelical moralism for an elite among the lay people: they adopted a strict observance of Sunday, a perfect loyalty in business, and they gave up all mundane pleasures, such as card playing, the theater, and dancing. Therefore, it is not deniable that moral principles of Evangelicalism had a very real influence in the course of the century. It started first by stressing the necessity of conversion. Evangelicals had kept this essential theme of Wesley's teachings. Well known is the story of the "grand old man" who experienced through the

---

[2] *Apologia*, p. 16.
[3] *Ibid.*, p. 17.

illumination of his "new birth" a very strong conviction that he was elected by God. Wesley would never separate an "experience" of this kind from the obligation to give testimony of the sincerity of one's conversion through the practice of good works. We know that several of his disciples broke away from this wise position, retaining the sufficiency of the subjective and transitory aspect of conversion for salvation. Some Methodists went as far as to deny the necessity of baptism; the "new birth" consequently became the main topic in their preaching, and it is not surprising to see the development at the end of the eighteenth century of a veritable organization of mass conversions.[4]

True Evangelicals avoided such excesses. For them, conversion was a much more discreet affair and the result of personal rather than collective fervor; the accent was put much more on the will than on the heart. The soul had done nothing if it had not taken into account its own misery; it was the essential requirement to discover the appeasing presence of Christ whose merits fill the conscience and bring to the soul the assurance of its conversion. In his *Autobiographical Memoirs*, Newman retraced the different stages of conversion: conviction of sin, terror, despair, news of free and full salvation, apprehension of Christ, sense of pardon, assurance of salvation, joy and peace, and so on to final perseverance.[5]

If Evangelical conversion is not as spectacular as the "Penitents' Dock," nevertheless, it leads to the same danger of a moral quietism. However, if men like Thomas Scott and Walter Mayers embraced Evangelicalism, it was because at a time when religious practices were at a low point, it was the only refuge[6] within the Established Church for them.

Taking advantage of the popularity of Methodism, Evangelicalism penetrated deep into the working classes. Soon, it extended its influence over the Established Church, thanks to the prestige of John Newton, friend of sinners and spiritual director, and thanks, too, to the success of Thomas Scott's works, whose *The Force of Truth* (1779) and *Commentaries on the Bible*, formed generations of clergymen. The poetry of Cowper and of Toplady, competing with the hymns of Charles Wesley, conquered the intellectual elite.

---

[4] Swarts, *Salut par la foi et conversion brusque*, p. 146 ff.
[5] *Autobiog.*, p. 80.
[6] K., p. 112 ff.

Another worthy achievement of Evangelicalism, perhaps its greatest, was to revive the missionary spirit at the beginning of the nineteenth century in an England that was negligent of its duty with regard to the conquered and colonized nations. Since 1784, when the first missionary bishop was consecrated, Evangelicalism was identified with the cause of missions abroad for several decades.

The name of William Wilberforce became famous in the campaign for the abolition of slavery. He was the father of Samuel, future bishop of Oxford, and Henry, intimate friend of Newman. In the meantime, the group of Clapham courageously devoted much effort to philanthropic endeavors, which were more generous than enlightened to tell the truth.[7]

However, in spite of these efforts, the final failure of Evangelicalism was predictable by reason of its doctrinal shortcomings and its inability to impose some authority over the Church. In the nineteenth century, the movement was not successful in giving great men to the Church. In spite of the powerful seeds of moralism it introduced among its adepts, it was incapable of carrying out profound reforms in society. At the time of Newman, Evangelicalism defined itself above all by its declared hostility to "Romanism." Its preaching was affected by this cant, a sort of edifying rhetoric that Hawkins, one of the Noetics of Oriel, denounced in the early stages of Newman's career.[8] The Evangelical movement moved closer to Methodism in order to combat the Tractarians, whose influence it feared and whose Catholic orientation it condemned.

[7] See the study by Rogers, "Anglican Background," in *A Tribute to Newman*, pp. 1-26.
[8] *Autobiog.*, pp. 73-79.

THE SPIRITUALITY OF THE OXFORD MOVEMENT

*T*HE HISTORIANS of the Oxford Movement have not yet outlined its ascetical trend, and an appropriate study of its spirituality is yet to be carried out.

For the most part, the monographs, no matter what opinion is expressed by the writer, limit themselves to the doctrinal or liturgical revival and do not go further. Indeed, the religious sources which produced this renewal and prepared its evolution are mentioned but they do not show the nature of the spirit that inspired the reform of the Church in the hearts of its promoters, nor in what direction it engaged its disciples.

Among the books which emerged from an abundant literary production, let us single out the excellent study by Brilioth, *The Anglican Revival: Studies in the Oxford Movement*, (Longmans, 1925). Brilioth was a Swedish Lutheran who sought to define the social and religious causes of this historical phenomenon which constitutes the Oxford Movement.

The author detects both the influence of the Wesleyan Movement and more especially, that of Evangelicalism. He sees in Newman the man who inspired the revival which expands the moral and ascetic tradition begun by Wesley in the preceding century.[1]

The arguments cited by Brilioth do not seem decisive: the analogy between the moral reform initiated by the Methodists and the one which inspired the Tractarian preaching, the historian concludes, reveals the close relationship between the two. This is not the place for us to discuss every claim made by Brilioth, but let us note the following:

---

[1] Brilioth, *op. cit.*, p. 6 (note), p. 211: This was a religious revival, very close to Evangelicalism which it continued and reshaped.

1. It would appear strange that the leaders of the Movement intended to continue the religious reform of Wesley. Indeed, Newman had long since detached himself from Evangelicalism, and Froude, Keble, and Pusey had scarcely any sympathy whatsoever for Wesleyan non-conformism.

2. The moral and ascetic preaching of the Tractarians can readily be explained by their biblical and patristic inspiration.

3. The attitude of Newman himself during the course of the Movement was one of severity towards the dissidents. He refused to perform a marriage ceremony for a dissident in his Church of St. Mary's at the risk of alienating a large group of people in Oxford.[2] In a letter to Froude, dated June 22, 1835, he makes his position clear with regard to this dissident party: "The church must not reconcile itself to it, yet must claim to have control over them."[3]

4. Finally and above all, the history of the Movement reveals three directions: dogmatic, liturgical, and hierarchical, which have no connection with the Methodist revival.[4]

These reservations having been noted, the study of Brilioth merits attention because it highlights the spirituality of the Movement. The spirit which animates the leaders and which motivates their boldness is one of a true moral reform, which leads the soul toward a rigorous asceticism. Newman and his companions wished to set the conditions for spiritual renewal by offering a very high ideal of perfection.

Historians had every right to admire the sacramental and liturgical reform that the Tractarians established under the cover of Anglicanism.[5] They also had to show that the point of departure of this reform came from something higher, which is their very idea of the Church's mission to save

---

[2] M. I, p. 98; also see text, Chapter IX, for greater details on this affair.

[3] Mozley, II, p. 98.

[4] This is the reason why we prefer the distinction established by Knox in *The Tractarian Movement* over Brilioth's assumptions: "Two reformist trends are found at the beginning of the nineteenth century: the first is Evangelicalism, which is progressive and humanitarian; the second, called "Tractarian," is conservative, respectful of order and hierarchy and yet influenced by a literary romanticism.

[5] The Anglo-Catholic ritualism is the direct result of the Tractarian Reform. See the principal works: Knox, *op. cit.*, and Lesly-Stewart, *A Century of Anglo-Catholicism*, very favorable to the liturgical restoration in the Movement. To the contrary, Brilioth, *op. cit.*, and Webb, *Religious Thought in the Oxford Movement*, insist on the close relationship between the Tractarian Movement and Evangelicalism. A third explanation

sinners. The strict attention that these Tractarians paid to the things pertaining to liturgy and discipline in the Church was matched only by their aspirations toward perfection.

It is not difficult to discover in the early history of the Movement these specific traits. With good reason, Brilioth studies, each in its turn, such outstanding documents as the sermons of Newman, Pusey, and Keble; he includes also those of Manning and a collection published in 1845, *A Course of Sermons Chiefly Bearing on Repentance and Amendments of Life*. One discovers in all of these works the familiar themes of the Newmanian moral preaching: the mysterious character of our spiritual life; the necessity to seek the truth; the personal vocation of the soul in quest of a personal rapport with its God; the duty to achieve moral progress, which Brilioth identifies with the Wesleyan conversion; the call for the highest sanctity of life to be found more in faith and union with God than in rituals and good works; and a strong preoccupation with one's own salvation, that Brilioth identifies as the doctrine of predestination.[6]

---

is offered by J.A. Froude, "Letters on the Oxford Counter-Reformation," in a collection: *Short Studies on Great Subjects*, v. IV, pp. 230-360. This writer, brother of Richard Hurrell Froude, former Tractarian and later a Latitudinarian, sought to show that the questions raised up by the Tracts were of secondary importance and that they oriented religious thinking in a direction sterile to the spirit. This unfair judgment was adopted and emphasized by Storr, a theologian of the liberal school, in his book: *The Development of English Thought in the 19th Century, 1800-1860*, cf. p. 270 ff. The Tractarian Movement, according to him, would have isolated religious life and higher theological reflection from modern thinking; it would have brought only a liturgical and devotional awakening to the Anglican Church.

[6] Each one of these teachings is true and is found in the preaching of the Tractarians. But Brilioth's interpretation is subject to discussion. The affinities with Evangelicalism and the reform of Wesley are not as evident as this writer suggests. Indeed, in the beginning, the Methodists were anxious to return to the tradition of the primitive Church and to define the limits of an ecclesiology, but "very quickly mixed elements established themselves: ritualism, asceticism, mysticism entangled themselves" (Aug. Léger, *La Jeunesse de Wesley*, p. 192). Very early, the preaching of Wesley took on a moral tone; he encountered more obstacles along his way and his reform ended in a separation from the Church. As a result, Methodism soon reduced the Church to an abstract notion, a divine idea, a pure means of sanctification through sacraments and liturgy, which were the only hierarchical and apostolic structures recognized. This aspect is essential to distinguish it from the Oxford Movement: the theology of the "Via Media" defines itself by its conception of the Church. See the work of Van de Pol, *De Kerk, in Bet leven en denken van Newman*. The author shows that the idea of justification prevailed in Newman's mind over the one of predestination which was at the root of his first conversion, and this idea of justification cannot be embodied anywhere else but in the Church, which is the instrument of salvation.

These two sentiments, the awareness of being a sinner and the need for ascetic practices, became more and more essential as the Movement evolved. It seems that after the failure of the "Via Media," Newman and Pusey sought refuge on the safer ground of asceticism and monastic life as a means to reach perfection. We know that Newman was first of all concerned about rediscovering the note of sanctity in his Church, and Pusey, after the defection of his companion, was to remain loyal to this generous effort of sanctification in his Church.[7]

There is no doubt that from the beginning of the Movement, its promoters had only this spiritual and moral renewal in view. Our conviction is based on several facts:

1. *The Ascetic and Moral Character of the Tracts*

The *Tracts for the Times* were a call for individual reform as much as a call for the reform of the Anglican Church.[8] Some tracts are of a dogmatic nature and define as a condition for reform, the return to the doctrine of Apostolic succession. But a number of the tracts are of a liturgical nature and therefore define the terms for public prayer and the liturgy as requirements for Christian perfection. See, in particular, tracts 3 and 9.[9]

Besides these tracts recalling the necessity for a true liturgy, there are others that invite clergymen and the faithful to positive and personal asceticism:

Tract 14, *The Ember Days*: The author recalls that it was the custom in the early Church to pray for the ordinands; this custom existed in the Anglican Church. It is necessary to restore it: "Each ought to consecrate

---

[7] See text, Chapter VIII, regarding the Oxford Movement. It is after the failure of the "Via Media," that Newman came to define the Church by the degree of sanctity of its members. Such a view lends itself to subjectivism, and Keble corrected his friend regarding the sermons in which he had expressed this viewpoint.

[8] See Thureau-Dangin, *op. cit.*, v. II, p. 93 ff.

[9] Tract 3, *Alterations in the Liturgy*: "In modifying things immaterial, we but elevate ourselves without satisfying a desire to correct ourselves."
Tract 9, *The Brevity of the Office*, is a protest against the tendency to shorten the Office; it recalls here the example of the early Church. See Liddon, *Life of the Rev. E.B. Pusey*, the titles and the authors of the *Tracts for the Times*.

these days whenever possible to prayer and meditation, joining to this, religious fasting if health permits." It concludes that personal sanctity of life is the very condition for a renewal of the Church.

Tract 16, *Advent*: We ought to prepare for the second coming of Christ.

Tract 18, a long tract by Pusey on *The Blessings of Fasting as Recommended by the Church.*

Tract 21: *Mortification of the Flesh as Defined by Scripture.*

Tract 32: *It is Necessary to Keep the Ordinances of Religion.*

2. The Diffusion of Spiritual Books

The leaders of the Movement sought to recover the masterpieces of devotional literature found in the Anglican or even in the Catholic heritage. Thus, Newman brought out a new edition of *Private Prayers* by Bishop Andrewes and it is the subject of Tract 78 (1840). In 1838, he re-edited the *Sacra Privata* of Wilson, then the *Godly Meditations upon the most Holy Sacrament of the Lord's Supper*, by Sutton. In 1839, he wrote the preface to another similar work of Sutton, *Learn to Live*; then he edited a quite unusual work by a parish priest, *The Rich Man's Duty to Contribute Liberally to the Building, Rebuilding, Repairing, Beautifying, and Adorning of Churches.*[10]

These works by Anglican writers were not the only ones to be widely diffused. In 1838, Newman and Keble together edited the *Remains* of R.H. Froude: one remembers, no doubt, what a shock these writings aroused in Anglican circles.

After that, Newman had proposed the publication of a collection of works, devoted to the lives of the English saints.[11] Pusey, who had just lost his little daughter in 1844, undertook the translation and editing of foreign

---

[10] All of the prefaces to these works were written by Newman. They were lent to us by Father Tristram from the Oratory.

[11] The lives of the saints were undertaken above all in order to satisfy the strong desire of the Oxford men of the younger generation: Oakeley, *The Life of St. Augustine*, Dalgairns, *The Life of St. Stephen Harding*, of St. Hilary, and of St. Aelred (cf. *Apologia*, p. 166). Newman himself composed several of these lives (*Apologia*, p. 165). The *Lives of English Saints* was re-edited by Hutton in 1900.

spiritual writings, such as: *The Spiritual Combat*, by Scupoli (seventeenth century), admired by Bishop Wilson in the eighteenth century; *Introduction to the Devout Life*, by St. Francis de Sales, that Laud had already introduced in England, although he expunged from it what he called "Roman corruptions"; the *Spiritual Exercises* of Louis of Grenada; *The Letters of John of Avila*, and some other works, already known in England, like those of Massillon and Fénelon.[12]

Between Newman and Pusey, a curious correspondence was established about these translations and their distribution on English soil. Pusey wanted their widest diffusion possible. He thought that although born in one particular branch of the true Church, they could be useful to the common good of the whole Church. But Newman, more aware of possible problems that might arise from these publications among undecided followers, was reluctant to allow too wide a distribution. He believed that the doctrine which they presented to the faithful was too rich a food to be absorbed without risk. A patristic publication undertaken together soon found him equally hesitant. Keble was on Pusey's side. Nevertheless, Newman finally consented to preface Pusey's publication and evoked his faith and confidence in the Anglican Church "in whose bosom we hope to die."[13]

He reacted differently to Pusey's initiative when he wished to provide a translation of the *Breviary* from Sarum, an Episcopal seat in England before the Reformation; Newman in 1828 contributed a long

---

[12] Pusey was not really innovative in view of the fact that in the seventeenth and eighteenth centuries, some of these books had already been known in English translations. In particular, the Quakers, then the reforms of Wesley, had allowed a pretty large distribution of these writings. Wesley had translated *The Letters of St. John of Avila*, and *The Life of M. de Renty*, by the Jesuit Saint-Jure. He had been acquainted very early with the *Imitation of Christ*, and William Law, whom he had consulted and who had recommended *The Spiritual Guide* of Molinos, the *Pensées*, by Pascal, and the *Cantiques*, by Antoinette Bourignon. Quite a variety as one can see! The Tractarians were better advised and more discreet! Wesley himself got lost in some of these mystical readings in which he was trying to relive his own experience. See Swarts, *Saved by Faith*, p. 75 ff.; Agnès de la Gorce, *Wesley, Maître d'un peuple*, p. 59; *La jeunesse de Wesley*, by A. Léger, p. 77 ff.

[13] *Life of E.B. Pusey*, by Liddon, v. II, p. 393 ff. Newman had advised against the translation and adoption of the *Guide du Carême*, by Avrillon but soon after, he gave his moral support to his discouraged friend in a letter of August 18, 1844: "Nothing is able to go against this fact that your undertaking has been pleasing to God" (*Ibid.*, p. 402).

preface to a selection of hymns drawn from the *Parisian Breviary*, and adapted them to the different seasons of the liturgical year.[14] Pusey's project was still more ambitious. He wanted to translate large extracts from the *Breviary* in order to enrich the devotional literature of Anglicanism. Newman did not give him any encouragement: "I do not feel that our system is able to support it. It is as if one tried to sew a piece of new cloth on an old vestment."[15] Pusey did not understand Newman's scruples and he went his own way; the translation of the *Breviary* was halted only under a threat from ecclesiastical authority.

3. The Return to Ancient Rules of Monastic Life

One of the most direct results of this spiritual renewal was to stimulate the generosity of the most dedicated followers of the Movement. Thus, its leaders found themselves, often against their will, invested with a moral responsibility which was in effect very close to directing the consciences of many. Spiritual direction was not entirely lost in England and John Wesley, before attempting his reform movement and undertaking his preaching, went to visit William Law, who was enjoying, in the beginning of the eighteenth century, an incontestable spiritual influence.[16] Froude himself had, early in his life, submitted to the spiritual direction of Keble. Newman had also a personal experience of it and Pusey would much later.

After the difficulties encountered by the "Via Media," many disheartened souls sought advice and counsel from the leaders of the Movement, especially from Newman. We see, already, in many parts of the correspondence, the practice of a sort of spiritual direction, in which is found both the confidence required from the faithful and the firmness

---

[14] This preface is found among the papers furnished by Father Tristram. It is dated, February 21, 1838, and contains a reflection on prayer that one finds in the other sermons of Newman and in the *Grammar of Assent* (p. 133 ff.).

[15] Liddon, *Life of Pusey*, II, p. 393 ff., Letter to E.B. Pusey, 2, Dec. 18, 1843; Cf. Ker, p. 282. It is to be noted that the solitaries at Littlemore utilized the translations of Pusey; a complete translation of the *Breviary of Sarum* was published much later by Cambridge University Press. On this question of the *Breviary of Sarum*, see Ollard and Cross, *Dictionary of English Church History*, Art. "Sarum Use," p. 544 ff.

[16] See Swarts, *op. cit.*, pp. 77-86.

expected from the director. The reputation of Keble for being too timid a
director does not apply to Newman. In a series of letters which he
addressed to a certain Miss H., in response to some specific questions
which she had asked, we discover a Newman clearly aware of the dangers
and possible deviations in spiritual life and a desire to find a remedy for
them.[17] This is an aspect of Newmanian spirituality still little known.

This generous person confided in Newman, seeking his advice about
the wisdom of binding herself by religious vows which would strictly
confine her to a life of piety, cut off from the world. Although Newman's
attitude was still overcautious on this subject, we can nevertheless detect
a profound desire for religious life that indicates a probable return to the
traditional forms of asceticism as they are expressed in religious orders.

In fact, Newman's preoccupation was not so much to restore
monasticism and other forms of religious life but to reorganize public
worship and good works in his own Anglican Church. A series of letters
at the end of the year, 1838, show us the problems encountered by Newman
in his attempt to organize a community of priests for the ministry in urban
centers. This project, which was dear to his heart, was also mentioned
much later in a letter to Pusey, dated March 17, 1840.[18]

As for Pusey, his ambition was to establish religious communities in
England; in 1840, he went to Ireland to study the necessary conditions for
the restoration of religious congregations of women. While traveling on
the Continent, some friends had sent him the rules of various orders; he
became so enthusiastic about this subject that his daughter, Lucy, was
caught up in this contagion for religious life; she resolved to devote her life
entirely to God in one of the religious congregations her father had
envisioned. She died early and Newman considered her to be a saint. Much
later, Pusey would see his hopes realized, and communities for women
would spread within the Anglican Church.[19]

---

[17] M. II, p. 311 ff. Is this Miss Holmes, with whom Newman would correspond for a long
time, even during his Catholic life? Cf. Ward I, p. 601. The most frequent themes in
these letters of spiritual direction are the following: a call for sanctity through purity of
intentions; meditations on humility and abandonment to the will of God; distrust of the
self; and a turning away from impatience and discouragement.

[18] *Life of Pusey*, II, p. 135. Newman wished to establish at Littlemore a community of
priests for the evangelization of the cities. Regarding the preceding incident, which was
opposed by Thomas Keble, see M. II, p. 239, Letter to John Keble, November 21, 1838.

Was not this a consequence of the spiritual revival born of the Oxford Movement since the publication of the first tracts? Brilioth had every reason to insist on the moral and religious character of the Movement above all. His mistake was to exaggerate the dependence of its leaders on Evangelicalism.[20]

---

[19] *Life of Pusey*, v. III, p. 5.
[20] Brilioth, *op. cit.*, p. 211.

Principal Events in the Life of Newman

February 21, 1801	John Henry Newman was born in London, son of a banker, John Newman, and of Jemima Fourdriner. The child was baptized on April 9 at the church of Saint-Benet Fink.
May 1808	Newman entered school at Ealing where he would remain until December 1816.
August 1816	During the school vacation, Newman remained alone at Ealing where he experienced his first conversion.
June 1817	Newman entered Trinity College, Oxford as an undergraduate.
April 12, 1822	He was elected fellow of Oriel College.
June 13, 1824	Newman was ordained a deacon in the Anglican Church and exercises his first pastoral ministry in the Church of Saint Clement at Oxford.
September 29, 1824	Death of Mr. Newman, father of John Henry.
January 20, 1826	Newman was named a tutor of Oriel. The beginning of his friendship with Richard Hurrell Froude.
January 5, 1828	Death of Mary, the youngest of the three Newman sisters.
March 14, 1829	Newman was named Vicar of the parish of St. Mary's Oxford.
December 1832	Newman, who just completed his first book, *The Arians of the Fourth Century*, embarked with the Froudes on a voyage to Italy and Sicily.
May 1833	Newman became ill with a strong fever and was alone in a deserted area of Sicily.
July 1833	Return to England. On the 14th of July, Keble gave the Assizes Sermon before the University. The 25th of July was the meeting of the Hadleigh Conference, which marked the beginning of the Oxford Movement.

1833 - 1841   Newman became the leader of the Tractarian Movement. In 1837, he published *Lectures on the Prophetical Office of the Church*. In 1838, *Lectures on Justification*. In this same year, he published Hurrell Froude's *Remains* with Keble. In February 1841, Newman published Tract 90, which ended with his disgrace among the University community and the Anglican Bishops.

September 1841   Newman retired to Littlemore, where he remained until February 1846.

September 1843   Newman resigned as Vicar of St. Mary's.

October 3, 1845   Newman gave up his Oriel fellowship.

October 9, 1845   Father Dominic Barberi received Newman and his disciples into the Church. The *Essay on the Development of Christian Doctrine* was published at the end of the year.

September 1846   The departure for Italy and Rome.

May 30, 1847   Newman was ordained a priest in the Roman Catholic Church.

February 2, 1848   Newman founded Maryvale near Birmingham, the first English community of the Oratory.

November 12, 1851   Newman was named Rector of the Catholic University of Dublin.

February 10, 1852   The Oratory was installed in the suburbs of Edgbaston.

November 12, 1858   Newman resigned the Rectorship of the University of Dublin.

1859 - 1860   Newman assumed the editorship of the review, the "Rambler," in which he published two articles which brought upon him the suspicion of Rome.

1864   Newman published the *Apologia Pro Vita Sua*.

1866   A letter to the Rev. E. B. Pusey on his recent *Eirenicon*.

1870   Publication of the *Grammar of Assent*.

1877   Newman was elected an honorary fellow of Trinity College, Oxford.

May 12, 1879   Leo XIII created Newman a Cardinal.

August 11, 1890   The death of Newman at Edgbaston.

BIBLIOGRAPHIC ABBREVIATIONS OF CERTAIN WORKS
FREQUENTLY CITED IN THIS TRANSLATION

M. I, II: *Letters and Correspondence of John Henry Newman*,
                 edited by Anne Mozley, Longmans, Green and Co.,
                 London, 1898.
W. I, II: *The Life of John Henry Cardinal Newman* by Wilfred
                 Ward, Longmans, Green and Co., London, 1912.
Apologia: *Apologia Pro Vita Sua*, ed. De Laura, W. W. Norton &
                 Company, New York, 1968.
K.:   *Correspondence of John Henry Newman with John Keble
                 and Others*, 1839-1845, Longmans, Green and Co., Lon-
                 don, 1917.
Par.:   *Parochial and Plain Sermons*, Ignatius Press, San Fran-
                 cisco, 1987.
Bouyer: *Newman: His Life and Spirituality*, P.J. Kenedy & Sons,
                 New York, 1958.
Verses: *Verses on Various Occasions*, Longmans, Green and Co.,
                 London, 1896.
Autobiog.:   *John Henry Newman: Autobiographical Writings*, edited
                 by Henry Tristram, Sheed and Ward, New York, 1955.
Diff.:   *Certain Difficulties Felt by Anglicans in Catholic Teach-
                 ings Considered*, Longmans, Green and Co., 4th ed.
Ker: *John Henry Newman: A Biography*, Clarendon Press,
                 Oxford, 1988.
Var. Occ.:   *Sermons Preached On Various Occasions*, Christian
                 Classics Inc., Westminster, Md., 1968.
Med. and Dev.: *Meditations and Devotions*, Burns & Oates, London,
                 1964.